11/2/72

PHILOSOPHY OF RELIGION SERIES

General Editor's Note

The philosophy of religion is one of several very active branches of philosophy today, and the present series is designed both to consolidate the gains of the past and to direct attention upon the problems of the future. Between them these volumes will cover every aspect of the subject, introducing it to the reader in the state in which it is today, including its open ends and growing points. Thus the series is designed to be used as a comprehensive textbook for students. But it is also offered as a contribution to present-day discussion; and each author will accordingly go beyond the scope of an introduction to formulate his own position in the light of contemporary debates.

JOHN HICK

Philosophy of Religion Series

General Editor: John Hick, H. G. Wood Professor of Theology,
University of Birmingham

Philosophy of Religion:
The Historic Approaches

M. J. CHARLESWORTH

HERDER AND HERDER

1972

HERDER AND HERDER NEW YORK

232 Madison Avenue, New York, N.Y. 10016

Library of Congress Catalog Card Number: 75–176367

Contents

vi

Introduction

What is philosophy of religion? The short answer is that it is simply philosophising about religion; but, like most short answers, this does not get us much further forward since it is not at all self-evident what exactly is meant by 'philosophy' and what by 'religion' and how the one can be concerned with the other. For, first, we have to engage in philosophising in order to define what 'philosophy' means, so that our view of what philosophy is itself involves taking up a philosophical position. In this respect, one's conception of the task of philosophy of religion will depend upon one's conception of the task of philosophy and this, as we have said, has to be argued for philosophically. And second, it is notorious that the definition of 'religion' – what is and is not to count as a religion – presents formidable difficulties.

If we investigate the complex set of phenomena that we call 'religion' in a *scientific* way, as a sociologist or anthropologist or a psychologist might, the object and method of that investigation are taken for granted and not put in question. Scientific investigators of religion may disagree about the conclusions they reach, but they do not disagree in any fundamental way about the validity of the method they are using or the nature of their task. But this is exactly what *does* occur with philosophers of religion. The difference between, say, Plato, Aquinas, Kant and a contemporary Wittgensteinian philosopher of religion, is not just a difference about the conclusions they severally reach about religion; it is also a difference about their respective conceptions of the nature and function of philosophy. Scientists do not put their method in question, but philosophers do, and it is precisely this that makes the definition of philosophy, and of the philosophy of religion, very difficult. In our attempt to delineate the main approaches that have been

vii

taken historically to the philosophy of religion we shall see that in each case a distinctive view of the nature and task and scope of philosophy is involved. Thus, for Plato and the neo-Platonists philosophy has a quasi-religious role in that its end is metaphysical vision or contemplation. The sage transcends reason through reason. For Aquinas, on the other hand, philosophy is strictly confined to the order of 'natural reason' and thus its job *vis-à-vis* the religious order of 'supernatural faith' is necessarily a defensive or apologetical one. With Kant, again, the metaphysical or transcendental pretensions of philosophy are even more severely curbed and consequently the philosophy of religion comes to be seen as a 'second-order' activity – 'making room' for religion by showing philosophy's own limitations. Finally, with the contemporary philosophers of analysis, philosophy becomes, in Wittgenstein's definition, 'the clarification of thoughts' and thus the philosophy of religion comes to signify no more than the 'meta-analysis' of the meaning of religious utterances – the 'therapeutic' clarification of the logical structure of religious discourse.

From one point of view, the philosophy of religion is largely an invention of the eighteenth century, for it was then that philosophers such as Hume, Kant, Lessing and Schleiermacher began to consider religion as a distinct phenomenon susceptible of being investigated in a critical and systematic way. It was then, we might say, that religion became a 'problem' explicitly for the first time, and that the philosophy of religion came to be seen as a distinct branch of philosophy alongside the philosophy of art and the philosophy of morals and the philosophy of knowledge. The Greek philosophers and their medieval followers had of course a good deal to say about philosophico-theological issues, but they did not ever consider them to constitute a distinct field of philosophical study. For Aristotle, and for Aquinas, the main branches of philosophy were logic, metaphysics, philosophy of nature, philosophy of mind, and ethics. Although for them religious questions came up in most of these spheres of philosophical inquiry, they were not separated off into a separate discipline. Aristotle indeed speaks of 'theology', but for him it is part of the general study of metaphysics – the investigation of 'being *qua* being'. There is an analogy here with the philosophy of knowledge or epistemology, for though both the Greeks and medievals concerned themselves with epistemological issues, knowledge and perception were not 'problems' for them in the way they came to be for Descartes and his heirs, and consequently they did not have a 'philosophy of knowledge' in the post-Cartesian sense.

If philosophy of religion is to be understood solely in the rather special sense it has been given since the eighteenth century, we would have to leave out of account both the Greeks and the medievals, for they do not have a philosophy of religion of this explicit and self-conscious kind. But if we understand philosophy of religion in a looser sense as meaning any philosophising about the general issues raised by religion, then fairly obviously we have to consider Plato and Aristotle and the neo-Platonists and their medieval successors (Jewish, Moslem and Christian), even though their philosophisings about religion are to be found scattered in their metaphysics, or their investigations into the nature of mind, or in their 'physics' or ethics.

If there are peculiar difficulties about defining 'philosophy', there are difficulties of another kind about the definition of 'religion', for it is impossible to specify clear and distinct criteria that any phenomenon must satisfy if it is to be accounted a specifically *religious* phenomenon. Even if our survey were limited to the major world-religions, it is well known that we cannot discern any very definite features common to them all. For example, if the concept of a unique and transcendent creator-God is central to the Judaeo-Christian religion, it is certainly not so in the case of Hinduism or Buddhism or Taoism, so that religion cannot be defined in terms of belief in and attitudes towards a creator-God. And the same objections may be made about other attempts to define religion in terms of a simple set of criteria. For example, Rudolf Otto's celebrated characterisation of religion in terms of what he calls 'the holy' or 'the numinous' (that reality that evokes a sense of mystery and awe and fascination) applies very nicely to Judaeo-Christianity but not to Theravada Buddhism (1).

Again, even within the Judaeo-Christian conception of religion there are profound differences between what might roughly be called the 'Catholic' tradition and the 'Protestant' tradition. Moreover, within those particular traditions there are very divergent views about the essence of religion. One need only think of the different approaches to religion of Aquinas, Pascal and Teilhard de Chardin on the Catholic side, and the differences between Kant, Kierkegaard, Karl Barth and Tillich in the Protestant tradition.

As William James pointed out long ago, religion is a 'complex' concept, like the concepts of 'government' and 'art', and it is futile to attempt to define it in a univocal way as though the word 'religion' stood for a 'single principle or essence' (2). We are able to point to clear or paradigm cases of religion, and we are also able to specify clear cases of non-religious views and attitudes; but there is a very large twilight in-between zone of world-views and ways of life which are difficult to characterise. It is not fanciful, for instance, to see Marxism as a quasi-religious world-view, even though it is, from another point of view, a deliberately anti-religious metaphysics.

It may be thought that the philosophy of religion is no worse off in this respect than, say, the philosophy of morals or the philosophy of art. It is, after all, just as difficult to define 'morality' or 'art' in any univocal way, and particularly in the case of art we have very much the same kind of borderline problems as with religion. For instance, we might ask whether Duchamp's 'objects' are *really* art or whether Cage's random noises are *really* music, in much the same way as we ask whether Braithwaite's 'agapeism' (being religious means adopting an attitude of Pauline charity or *agape*) is *really* religion? But the philosophy of religion is in an even worse situation, for the phenomenon of religion is open to doubt in a way in which the phenomena of morality and art are not. In Wittgensteinian terms, the 'language-games' of morality and art are indubitably 'played', and the only difficulty is that of giving an adequate analysis and account of them. But it is certainly not so clear that there is a religious 'language-game' at all, for it seems to be quite meaningful at least to hold that religion is possibly an illusion and that what there is of substance in it belongs to, or is reducible to, metaphysics or to ethics. Prima facie, 'reductionism' is logically possible in the matter of religion in a way in which it is not possible with respect to morality or art.

What is meant therefore by the philosophy of religion is something very loose and imprecise. If it is defined as the philosophical investigation of the issues raised by religion, we have to realise that what a 'philosophical investigation' is on the one hand, and what 'religion' is on the other, remain undefined save within the very wide limits just indicated. We must not think, then, that in tracing the history of the philosophy of religion and of the various ways in which it has been seen in Western thought, we are dealing with something as clear-cut as the history of the philosophy of science or even the history of ethics or aesthetics.

There are two distinct ways in which the history of the philosophy of religion might be approached, the one mainly historical and the other 'critical' (in the Kantian sense) or philosophical. Thus, one could outline the chequered career of the relations between philosophy and religion in Western thought and, in the manner of the historian, discern patterns in that historical record very much as Jaeger has done apropos the various theological ideas of the pre-Socratics, and Gilson apropos the natural theology of the medieval philosophers (3). Some properly philosophical conclusions might possibly emerge from such an essay in the history of philosophico-theological ideas, but they would be the incidental by-products of the investigation.

On the other hand, one could attempt to survey the history of philosophy's dealings with religion in a philosophical way, with the object of discerning the possible moves and gambits and of analysing the 'logic' of the various possible positions. Even though one might identify these possibilities with concrete historical views, and relate their analysis to what actual philosophers of religion have said, the whole interest of the exercise would be philosophical. Aristotle has been much maligned for his account of his predecessors' views in his various works, on the ground that his judgements are often unhistorical. But this kind of criticism misses the point of Aristotle's philosophical 'history', for it is concerned not with the mere chronicling of the ideas of past thinkers, but rather with the delineation of the main possible positions on a given topic or problem, and with what I have called the analysis of the 'logic' of those positions. No doubt it is all too easy to distort history (as Aristotle sometimes did) if one approaches it in this *a priori* way; but this need not necessarily happen.

It is, at all events, in this philosophical or (in the Kantian sense) 'critical' way that I have approached the history of the philosophy of religion in this book. Thus, I have tried to delineate four main positions, or four distinct conceptions, of the nature and scope of philosophy of religion, and then to analyse the logical structure of each of these conceptions, attempting to show their respective presuppositions and consequences, as well as their respective strengths and weaknesses. And in all this I have been mainly interested in the philosophical lessons that emerge from this inquiry, rather than with tracing out the purely historical development and interplay of certain ideas.

I begin first with that conception of the philosophy of religion which argues that it is the business of philosophy to lead men to a quasi-religious vision of reality and even to a quasi-religious way of life. In this view philosophy is in a very real sense continuous with religion. One might say, indeed, that this position makes a religion out of philosophy. Though there are intimations of this conception of the philosophy of religion in the pre-Socratic philosophers, it is above all with Plato and his heirs that it is made fully explicit. However, it is not only the Platonists (among whom, in this respect, we can include Aristotle) and the neo-Platonists, including certain medieval Islamic philosophers, who adopt this view, for it also emerges in modern philosophy with Spinoza and, in quite a different context, with Hegel.

The second conception of the philosophy of religion to be

considered is associated with the name of the great medieval thinker, St Thomas Aquinas, who sums up a long tradition of thought that begins with the Jewish sage Philo of Alexandria in the first years of the Christian epoch, and passes through thinkers as various as Origen, St Augustine, Abelard and Moses Maimonides. For Aquinas and his predecessors the task of philosophy of religion is above all a defensive or apologetical one, justifying the 'preambles' of religious faith and defending the 'articles of faith' by showing their 'negative possibility' or prima facie non-self-contradictoriness.

For Kant and the movement of thought he represents, on the other hand, philosophy has no justificatory role with regard to religion. Rather its function is to establish the conditions of possibility of religion and, in a negative way, to make room for religious faith. With Kant (at least according to one interpretation of his thought) the limitations of 'pure reason' *vis-à-vis* religion come to be heavily emphasised and philosophy's task is seen as that of pointing towards the possibility of religion by showing its own inadequacies. Kierkegaard and later Protestant thinkers exploit this view in a very radical way. This is the third conception of the philosophy of religion that we have to consider.

The fourth conception sees the philosophy of religion as being a purely 'analytical' or 'meta-logical' enterprise. For Wittgenstein and for the movement of analysis (if the very diverse philosophical strands that are usually included under this title can be called 'movement') it is not the business of philosophy to engage in metaphysical or transcendental speculation, but rather to analyse the conditions of meaningfulness of various kinds of 'languages' or areas of discourse. Thus philosophy of religion becomes the analysis of the function of religious language, investigating whether, for example, religious utterances are primarily descriptive and so true or false, or whether they function rather like moral utterances, or even poetic utterances, in that they express attitudes to life or evince feelings, or whether they have some quite peculiar function of their own.

As I have said, it is with the logical structure of each of

these conceptions of philosophy of religion that I am primarily concerned. However, this inquiry would be altogether abstract and bloodless if we were not able to see this 'logic' working itself out in the actual or 'live' speculations of philosophers of religion. It is for this reason that a good deal of attention has been given to the details of the thought of certain typical philosophers of religion, although I am very much aware of how selective my choice of 'types' has been, and how schematic my discussion of them must seem. However, if my approach is *a priori* and highly selective I would also want to claim that I have nevertheless not done violence to the thought of the philosophers whom I use as illustrations here, nor, I hope, engaged in too much Procrustean lopping of limbs in order to fit them into my four schematic beds.

1 Philosophy as Religion

(a) Introduction

In this work we will be mainly occupied with the philosophy of religion in the Western tradition and only incidentally with Eastern thought. This is, first, for the sake of convenience, for the study of Eastern religions would take us too far afield; and second, because the philosophy of religion is a peculiar creation of Western thought and occurs, in a pure form at least, only within that tradition. There are, no doubt, some Eastern thinkers – Sankara and Ramanuja, for example – who are concerned to speculate about religious themes in a quasi-philosophical fashion; but it remains true that in Eastern thought generally philosophy is never really disengaged from religion in the explicit way in which it has been separated out within the Western tradition. Some may see this lack of differentiation as an advantage and as a mercy to be grateful for, while at the same time judging the distinction between philosophy and religion that began with the Greeks, and that has persisted in Western thought ever since, as some kind of unfortunate original sin or 'fall'. However, unless philosophy or 'pure reason' is accorded some kind of autonomy or independence, then there cannot be a philosophy *of* religion. All that we will have, as in Eastern thought, is religious speculation, with a more or less philosophical colouring, where the final arbiter is religious revelation and faith and not pure reason.

However, if it is the Greeks who are the first to separate off philosophy from the popular mythical religious speculations of their time, they are also the first to attempt the invention of what one might call a philosophical religion – the construction of a religion out of philosophy which is intended to take the place of 'mythical' religion. Thus, for Plato and his later followers it is the task of philosophy to lead the sage to a supra-mundane vision and illumination; indeed, religion in this sense is the culmination of philosophy in that the end of philosophical wisdom is coterminous with the end of religion. In contrast with Eastern thought where philosophy is absorbed into religion, with the Greeks religion tends to be absorbed into philosophy, though philosophy itself suffers a change in the process. Here the task of philosophy is not to analyse religion as something already given, but rather to invent and constitute religion and, as it were, to serve the purpose of religion.

Since the Protestant Reformation, with its rejection of natural theology and its suspicion of the pretensions of philosophy with regard to religion, the very idea of a philosophical religion has come to be seen as almost self-contradictory, for if religion is the invention of man's unaided and 'natural' reason, it cannot by definition be religion. In Christianity there has always been a sharp distinction made between what we may discover by natural reason and what by supernatural religious faith – the latter going beyond and transcending philosophical reason. God's revelation is precisely a disclosure or revealing, on God's own initiative, of what cannot be known by pure reason alone. And with the Protestant tradition this disjunction between faith and reason, the natural and the supernatural, what man can know by his own efforts and what he is given to know by God's gratuitous revelation or disclosure, is so understood that it comes to be taken as self-evident that there cannot be any commerce between philosophy and religion, let alone any identification of the two. So Karl Barth, for example, attacks the idea of natural theology because of its very nature it involves reducing religion to philosophy and so denaturing it. Again, it has been argued that commitment to a religious revelation involves that one cannot accept the possibility of any human judgement on this revelation, otherwise it would not be a religious revelation. We cannot expect a religious revelation to fit in with our ordinary canons of knowledge, for 'everything that did fit in with these canons could be known ipso facto not to be revelation' (1). In much the same vein Rudolf Bultmann argues that if we

2

admit that we can have a 'natural' knowledge of God in the light of which we may judge the Christian view of God, then 'we have given up our Christian belief from the start; for it would be given up by the admission that its authenticity could be decided from a standpoint outside itself' (2).

Within this context, the mere idea of a philosophical religion is rejected out of hand in that it is alleged to involve a gross confusion between philosophy and religion. In such a conception of philosophical religion there can be no room for the dimension of the supernatural, or for revelation, or faith, or grace, and a religion which has no place for these concepts can scarcely be thought to be a religion at all.

Quite apart from these objections made from within the Christian or 'supernaturalist' conception of religion (and to that extent limited in their force and scope), there are other more general objections that seem to make the identification of philosophy and religion an impossible undertaking. For instance, the late-nineteenth-century French philosopher Édouard Le Roy criticises all philosophical or 'intellectualistic' forms of religion in that they make religion into a matter of speculative or theoretical assent and belief rather than of practical commitment. Le Roy, along with a good many other thinkers both ancient and modern, claims that it is of the essence of religion that it should provide a 'way' of life. Religion is of its very nature practical, and whatever theoretical content a religion may have is strictly subordinate to this practical purpose – the 'conversion' of men's lives. This is, in fact, the great difference between religion and philosophy, for while the latter is concerned with speculation for speculation's sake (philosophy is useless, as Aristotle remarked), religion is pre-eminently concerned with action and practice. For Le Roy, then, any religion that merely exacted speculative assent to a number of doctrinal propositions, or that consisted solely in philosophical contemplation, would precisely not be a religion, save in the most attenuated sense (3).

There is another consequence of this philosophical or intellectualistic conception of religion, namely, that it leads to a kind of religious élitism or esotericism. For, as only the

3

few intelligent or philosophically wise can assent to the truth of a philosophical system, if religion depends upon philosophy only a choice few will be able to be religious in the full sense, just as in Plato's 'Republic' only the philosophical élite can know what 'the Good' is and so be moral in the full sense, and just as for Aristotle only the fortunate few can be fully happy (4). In this view, ordinary non-philosophical people have to rest content with a lower-level morality and a lower-level religion. But, Le Roy claims, this once again demonstrates the impossibility of a philosophical religion, for if philosophy is incurably élitist or esoteric, religion cannot be so and still remain religion in the full sense. Religion is essentially popular or universalist, that is to say it must be within the reach of everyone, lettered and unlettered. It is not 'relative to the variable degrees of intelligence and knowledge; it remains exactly the same for the scholar and the unlettered man, for the clever and the lowly, for the ages of high-civilisation and for races that are still barbarous' (5). There have, of course, been ventures in religious esotericism – Gnosticism in Christianity, Ibn Rushd's 'Two Truths' doctrine in Islam, élitist forms of Buddhism – but it may be argued that these are very much exceptions that prove the rule, for these experiments have usually been rejected by the mainstream of religion and regarded as aberrations. To demonstrate that any form of religion implies, or leads to, this kind of philosopher's religion is therefore in effect to question its validity as authentic religion.

There is a good deal of force in these objections against the idea of a philosophical religion and they are objections that weigh very much with us at the present time (heirs of the Reformation that we are) and that prevent us from viewing sympathetically the strain of philosophical theology we are about to consider. However, whatever the objections, it is a brute historical fact that there is a substantial and important tradition in Western thought which identifies philosophy with religion and which sees religion as the culmination or highest realisation of philosophy. We can, of course, simply deny that this represents genuine religion

4

by insisting upon the sharp and irreducible distinction between the natural and supernatural, and by defining religion in terms of supernatural revelation, faith and grace – the gratuitous, unmerited intervention of God. Or again, we can define religion as practical in mode so that the notion of a philosophical or speculative religion becomes self-contradictory. But the 'intellectualistic' tradition is too large and central to be dismissed in this way (6), for it includes Plato and Aristotle, Plotinus and the neo-Platonic school, including the sixth-century Christian Pseudo-Dionysius (who had such a large effect upon the thought of the Middle Ages). Again, it is manifested in the philosophical theology of certain of the great Moslem thinkers such as Ibn Rushd in the twelfth century and, in quite a different context, in the thought of Spinoza and the deists of the Enlightenment in the seventeenth and eighteenth centuries, and of Hegel in the nineteenth century. Even within the Christian tradition, at least up until the Reformation, there is a persistent inclination towards 'intellectualism', despite the theological condemnations of it as being destructive of the distinction between nature and the supernatural, faith and reason. This tendency can be traced in the early thought of St Augustine (354–430) for example, and certainly in Boëthius's (480–524) 'De Consolatione Philosophiae'. The 'De Consolatione' had enormous influence upon subsequent Christian thought, and yet it is a work in which philosophy is seen as a way of life that culminates, without any kind of break, in religious enlightenment. Again, in the so-called 'dialectical' movement in the eleventh and twelfth centuries in the Christian West, there is this same tendency (though often ambiguously expressed) to identify 'true philosophy' with faith. It is indeed against this movement that St Peter Damian and St Bernard of Clairvaux, for example, protest so violently, and the violence of their attacks on the religion of the philosophers or dialecticians bears witness to its reality and importance. Even such orthodox Christian thinkers as St Anselm of Bec have a strong dose of intellectualism in their theology, though in practice they make the necessary reservations and qualifications about supernatural faith

5

being discontinuous with philosophical reason (7). Finally, contemporary with Aquinas in the thirteenth century there is the movement of 'Latin Averroism' which holds the philosophical life to be the highest state available to man, and which is important enough to earn ecclesiastical condemnation (8).

It is, therefore, very difficult to define away this conception of the philosophy of religion simply by claiming that, within the Judaeo-Christian context, it represents a kind of contradiction in terms. For this way of viewing the philosophy of religion has in reality been of very great moment in the history of Western thought, and though it may be difficult for us to take it seriously and sympathetically we must nevertheless make the attempt. We shall, therefore, look critically at some typical essays that have been made in this kind of philosophy of religion. Once again, we shall not be concerned to present a complete history of this tendency in Western thought, but rather to understand its motivation, its logical structure, and its implications both for philosophy and religion.

(b) Plato's philosophical religion

Plato's philosophy of religion is elaborated by way of reaction against the mythological and superstitious character of the popular religion given credence by poets such as Homer and Hesiod, and supported by the priests and religious 'professionals'. Plato argues that this kind of mythical religion lacks any rational basis in that no proofs or reasons are offered by its devotees for what they believe (9). Nor, again, does it give a true and adequate account of 'the divine', for the infantile stories of popular religion show the gods engaging in all kinds of morally dubious behaviour and as being subject to change and multiplicity (10). This view of the divine is childishly anthropomorphic and the first task of the philosopher is to demythologise the traditional theology and to replace it by a true, rationally based, theology. So Plato forbids the poets to speak of Zeus giving

6

portions of good and evil to men, because he wants to make it clear that since God is good, he cannot be the cause of evil (11). Again, he forbids the poets from talking about the various metamorphoses of the gods, for God is immaterial and cannot change; likewise he is truthful and cannot deceive us. Thus, as it has been put, 'Plato's religion . . . is above all based upon rational convictions, on intellectual beliefs, on truths', (12).

Apart from demythologising the popular anthropomorphic and irrational religion and substituting a purified rational religion in its place, the philosopher also must combat the atheism of those, like Empedocles, for whom God is an unnecessary hypothesis since the workings of nature are explicable in purely materialistic and mechanistic terms. In these atheistic views everything in nature comes about by chance, and religion, together with human morality and social institutions, are claimed to be mere products of convention (13). For Plato, both the atheistic philosophers and the exponents of mythological religion have this in common – neither see that the world is the effect of an intelligent cause or principle. So in the celebrated passage in the 'Phaedo' Socrates recounts his disenchantment with Anaxagoras's philosophical system which allowed no place for teleology and thus for a designing Intelligence. In fact, Socrates argues, we cannot explain the workings of nature in mechanistic terms, for the order and design of things and the adaptation of part to part in organic wholes implies purposiveness, and this in turn implies a purposing Intelligence.

As has often been remarked, Plato is here exploiting ideas that were in the air long before his time. Diogenes of Appolonia, for example, had put forward a finalistic proof of a supreme Intelligence in very much the same terms as the proof in the 'Phaedo': 'No,' Diogenes argues, 'this would never have been possible without an Intelligence – this distribution that regulates the measures of all things, summer and winter, night and day, the rains, winds and sunshine. So also for everything else: anyone who wishes to consider things will find in them the most complete order' (14).

7

Equally, as Jaeger shows, Plato's philosophical religion is foreshadowed in certain of the pre-Socratics. Thus, for example, he says: 'Anaximander's explanation of nature is something more than mere explanation of nature: it is the first philosophical theodicy' (15). Jaeger gives Xenophanes a major role in the demythologising of popular religion and its replacement by a philosophical religion (16), and he sums up this new approach to religion with the profound remark: 'Though philosophy means death to the old gods, it is itself religion' (17).

With Plato, however, the transcendence of the divine order becomes clearly marked for the first time. The earlier philosophers had spoken of the basic stuff out of which the world was made as being 'divine'. But Anaximander's 'Air' and Herakleitos's 'Fire' belonged to the world of 'becoming' and so could not really be 'divine'. For Plato it is rather the immutable, eternal, universal objects of pure intelligence – the Forms – that are divine in the strict sense. The totality of the intelligible Forms (together with the supreme Intelligence that contemplates the Forms) makes up 'the divine, the immortal, the intelligible, the indissoluble, the eternally identical' of which the 'Phaedo' speaks (18). Plato calls this totality the universal Being, Being without limitation, Being that is totally being, the Whole, and for him it is this alone that is divine in the strict sense, and not the physical world of the pre-Socratic philosophers (19).

If the intelligible world is coterminous with the order of the divine, then the Form of the Good, upon which all the other intelligible realities depend, will be the quintessence of divinity. So Plato says in the 'Republic' (20) that the Form of the Good is Goodness itself, Being itself, Justice itself; it is not a member of the class of good things, or of the class of beings – rather it is that by which things are good, existent, just and so on. (This is an idea that the medieval philosophers will take up and powerfully exploit later on.) We can say indeed that the Form of the Good transcends existence and goodness, for that which is the principle of existence and goodness cannot itself be called existent or

8

good, any more than, to use a modern analogy, the standard metre in Paris (that by approximation to which any length is called a 'metre') can itself be called a 'metre'. (Once again, this is an idea that will be taken up and developed by the neo-Platonists.) Again, for Plato, the Form of the Good is mysterious not through any obscurity or unintelligibility attaching to it, but rather through its own excess of intelligibility. Just as we cannot look directly at the sun, which is the source of the light by which we see other things, so also we cannot look directly at the source of intelligibility by which we understand everything else. This pregnant idea, that the mysteriousness of God springs from his super-intelligibility, will also subsequently have a very deep influence upon both the neo-Platonists and the medieval philosophers of religion. If Plato's God is a hidden God he is that only in the paradoxical sense that he is so obvious and luminously clear that we find it difficult to see him. The obscurity is not in him but is due to the limitations of our intelligence.

This is a truly extraordinary conception and it represents a revolutionary development in human thinking about God and the religious order in general. It is, of course, intellectualism of the boldest and most uncompromising kind, for the divine is seen not as being discontinuous with the rational order (the sphere of philosophy) but rather as being completely continuous with it. In fact, the divine represents an intensification or deepening of the intelligible realm accessible to philosophical reason. And, as we have seen, its mysteriousness derives from an excess of intelligibility rather than from a limitation of it or from a break with the intelligible order, as is the case with primitive religion where the divine is held to be mysterious precisely because it is not accessible to reason. If it is possible to speak of Plato's 'mysticism' (21) then it is very much a mysticism that is the fruit of philosophical contemplation and vision, for the supra-rational is attained only through the intensification of the rational (22).

For Plato, therefore, the sphere of the divine is not discontinuous with the rational order. Rather it is by carrying

9

through the activity of intelligence to its ultimate limit or highest point that we reach the divine. As has often been remarked, for Plato the 'divine' is a kind of continuum covering the intelligible world as a whole (23), the degree of divinity being proportionate to the degree of reality and the degree of intelligibility. Thus the philosophical ascent of the mind from the sense world to the intelligible world is also at the same time a religious ascent. For Plato, it has been said, 'Reason – as well as Soul, is found in the Universe and is due to the action of God, who is himself identified with Reason. In other words, the universe is rational and good in so far as God's rational nature and goodness are imparted to it; it is irrational and bad in so far as God's rational nature and goodness are not wholly imparted to it' (24).

Plato is quite willing to accept the élitist consequences of this severely intellectualistic view of religion, and it is clear that for him the truly moral life and the truly religious life are only for a few choice souls and not for the many 'lovers of sights and sounds' who remain imprisoned in the world of *doxa*. Just as the philosophers are the only ones capable of true wisdom and of morality in the full sense, and so of political guardianship, so also they are the only ones capable of attaining to true religion. The Guardians are then both philosopher rulers and religious leaders. As Plato says in the 'Laws': 'The care of the State cannot be entrusted to those destined for this task unless they take steps to acquire all the knowledge that can be had of the Gods' (25).

Again, as we have seen, Plato's view of the religious state is a purely speculative or visionary or contemplative one; religion for him is very much a concern of the intellect and not of the will or the desires. As he expresses it in the magnificent passage in the 'Timaeus' (26):

If the heart of man has been set on the love of learning and true wisdom and he has exercised that part of himself above all, he is surely bound to have thoughts immortal and divine, if he shall lay hold upon truth, nor can he fail to possess immortality in the fullest meaning that human nature admits; and because he is always devoutly

10

cherishing the divine part and maintaining the guardian genius that dwells with him in good estate, he must needs be happy above all (27).

With Plato we have the first systematic attempt to construct a philosophical religion that will take the place of popular or 'mythical' religion. The great merit of such a philosophical religion for Plato is precisely that it is rational and intelligible and thus worthy of man at his best and most human. Mythical religion, on the other hand, is irrational and unintelligible and unreal, and so is suitable only to children or to the ignorant multitude who cannot rise above the world of dreams and illusions. The price we pay, however, for this is, first, that religion is wholly dependent upon philosophy and is only as valid as the philosophy on which it depends; second, that such a philosophical religion is inevitably élitist in that it is only the fortunate few sophisticated intellectuals capable of philosophical speculation who will be able to be religious in the full sense; and third, this kind of intellectualistic religion is predominantly speculative or contemplative in character.

However, Plato is quite prepared to pay this price and we cannot plausibly claim that because his conception of religion is based upon (indeed, issues from) philosophy, and thus is subject to philosophical verification, as well as being élitist and intellectualistic, it is therefore not a religion at all.

We may conclude with the words of one of the most perceptive Platonic scholars: 'There is certainly such a thing as Plato's religion. It derives from his philosophy, it obeys the same principles and expresses the same aspirations, and it is, so to speak, the culmination and the flower of that philosophy' (28).

(c) Aristotle: The contemplative ideal

At first sight Aristotle's philosophy seems notably to lack the religious orientation that is so marked in Plato. Certainly the gods and the general realm of the 'divine' occur as a constant feature of Aristotle's thought right from his early

11

'Platonic' treatise 'On Philosophy' up to his later and more mature works. But, as Pascal complained of Descartes's God, the Aristotelian divinities appear to be dragged in to fill philosophical gaps, or to put the finishing touch upon a purely philosophical construction. Aristotle's theology, it has been said, seems to be a 'sort of appendix to physics, and to his particular physical theory' (29). Thus, it has often been claimed that both the Prime Mover of the 'Physics' and the ever-active Mind of the 'Metaphysics' are wholly unconcerned with the affairs of men or with the world in general, and the impression that one gets is that the Aristotelian God is a cold and bloodless abstraction, the 'self-absorbed object of unreciprocated love' (30). Aristotle's God is one to whom we assent speculatively, the supreme object of philosophical contemplation; but he (if we can even call Aristotle's divine entity 'he') is not one whom one could love and trust and pray to. Commenting on Aristotle's observation in the 'Poetics', that the tragic dénouement should spring from the hero's character and not be facti-tiously engineered by the gods, a recent commentator has this to say: 'Nothing could show more vividly how things have changed. The Gods are gone, except as a curtain raiser, and there is nothing to replace them except an Aristotelian Prime Mover sitting forever beyond the heavens' (31).

Jaeger's view of Aristotle's religious ideas goes even further than this, for according to him Aristotle's philo-sophical development or evolution was away from a pre-occupation with the supra-sensible world and the sphere of divinity (characteristic of his early Platonising phase) to a growing interest in the physical sciences. So in this view Aristotle's early metaphysics and theology, of a quasi-Platonic kind, give way to a philosophy of a strongly empi-ricist bent that is wholly unconcerned with theology (32).

Nevertheless, despite these unpromising first appearances, there is in reality a definite and strong religious or theo-logical orientation to Aristotle's philosophical system as a whole, and it is not too much to say that we find in Aristotle very much the same attempt to make religion the conclusion

12

of philosophy as we have already noticed in Plato. In fac t the notion of God is intimately involved in Aristotle's metaphysics, his psychology, his ethics, and his philosophical astronomy.

In Book VIII of the 'Physics' Aristotle sets out an elaborate argument to show that the change or mutability that is of the essence of the material world cannot be explained without reference to an extra-physical cause of change which is not itself subject to change or mutability. Given that, for Aristotle, change or mutability is explained in terms of potentiality and actuality, this means that the unchanging cause of change is not itself subject to potentiality of any kind but is rather a purely actual thing. It *is*, and it cannot be otherwise than it is; and it is purely and ceaselessly active or dynamic without any kind of passivity or receptivity (33). Aristotle's God, then, is full of life and energy to the highest degree – 'boiling with life', as Plotinus is to say later. Again, Aristotle's Prime Mover is not any kind of absentee landlord, or – to vary the analogy – a deistic God who winds the world up like a clock and then leaves it to run itself, for the influence of the Prime Mover upon the material world is direct, instantaneous and constant.

In Book X of the 'Metaphysics' the nature of God's operation on the world is described in some detail. It is as a final cause that God acts on the world of mutability, and all the various changes in the universe, from the rotations of the heavens to the changes of material sublunary things, are seen as attempts by matter to approximate as far as possible to the perfection of God's eternal and immutable activity or dynamism. For Aristotle the circular movements of the planets are the most impressive manifestation of this approximation to the divine – so much so that he holds the contemplation of the movement of the stars to be one of the main sources (together with the prophetic power of the soul in dreams) of the religious impulse in man (34).

Indeed this is for Aristotle the one tenet of popular religion that the philosopher can retain in his account of the divine. As he puts it at the end of Book X, chapter 8, of the 'Metaphysics':

It has been handed down from the dim ages and left to posterity in the form of myth, that these principles [the stars] are gods, and all Nature is set round with the divine. The rest is mythical accretion designed to cajole the popular mind and to be used in the interests of law and utility .... But if we strip this off and take the central fact alone, that they called the primary substances gods, it may well be thought god-inspired .... So far, and so far only, are the beliefs of our society and those handed down to us by our ancestors, plain and true for us (35).

Aristotle's low-keyed and modest prose in the 'Physics' and 'Metaphysics' conceals the very radical conception that he has of the relationship between God and the world – a world maintained in a state of dynamic process out of theo-centric desire to imitate or approximate to the eternal energy or activity of God. The same idea is implied by his remark that God brings about order and goodness in the world just as the leader brings about order in the army (36). 'The image of the leader', says a commentator on this passage, 'shows that the principle of order not only transcends the world as a model of perfection but also pervades the world as a force exercised by the supreme power' (37).

This theocentric character of Aristotle's metaphysics is also evidenced in his account of the relationship between 'first philosophy' or metaphysics and 'theology'. Thus Aristotle certainly suggests on occasion that the object of 'first philosophy' – 'being *qua* being' – is identical with the divine in that it is only God that exists or has being in the fullest sense. As Professor Merlan has put it:

> When Aristotle speaks of being *qua* being, ancient readers up to the time of Plotinus seem to mean: only of God can it be said that He is, whereas everything else is not only being but also becoming. Right or wrong, they seem to take the phrase 'being as being' as a kind of definition of the divinity. Therefore they do not see any essential difference between Plato and Aristotle in this respect (38).

14

The theocentric character of Aristotle's psychology is certainly much less clear than that of his metaphysics but, in his enigmatic observations on *Nous* in the 'De Anima' (39), there is the hint that human thinking depends upon the Supreme Mind or *Nous*. Alexander of Aphrodisias, at any rate, interprets the passage in the 'De Anima' as meaning that the human mind cannot engage in the activity of thinking without in some way participating in the ever-active divine *Nous*. In fact, he suggests that in so far as it is active (and not just receptive or passive) it is assimilated to the divine Mind and is 'divinised' (40).

At first sight, Aristotle's ethics does not seem to have any explicitly religious dimension, for the portrait of the good man that emerges from the 'Nicomachean Ethics' is hardly that of a religious mystic, but rather that of a 'well-rounded personality' who knows how to pursue his enlightened self-interest. Again, Aristotle does not see God as the origin of moral values nor as the sanction of them. Nevertheless, he clearly acknowledges that the culmination of the good life is the life of contemplation, and that this also represents the closest imitation of, or approximation to, the life of God of which men are capable. Thus in the famous passage in the 'Nicomachean Ethics' (41), Aristotle says that the highest form of happiness lies in the activity of *theoria* or pure contemplation, and he goes on to claim that the activity which brings the greatest happiness to man must be that which imitates the activity of God (42). Now God's activity cannot be either of a practical or productive kind, for it would be absurd to think that God needed to be courageous or temperate or that he needed to make artefacts. But 'if you take away from a living being action, and still more production, what is left but contemplation? Therefore the activity of God which surpasses all others in blessedness, must be contemplation; and of human activities, therefore, that which is most akin to this must be happiness' (43). If, then, this contemplation, which is the highest point of the moral life, is not strictly speaking *religious* contemplation (44), nevertheless through this *theoria* man imitates the divine life in the closest way possible to him. Reason (*nous*),

15

as Aristotle says, is 'the best thing in us' and the most divine element in our nature (45), and in its most intense form of activity (contemplation) we approach closest to the divine. Thus Aristotle argues:

> If the Gods have any care for human affairs, as they are thought to have, it would be reasonable both that they should delight in that which was best and most akin to them [i.e. reason] and that they should reward those who love and honour this most, as caring for the things that are dear to them and acting both rightly and nobly. And that all these attributes belong most of all to the philosopher is manifest. He therefore is dearest to the gods. And he who is so will presumably be also the happiest, so that in his way the philosopher will more than any other be happy (46).

This theistic orientation of Aristotle's ethics is even more marked in the 'Eudemian Ethics' where good and bad are defined in terms of that which leads to the contemplation of God and that which hinders the contemplation of God respectively (47).

Despite these religious implications of Aristotle's metaphysics, his psychology and his ethics, there are, however, two great lacunae in Aristotle's conception of religion. The first is that Aristotle has no doctrine of personal immortality, and the second is that Aristotle's conception of God seemingly excludes any kind of providential interest and concern for the world and for human beings. With regard to the first, it seems that for Aristotle the contemplation of God (or the contemplation that imitates God's contemplation) does not continue after death since the individual intellective *psyche* or soul is not capable of existing independently of the body of which it is the 'form'; although *Nous*, which is not bound up with a bodily organ and which enters the human *psyche* 'from without', is eternal and immortal (48). However one may interpret the relation between *psyche* and *Nous*, it is clear enough that Aristotle did not envisage that the individual psyche could survive the death of the body and that Ibn Rushd's later interpretation of Aristotle's mys-

and providence with regard to man, must inevitably be a cold and heartless kind of religion, has only to read Plotinus's 'Enneads' in order to realise his mistake. For the 'Enneads' shows once and for all that a philosophical religion is not, as has so often been alleged, some kind of unviable monstrosity. In its own way, indeed, the One of Plotinus and his followers perfectly fits the definition of the central religious reality which Rudolf Otto calls 'the Numinous', and which he defines as 'mysterium, tremendum et fascinans'. Again, the example of the great neo-Platonists' lives is significant in this respect. For the life of Plotinus, as his disciple Porphyry recounts it, shows a seriousness and devotion and sense of vocation that is very similar to that of the Eastern religious sages. And the same is true of Porphyry himself and of Proclus. Thus it has been said that 'philosophy produced some of the most striking ideal types, the saints of antiquity. Around all the prominent figures who founded or developed schools there grew not only anecdotes but also haloes' (60).

This merging of philosophy and religion, entailing as it does a denial of any distinct supernatural order, is of course very difficult to reconcile with Christianity. But it is surprising how much this intellectualistic view of religion persists even within the Christian tradition. Thus, although the early Christian thinkers in practice make the necessary reservations in order to safeguard the distinction between what is supernaturally revealed and accessible to faith and what is accessible to philosophical reason, there is a tendency in Christian neo-Platonists such as Origen (185–254), St Gregory Nazianzen (330–90) and St Gregory of Nyssa (330–95) to see the end of Christian wisdom and of 'true philosophy' as identical. Speaking of St Augustine, a recent commentator says that 'he does not appear to have felt any sharp need, at the time of his conversion, to disentangle the teaching of Christianity from that of the 'Platonists'. It was easy to pass from the atmosphere of Plotinus and Porphyry to that of St Paul and the Fourth Gospel, and Augustine had no sense of any radical transition' (61). The same writer goes on to say that 'in the works written at the time of his conversion to Christianity and immediately

21

following it, Augustine interpreted his conversion as the result of his quest for wisdom, and often speaks of having arrived in the "haven of philosophy". "Christianity" and "true philosophy" are practically synonymous terms' (62). So, in the famous passage in the 'Confessions', Augustine describes his conversion from rhetoric to philosophy in wholly religious language:

> Among these people, being not yet in manhood's strength, I was learning books of eloquence, in which I wished to shine with a purpose flighty and to be condemned, in the joy of human vanity. In the usual order of studies I had come to a book of a certain Cicero, whose speech is admired by almost all though his heart is not. But that book contains his exhortation unto philosophy and is called 'Hortensius'. Now that book changed my affections and turned my prayers to Thee thyself, O Lord, and made my wishes and desires quite other. Suddenly all vain hopes grew cheap in my eyes and I yearned for the immortality of wisdom with a burning zeal which passes belief and I began to rise that I might return unto Thee (63).

It is, however, in the work of the Christian thinker Pseudo-Dionysius that this neo-Platonic religious intellectualism is given its most extravagant expression. Pseudo-Dionysius was a Christian thinker of the sixth century who put forward a Christianised version of Proclus's thought under the name of Dionysius the convert of St Paul (64). With Pseudo-Dionysius indeed it is difficult to know whether he is putting forward a neo-Platonic view of reality illustrated by Christian themes, or whether he is proposing a Christian world-view in neo-Platonic categories. Pseudo-Dionysius himself would probably not have seen the difference between the two, for seeing philosophy as religion, or religion as philosophy, would for him have come to one and the same thing (65). Pseudo-Dionysius had enormous influence upon medieval thinkers – Erigena, Simon of Tournai, Bonaventure, Aquinas – and there is no doubt that his religious intellectualism rubbed off on them to some extent.

22

The same tendency to identify Christianity and 'true philosophy' occurs in a different context in the great and influential work, the 'De Consolatione Philosophiae' of the sixth-century Christian thinker Boëthius. The aim of the 'De Consolatione' is precisely to show that philosophy leads the soul to God, and though the teaching of the work harmonises generally with Christian teaching about God, man and human freedom, there is no explicit reference to Christianity in it. Indeed, it has been claimed that Boëthius wrote the 'De Consolatione' at the end of his life when he had abandoned Christianity and returned to philosophy as a secular way to salvation (66).

Despite this infiltration of Platonic religious intellectualism into early Christian thinking, it remains true that in the last resort, Christianity sees the sphere of natural reason and of philosophy as distinct from the supernatural sphere of religious faith. In other words, one can never attain to religious faith simply by intensifying the exercise of pure reason. It is this realisation that forces the medieval Christian thinkers to formulate a completely new conception of the philosophy of religion.

(e) Medieval Islamic thought and the 'Two Truths' theory

The philosophical religion whose career we have been tracing among the Christian neo-Platonists also has interesting echoes in the tradition of thought that springs from the meeting of neo-Platonic philosophy and the religion of Islam. Apart from the orthodox Moslem apologists – the *mutakallimun* – who use philosophical instruments to defend and explicate the Islamic faith proposed in Mohammed's revelations in the Qur'an, there is a line of philosophers who seek to construct a purely philosophical theology of much the same kind as they find in their Greek masters, Plato, Aristotle and the neo-Platonists (67).

Thus, for example, a Persian Platonist of the ninth century, Al Razi (Rhazes, 865–925), puts forward a purely rationalistic view of religion in the following words: 'Philosophy', he says, 'is the imitation of Almighty God so far as

23

lies within man's power' (68). The revealed religion of the prophets, Moses, Jesus and Mohammed, is superstition, and philosophy is the only true and universal way to salvation. 'God, glorious is his name, has given us reason in order to obtain through it from the present and future the utmost benefits that we can obtain; it is God's best gift to us . . . . By reason . . . . we succeed to the knowledge of God, which is the highest knowledge we can obtain' (69).

Similarly, the great Al Farabi (870–950) attempts to reconcile the Islamic religion and Platonic–Aristotelian philosophy by arguing that religion simply presents in a symbolic and limited form what philosophy presents more adequately and universally. As he puts it, the philosopher alone knows the truth in the full sense, and it is made known to others 'through symbols which reproduce it analogically' (70). This idea is of course a very old one; it is found, for instance, in Plutarch of Chaeronia in the second century in his 'De Iside et Osiride'. 'There is one divine mind', he says, 'which keeps the universe in order and one providence which governs it. The names given to this supreme God differ; he is worshipped in different ways in different religions; the religious symbols used in them vary, and their qualities are different; sometimes they are rather vague and sometimes distinct' (71). The same equation of the religious with the symbolic will also, as we shall see, have a long history in subsequent speculation right up to the present times (72).

According to Al Farabi, philosophical theology is the outcome of human reason alone and is, as such, universally valid. The symbolic expression of religious truths in the various 'revelations', however, are valid only for those who accept them and who understand the particular set of symbols they employ. It is worth while citing Al Farabi on this at length since he provides the first expression in Islamic thought of what has been misleadingly called the 'Two Truths' theory – in other words, the theory that philosophy and religion express the same truth in two different ways and at two different levels. Thus Al Farabi writes:

. . . According to the ancients, religion is an imitation of philosophy. Both comprise the same subject and both give an account of the ultimate end for the sake of which man is made – that is, supreme happiness – and the ultimate end of every one of the other beings. In everything of which philosophy gives an account based on intellectual perception or conception, religion gives an account based on imagination. In everything demonstrated by philosophy, religion employs persuasion. Philosophy gives an account of the ultimate principles ... as they are perceived by the intellect. Religion sets forth the images by means of similitudes of them taken from corporeal principles. (73)

It may seem that Al Farabi's position is one of religious scepticism, but this would be to misunderstand him, for he clearly thinks that he is giving an account of true religion superior to that of the *mutakallimun*, and that it is only through philosophy that one can achieve salvation and eternal bliss in the next life.

Ibn Sina (Avicenna, 980–1033), perhaps the central figure in Islamic philosophy, also maintains very much the same view of religion and philosophy though he is, perhaps, less severely 'reductionist' in his account than Al Farabi. In other words, he does not reduce the teaching of the Qur'an to a set of philosophical truths, without remainder, but rather attempts to harmonise the basic tenets of Islamic religious faith with Aristotelian and neo-Platonic philosophy. There is no doubt, however, that for him philosophy has the final say with regard to any conflict between faith and reason. Again, for him mystical contemplation is identified with philosophical insight. Thus a recent commentator writes: 'The highest form of the ritual prayer of the mystic is for Avicenna identical with the silent contemplation of the neo-Platonic philosopher which is the outcome and the culmination of intense and protracted philosophical studies' (74).

A more nuanced version of the 'Two Truths' theory is put forward by the great twelfth-century Spanish Moslem, Ibn Rushd (Averroës, 1126–96), who had considerable influence upon the Christian thinkers of the Middle Ages, especially Aquinas. The Qur'an, according to Ibn Rushd, is not opposed to philosophy. In fact, since it is the function of philosophy to lead men to the knowledge of God, the Qur'an implicitly commends philosophy. Again, we can only know the inner meaning of the Qur'an through philosophy, so the Qur'an cannot be opposed to philosophy as the religious fundamentalists pretend. There are three different levels of interpretation and understanding of the religious revelation contained in the Qur'an. First, there are those capable of understanding the latter through strict philosophical demonstration, and there is no doubt that for Ibn Rushd this is the highest and noblest form of religious understanding. Second, there are those who assume the truth of the Qur'an and argue for it dialectically. These are the theologians, and their understanding is inferior to that of the philosophers since it rests upon undemonstrated assumptions. Third, there are the 'people of rhetoric', or ordinary unsophisticated believers, who understand revelation through poetic analogies and metaphors. Thus, it has been said, for Ibn Rushd, 'there is absolute and esoteric rationalism for the philosophers; absolute and exoteric fideism for the ordinary people; and semi-rationalism and semi-fideism for the theologians, who form a hybrid class' (75). And the same commentator concludes that for Ibn Rushd 'religion does not teach any truth that the reason of the philosopher is not able to discover for itself. It is strictly only a system of symbols for the use of the masses who alone have to take them literally' (76).

Though the 'Two Truths' theory had indirect antecedents in early Christian thought with the distinction between the theologians who have 'knowledge' (*gnosis*) of the true meaning of the gospels and the 'simpler' Christians (*simpliciores*) who are capable merely of 'belief' (*pistis*) (77), there is nothing in medieval Christian thought to compare with the radical kind of religious intellectualism to be found in this line of Islamic thinkers. Though they were attacked by orthodox theologians and other philosophers, such as the remarkable Al Ghazzali (1058–1111), who opposed their reduction of Islamic revelation to Platonic–Aristotelian

26

philosophy, they themselves do not see their work in this light or as being sceptical in intent. In fact, it is clear that they thought that, by showing the concordance between the essentials of Islamic religion and the philosophico-theological conclusions of Greek philosophy, they were saving religion and making it respectable in that it could now be seen to be intrinsically rational. For them, as for their Greek masters, to rationalise religion was not to destroy it but rather to enhance and ennoble it and make it more fully worthy of man's attention. For if religion were not the expression of philosophical reason, it would be irrational and unintelligible – a tissue of imaginative myths with no more truth-value than poetry. The 'Two Truths' theory enables us to see what is of universal value in the Qur'an and other religious revelations, and at the same time makes it possible for the philosopher to be a religious man in the fullest sense.

(f) The Enlightenment: Pure reason and religion

Though, as we have already remarked, the kind of religious intellectualism we have been examining has some repercussions in the philosophico-theological thought of the medieval Christian West, medieval thinkers such as Aquinas formulated a distinct position of their own according to which philosophy plays a defensive or apologetical role with respect to religious faith, the latter being seen as transcending philosophy or 'natural reason'. We will examine the structure of this position in the next chapter.

With the break-up of the medieval synthesis, however, and the emergence in the seventeenth century of a new rationalistic style of philosophy, there was a curious reversion to, or reinvention of, the older conception of the philosophy of religion. Thus, though Leibniz (1646–1716) and Spinoza (1632–77), for example, operate within a philosophical and religious context profoundly different from the Platonic/neo-Platonic tradition, they nevertheless, in their own way, also see religion as the culmination of pure reason.

27

Or, to put the matter more exactly, philosophy for them expresses in a rational mode, accessible to the intellectually sophisticated few, the substance of what religion expresses in a symbolic or mythical mode accessible to the simple-minded many. And later on, Hegel (1770–1831) – although his philosophical perspectives are different again from those of Leibniz and Spinoza – adopts very much the same point of view. As Hegel puts it: 'The substance of the Christian religion, the highest developmental stage of any and all religion, coincides completely with the substance of true philosophy' (78).

There is of course a large difference between the philosophy of religion of these thinkers and the philosophy of religion of the Greeks and their direct descendants. The distinction between turning philosophy into religion and turning religion into philosophy is a very fine one, but it could perhaps be said that, whereas for the Platonic/neo-Platonic tradition philosophy comes to have a religious dimension, for Spinoza and Hegel, on the other hand, religion tends to become a branch of philosophy. It is this, no doubt, that led Croce to remark of Hegel that he is at once the most religious and the most irreligious of philosophers, and that caused some of Spinoza's contemporaries to condemn him as an atheist, even though his philosophy culminates in the 'intellectual love of God'.

It is difficult, however, to make this point without aiding and abetting the usual misleading criticisms that are made of the rationalist philosophers (and, in another way, of Hegel), namely, that they were deists who arbitrarily introduced God into their philosophical systems in order to extricate themselves from difficulties and paradoxes or, even more damagingly, that they gave their philosophy religious trappings to escape sanctions from the ecclesiastical and civil powers. Pascal has expressed the first kind of criticism in his famous remark apropos Descartes: 'I cannot forgive Descartes. He would have liked, in the course of his philosophy, to by-pass God. But he could not help making Him give a shove to set the world in motion; after that he has nothing further to do with God' (79).

28

But Descartes's God is not really a *deus ex machina*, and neither are the Gods (all very different) of Leibniz, Spinoza and Hegel, for in all these philosophical systems God is a necessary and indispensable element. Of course Spinoza's God – the object of 'intellectual love' – and Hegel's God – the Absolute Self-Conscious Spirit – are very far removed from the God of Judaeo-Christianity, and their conception of popular religion as giving mythical or symbolic expression to truths known in their fullness by philosophy is equally at odds with traditional Christianity. But unless we arbitrarily define 'God' and 'religion' exclusively in traditional Judaeo-Christian terms, we cannot protest that Spinoza and Hegel are not 'really' talking about God or religion at all (80).

Again, there is no reason to doubt these thinkers' personal religious concern. Leibniz was deeply interested in religion and religious affairs all through his life; Spinoza was described by Novalis as a 'God-intoxicated man'; and it has been said of Hegel that he is 'in a sense the most Christian of thinkers, for while the official defenders of Christianity have usually borrowed their logic and the cast of their thought from Aristotle or from other sources, Hegel alone among thinkers has borrowed the whole cast of his thought from Christianity' (81).

It is of considerable interest to see in the strain of thought represented by Leibniz, Spinoza and Hegel very much the same moves being made as in the older Platonic/neo-Platonic tradition. There is, for instance, the same denial of any distinction between the 'natural' order of reason and the 'supernatural' order of religious faith. Leibniz does indeed give lip-service to this distinction, but in practice he constructs a philosophical religion quite independently of revelation.

Leibniz [it has been said] writes with perfect seriousness and decency about the Christian scheme of redemption, but it hardly looks like being for him a crucial deliverance from perdition. It is not the intervention of Mercy by which alone he possesses himself of us: it is one of the

29

ways in which supreme Benevolence carries out a cosmic policy; and God's benevolence is known by pure reason, and apart from Christian revelation (82).

The same denial of the supernatural dimension of faith is also made even more firmly and explicitly by Spinoza and Hegel.

Again, these philosophers of religion betray the same religious élitism or esotericism already noticed in the older religious intellectualists. In other words, for them it is only the few intellectual experts who can grasp the true substance of religion in its rational mode. As Hegel expresses it in the celebrated conclusion to his 'Lectures on the Philosophy of Religion':

For us philosophical knowledge has harmonised this dis-cord [about religious belief], and the aim of these lectures has just been to reconcile reason and religion, to show how we know this latter to be in all its manifold forms necessary, and to rediscover in revealed religion the truth and the Idea. But this reconciliation is itself merely a partial one without outward universality. Philosophy forms in this connexion a sanctuary apart, and those who serve in it constitute an isolated order of priests, who must not mix with the world and whose work is to protect the possession of Truth (83).

Spinoza also makes a sharp distinction between the philosopher's knowledge of God and the belief of the ordinary *croyant*. The philosopher attains to the 'greatest good of the mind' which is the knowledge of God (84), and he enjoys the satisfaction and spiritual pleasure that goes with this knowledge (85). This 'intellectual love of God', which Spinoza describes in terms analogous to those appropriate to religious mysticism, is 'the very love of God with which God loves himself, not in so far as he is infinite but in so far as he can be expressed through the essence of the human mind, considered under the species of eternity' (86). On the other hand, the ordinary man's approach to religion is a completely non-speculative one. Faith at this level is a matter of 'obedience' to God's moral commands and a man is to be accounted religious in so far as he does good works. As Spinoza puts it: 'It follows that we can only judge a man faithful or unfaithful by his works. If his works be good, he is faithful, however much his doctrines may differ from the rest of the faithful: if his works be evil, though he may verbally conform, he is unfaithful' (87). The imaginative utterances of the religious prophets, so Spinoza implies, are neither true nor false; they are simply more or less rhetorically effective in that they lead us to that love of our neighbour that is the heart and soul of religion. So he says, 'the sphere of reason is truth and wisdom . . . the sphere of theology is piety and obedience' (88). 'It is not true doctrines', he goes on, 'which are expressly required by the Bible, so much as doctrines necessary for obedience, and to confirm in our hearts the love of our neighbour, wherein (to adapt the words of John) we are in God and God in us' (89). This practically oriented religion is 'adapted to the understanding and established opinion of the multitude' (90), and although Spinoza is sympathetic to the value of this popular religion, there is no doubt that for him it is inferior to the philosophical religion that culminates in the intellectual love of God (91). Later on, Schopenhauer (1788–1860) mocks this distinction between the philosophical religion of the few and the allegorical or mythical religion of the vulgar. Thus in his dialogue 'On Religion', his *alter ego* Demopheles speaks of 'philosophers for the few, the emancipated; founders of religions for the many, for mankind as a whole'.

Religion [he goes on] is the metaphysics of the people, which they absolutely must be allowed to keep: and that means you have to show an outward respect for it, since to discredit it is to take it away from them. Just as there is folk-poetry and, in the proverbs, folk-wisdom, so there has to be folk-metaphysics: for men have an absolute need for an *interpretation of life*, and it has to be one they are capable of understanding. That is why it is always clothed in allegory; and, as far as its practical effect as a guide to behaviour and its effect on morale as a means of

31

consolation and comfort in suffering and death are concerned, it does as much perhaps as truth itself would do if we possessed it . . . . The people have no direct access to truth; the various religions are simply schemata by which they grasp it and picture it, but with which it is inseparably linked. Therefore, my dear chap, I hope you'll forgive me for saying that to ridicule them is to be both narrow-minded and unjust (92).

In his own way, Hegel makes much the same kind of distinction between philosophical religion and popular religion. The philosopher knows that God is not an independent objective entity, but is rather identical with the self-conscious Spirit which is becoming manifest in mankind as a whole. This does not mean that for Hegel God is identified with man, so that religion becomes a kind of humanism, but it does mean that the traditional 'theistic' God has to be done away with and that in this sense we may say that 'God is dead' (93).

Popular religion, on the other hand, involves 'representational thought'. 'Representation' (*Vorstellung*) for Hegel does not simply mean thinking by means of images or mental pictures conjured up in the imagination. An image is always particular and so has no rational content, since rationality and universality are synonymous. A 'representation', however, is involved in a pictorial way of thinking which presents some universal, and so rational, truth. Thus, for example, the popular idea of God creating the world is a 'representation', for it represents, in an image taken from human making, the origin of the world as an event taking place in time (though for philosophical understanding, of course, the creation of the world is not an event, nor does it take place in time) and so gives us some dim idea of the philosophical truth that the Idea externalises itself by an eternal and timeless process (94). This kind of representational thought is typical of popular religion and is of course accessible to the majority of non-philosophical men; but the inner meaning of what is represented by religious representations is available only to the 'isolated priesthood' of philosophers.

32

We may remark as well that for both Spinoza and Hegel philosophical religion is essentially speculative or visionary, as contrasted with popular religion which is above all concerned with moral practice. Thus, Spinoza expressly rejects any reciprocity in our intellectual love of God. We love God, in so far as we intellectually contemplate him, but God certainly does not love us in return. 'He who loves God', Spinoza says, 'cannot endeavour to bring it about that God should love him in return' (95); indeed, for a man to want God's love would be tantamount to desiring that 'God whom he loves should not be God' (96).

Hegel also proposes the same severely intellectualistic view. 'The aim of philosophy', he says, 'is to know the truth, to know God, for he is the absolute truth, inasmuch as nothing else is worth troubling about save God and the unfolding of God's nature' (97). Thus, for Hegel, all the doctrines of Christianity, despite any 'practical' appearance they may have, are translatable into speculative or theoretical terms. His account of the meaning of the death of Christ (the doing away of the human side of Christ's nature) is typical in this regard. 'The real point of importance', he says, 'is an infinite relation to God, to God as actually present, the certainty of the Kingdom of God, a sense of satisfaction not in morality, nor even in anything ethical, nor in the conscience, but a sense of satisfaction beyond which there can be nothing higher, an absolute relation to God himself' (98).

In addition to these characteristics which Leibniz, Spinoza and Hegel share with the older religious intellectualists, they bring out very vividly another aspect of the 'logic' of this position. For Leibniz, Spinoza, and Hegel it is what is necessary and universal and essential and eternal that is of primary value in true religion, so that the contingent, particular, accidental and temporal features of religion are disregarded as being of no real significance. There are elements of this 'necessitarianism' in the neo-Platonists and, as we have seen, in certain of the Islamic thinkers who contrast the particular and limited character of the various historical revealed religions with the universal

33

and eternal character of philosophical religion. But with Spinoza and Hegel this tendency is strongly emphasised. For them the historical facts of Christianity – that, for example, Christ was born at a certain time and place; that he lived, suffered and died and rose again from the dead – are, as historical facts, of no relevance to religion at all. Thus Spinoza writes that 'it is not entirely necessary to know Christ according to the flesh, but we must think far otherwise of the eternal son of God, that is the eternal wisdom of God which has manifested itself in all things, more especially in the human mind, and most of all in Christ Jesus. For without this wisdom no one can attain to a state of blessedness' (99). Again, Hegel says that we must distinguish between the 'outward history' of Christ, and the universal and necessary meaning of the events of His life, this latter being the concern of true religion (100).

This radically a-historical conception of religion, which derives from Hegel's whole conception of philosophy (101), is brought out very dramatically in a remarkable essay by the English neo-Hegelian, F. H. Bradley, and it is worth while citing him at some length:

Suppose (let us say) a man convinced of the truth of Christianity, and rightly or wrongly to understand Christianity as the unity of God with finite souls, a reality at once consummated and eternal and yet temporal and progressive. Christianity is to such a man a main aspect of the Universe, conscious of itself above time, and yet revealing itself in the historical growth of spiritual experience. And imagine the same man asked to compare with this principle the truth about some happening in time. I will not instance such events as the virgin birth and bodily ascension of Jesus of Nazareth, but I will take the historical assertion that Jesus actually at a certain time lived and taught in Galilee and actually died at Jerusalem on the cross. And by 'actually' I mean so that, if *we* had been there, we should have seen these things happen.

'All such events', our supposed man might reply, 'are if you view them as occurrences, of little importance.

Inquire by all means whether and how far there is good evidence for their happening. But do not imagine that Christianity is vitally concerned with the result of your inquiry. Christianity, as I conceive it, covers so much ground, fills such a space in the Universe, and makes such a difference to the world, that, without it, the world would be not so much changed as destroyed. And it counts for much that this eternal truth should have appeared on our planet (as presumably elsewhere), and should here (we hope) be developing itself more and more fully. But the rest, if you will take it as mere event and occurrence, is an affair so small – a matter grounded by the very nature of its world on so little – that between the two things there can be hardly a comparison' (102).

(g) Summary and evaluation

So far we have attempted to expose the anatomy of this view of the philosophy of religion which sees philosophy as leading to and issuing in religion. There is, it will now be clear, a kind of logic operating in this position in the sense that, given the identification of philosophy with religion, the other aspects of this position follow with a kind of necessity, and are also interconnected. Thus, for example, this kind of philosophy of religion results in an austerely contemplative or speculative approach to religion; it involves the denial; or at least the blurring, of the distinction between the sphere of natural reason and that of supernatural faith; it results in religious esotericism; and finally, it leads to a radically a-historical approach to religion. Let us look at each of these aspects in more detail.

First, according to this position, religion is defined as consisting essentially in the intellectual vision or contemplation of 'God'. The latter, as we have seen, has been variously understood as the Form of the Good (Plato); the purely and eternally actual and dynamic source of change and mutability, and the ever-active *Nous* or Mind (Aristotle); the one transcending all our finite categories (Plotinus and the neo-Platonists); the creative and providential God of Islam;

35

Spinoza's infinite substance (*Deus sive Natura*) of which finite beings are 'modes'; and Hegel's Self-Conscious Spirit working itself out in the world. And the intellectual apprehension and contemplation and enjoyment of God, in these several senses, is held to be of the essence of 'religion'.

In each case, no doubt, the philosophical knowledge and contemplation of God is accompanied by practical or ethical effects, so that, for example, through his contemplation of God a man will be led to live virtuously and to be morally happy. But it remains true that the speculative aspect is primary, and the ethical aspect merely secondary. Spinoza expresses this order of precedence between the speculative and practical very nicely in one of his letters: 'I know (and this knowledge gives me the highest contentment and peace of mind) that all things come to pass by the power and unchangeable decree of a Being supremely perfect' (103). Here it is the vision of the supremely perfect God on whom all else depends that is central, the resulting contentment and peace of mind being seen as an incidental concomitant.

It has been said, apropos Spinoza's 'intellectual love of God' (and it could be said also of the other forms of speculative religion), that 'the love in question is more akin to the pleasure or mental satisfaction accompanying a scientist's vision of a complete explanation of Nature, rather than to love in the sense of love between persons' (104). But perhaps it would be more enlightening to see the speculative vision of God as analogous to aesthetic appreciation. Aesthetic appreciation is primarily non-discursive or contemplative, though it may have concomitant emotional and even moral repercussions; it is disinterested or impracticable or 'useless', and it is non-reciprocal in that it does not expect any response from the object contemplated; and finally, it is 'ecstatic' in that through intellection we are, as it were, led beyond intellection. It is, at all events, these aspects of philosophical knowledge—its non-discursive or contemplative character, its disinterestedness, and its ecstatic dimension – that the philosophers we have been considering wish to stress.

If then it should be objected that the identification of

religion with philosophy makes religion too abstract and coldly intellectual an affair, we ought to remember that it is philosophy in the above sense that is in view. Aesthetic appreciation, it could be argued, is not cold and abstract, even though it is a form of intellectual contemplation, and if our analogy holds any water, the same could be argued of the intellectual contemplation of God. The prejudice (deriving from the Romantic movement) that the intellect is 'cold', as against the heart and passions which are 'warm', is really no more than a prejudice, for the intellect can be warm just as the heart can be cold.

Again, aesthetic appreciation does not have any direct practical or ethical implications, but it is not therefore without human value of its own. And in the same way, it might be urged, religious contemplation may very well have its own value even though it does not have any direct practical effect.

Objections against this kind of intellectualistic religion, on the ground that it must inevitably be abstract, and of no immediate practical concern to men, do not then seem to be fatal. In other words, there is nothing bizarre, as has often been alleged, about the notion of a philosophical religion which, to use Hume's words, 'affords no inference that affects human life, or can be the source of any action or forbearance' (105).

In the same way, we may agree that this concept of philosophical religion involves a denial of the distinction between the natural and supernatural, and so renders otiose the whole notion of 'revelation' as the gratuitous disclosure by God (through prophets and 'inspired' agents) of truths inaccessible to natural reason. And in this way it would seem that philosophical religion cannot be squared with any form of religion, such as traditional Judaeo-Christianity, in which the notion of a supernatural revelation has a central role (106). But it does not follow that philosophical religion is incompatible with forms of religion other than traditional Christianity, or even with forms of 'liberal' Christianity which do not hold a strictly supernaturalist view of revelation. It seems to be quite possible to have a religion without

37

the notion of a supernatural revelation, and in this sense a 'religion within the limits of reason alone', to use Kant's famous title, is not something that is repugnant either to religion or to reason.

Very much the same reply might be made to objections against the inevitable esotericism of philosophical religion. It is, doubtless, very difficult to reconcile élitism or 'gnosticism' with any form of religion that emphasises the possibility of salvation for all men. But, once again, there seems to be no necessary reason why there cannot be a religion which would be accessible only to a choice few 'in the know'. There have, after all, been many esoteric religious sects, such as the various forms of Manicheism which made a sharp distinction between the 'pure' or the initiate and the ordinary second-class believers (107), and again there have been certain forms of Buddhism that are frankly élitist (108). The fact, then, that esotericism is at odds with religions such as Christianity, does not mean that it is at odds with religion *tout court*. Again, no matter how much importance is to be given to the requirement that religion be universally accessible, it surely cannot outweigh the requirement that it be *true*. If a religion is true and universally accessible in addition, that is all to the good; but if it is true in such a way that it is available only to the intellectual few, then, no matter how unwelcome a fact this may be to us, we cannot on that account refuse it the name of religion. The early twentieth-century Cambridge philosopher, John McTaggart, has written very aptly, and very nobly, on this very point.

No dogma – at any rate, no dogma of religion – is asserted which is not also denied by able students.

It follows that a man is not entitled to believe a dogma except in so far as he has investigated it for himself. And since the investigation of dogma is a metaphysical process, and religion must be based on dogma, it follows further that no man is justified in a religious attitude except as a result of metaphysical study. The result is sufficiently serious. For most people, as the world stands at present, have not the disposition, the education, and the leisure necessary for the study of metaphysics. And thus we are driven to the conclusion that, whether any religion is true or not, most people have no right to accept any religion as true . . . .

We are here confronted [McTaggart goes on] with one of the great tragedies of life. Many men desire passionately to know the truth as to the great problems of religion. And no man may believe any solution of these problems to be true unless he has tested it himself. Even if he tests for himself, and comes to some conclusion, his conclusion must lack that confirmation by the unanimous agreement of inquirers which plays so great a part in knowledge elsewhere.

This is sad, and would be sad even if dogma were not essential to religion. For whether dogma is essential to religion or not, it is clear that many men do desire, and will desire, to know the truth about such dogmas as the existence of God and the immortality of man . . . . It is sad, but I do not know why it should be thought strange. Is knowledge so easy to get that the highest and deepest of all knowledge is likely to be had for the asking? Or is everything good so common, that we should expect that religion – almost the best of all earthly things – should be never absent where it is desired?

McTaggart ends by citing Spinoza's famous apology for his own philosophical (and esoteric) religion: 'If the way which I have pointed out as leading to this result seems exceedingly hard, it may nevertheless be discovered . . . . But all things excellent are as difficult as they are rare' (109).

There is, finally, the question of the a-historical character of religious intellectualism. As Kierkegaard protested against Hegel, the rejection of the historical dimension of religion as irrelevant is incompatible with any religion such as Christianity which is based upon historical claims. St Paul's firm statement, 'If Christ be not risen from the dead, then all our hopes are vain' (110), is a dramatic expression of the importance of historical fact in the Christian religion. It was for this reason that Hegel's attempt to translate the

39

substance of the central Christian doctrines – the Incarnation, the Trinity, etc. – into the categories of his own philosophy, and so to show that they really represented metaphysical necessities, seemed so outrageous to Kierkegaard and his sympathisers.

However, while this is true of traditional Christianity, there are religions such as Buddhism where historical claims play very little part. Thus for a Buddhist it is not important whether Buddha ever actually lived, or whether he did what he is said to have done. What matters in Buddhism is the timeless and universal doctrine of the Buddha. From this point of view, then, a religion that is in effect a system of quasi-necessary truths, with no place for the contingent or historical dimension, is not a contradiction in terms.

These various objections against religious intellectualism are therefore all inconclusive. However, there is a more fundamental and serious complaint against this view, that stems not from the nature of the intellectualistic religion it proposes but rather from the conception of the nature and scope of philosophy that it assumes. In other words, one might say that what is wrong with this whole philosophy of religion is not so much its view of religion as its view of philosophy, for it presupposes a high metaphysical conception of philosophy which is formidably difficult to defend. In this conception philosophy is held to be capable of transcending the spatio-temporal world of our immediate experience and of providing knowledge of immaterial and timeless entities (like Plato's Forms) or some kind of Absolute substance (like Spinoza's God or Hegel's Spirit).

This was, of course, the kind of overweening metaphysics that Kant set out to destroy once and for all in the 'Critique of Pure Reason', and the whole tendency of post-Kantian philosophy – with the great exception of Hegel – has been against this kind of 'transcendent' metaphysics, in favour of a much more modest 'descriptive metaphysics' – a conception of philosophy which would hardly lend itself to playing a quasi-religious role. Even before Kant, St Thomas Aquinas in the thirteenth century had proposed a much

40

more limited view of the nature of metaphysics than that of his classical masters (Aristotle and the neo-Platonists). One could say indeed that for Aquinas, philosophy, given his conception of its nature and scope, could not plausibly be identified with religion, in the way in which Plotinus's philosophy, for example, could easily be so identified.

As we remarked before, the great strength and advantage of this view of the philosophy of religion is that it makes religion into a rational enterprise and so worthy of man at his best and most human. But this is also its weakness, for it means that religion is only as good or valid as the philosophy of which it is the issue. This point has sometimes been made in the following way: if religion is identified with philosophy then it necessarily becomes subject to the same kind of doubting and questioning to which any philosophical position is subject. But, so the objection goes, whereas assent to a philosophical position is always subject to questioning and is thus tentative and revocable, religious assent implies that we commit ourselves absolutely and irrevocably without any doubts or *arrières pensées*. In an act of religious faith I 'stake my life', whereas in an act of philosophical assent I do nothing of the kind. Thus, Professor Price has argued that if the religious believer's faith is based upon arguments, then 'his faith would have to be a kind of opinion . . . and if adverse evidence turns up, one ought to feel less confidence in one's opinion or even to reject it altogether. Now whatever religious belief may be, it is quite different from opinion. In face of adverse evidence, a man sticks to his faith, but he abandons an opinion' (111).

There is some force to this objection; but unless some kind of philosophical relativism is being assumed, so that all philosophical positions are held to be dubitable and tentative and never capable of exacting absolute and unqualified assent, it is difficult to see that religious assent differs essentially from philosophical assent. Men have, after all, staked their lives on philosophical positions just as much as on religious positions. And, from another point of view, commitment to religious faith is just as revocable and tentative in its way as a philosophical commitment. It is

41

often said that if a person truly loves then he cannot fall out of love ('Let me not to the marriage of two minds admit impediment'); and in much the same way it seems to be implied that if one makes a religious commitment or assent then one cannot envisage the possibility of going back on it. But the notion of irrevocability is no more contained in the notion of religious assent than it is contained in the notion of love. As McTaggart has put it: 'On matters of dogma we cannot dispense with proof . . . . This will leave all questions of dogma more or less problematic, and many quite unanswered. And this is doubtless unpleasant. But unpleasant things are sometimes true' (112).

However, what is true in this objection is, as we have remarked, that the intellectualistic position does depend upon a certain conception of the nature and scope of philosophy being valid. And, for strictly philosophical reasons, it is difficult to see how that conception can be made valid.

Despite the general decline of this view of philosophy and of the philosophy of religion which derives from it, there are still some echoes of it in certain contemporary philosophers of religion. Apart from the influence of Hegel in liberal theology, there are hints in the philosophy of A. N. Whitehead that point towards an identification of religion with philosophy. Thus, at the end of 'Process and Reality', Whitehead considers 'God and the world' and he makes the pregnant observation that 'God is not to be treated as an exception to all metaphysical principles, invoked to save their collapse. He is their chief exemplification' (113). Again, perhaps it is not too fanciful to see a tendency towards an intellectualist philosophy of religion in the evolutionist speculations of Teilhard de Chardin (114).

We may conclude, then, that if this whole conception of the philosophy of religion, which has had such a long and varied and important career in Western thought, is now more or less dead, it is nevertheless not altogether lying down. It may be, perhaps, that with the movement towards rapprochement among the great world religions, it will even undergo a revival of some kind, since such a rapprochement will probably involve an emphasis on the universal and

42

'necessary' elements in the world-religions and a soft-pedalling of their particular and historically contingent aspects. But, as we have said, it is not easy to see how we could now reconstruct a conception of philosophy that could adequately play a religious part or assume a religious mantle.

2 Philosophy as the Handmaid of Religion

(a) Introduction

Judaeo-Christianity is a religion, we have said, which is difficult to square with the demands of philosophical religion, since for both classical Judaism and Christianity the very concept of religion implies a God-given disclosure of truths about the divine order, as well as about the divinely ordained 'way of life' leading to salvation, inaccessible to ordinary reason. There have, of course, been many attempts within Christianity to elaborate a form of Christian intellectualism or 'gnosticism', where Christianity was made to appear as the issue of a philosophical world-view; but all these essays have involved some kind of reductionist violence being done to the Christian religion.

For the Jew or Christian of antiquity, then, wishing to give full due to the impressive tradition of the Greek philosophy of religion, while at the same time maintaining the essentially revelatory character of the Judaic Law and prophetic tradition and of the Christian Gospel, a new conception of the philosophy of religion had to be invented. Once again, the working out of this view of philosophy's relationship with religion was a long and chequered process (1). It received its first impetus from the Jewish-Hellenistic thinker, Philo of Alexandria (d. A.D. 40) at the beginning of the Christian era. Philo's ideas were taken up by the early Christian Platonists, Clement and Origen, in the second and third centuries, and were further refined by St Augustine (350–430) and by the Boëthius (470–525) of the 'Theological Tractates'. In the Middle Ages proper Peter Abelard gave the new theory more precise expression and St Anselm also contributed original elements, as did the Jewish

Aristotelian Moses Maimonides. Then finally, with St Thomas Aquinas in the thirteenth century, the theory received its definitive expression. It was also in Aquinas's formulation that the difficulties of this account of the functions of philosophy with regard to religion became apparent and pressing.

(b) Philo of Alexandria

Philo was a member of the Jewish community in Alexandria at the time of the founding of Christianity. Devoutly Jewish and equally devoutly committed to Greek philosophy, Philo attempted a synthesis which would enable him to have the best of both worlds. It is proof of the originality of his thought that his main ideas on philosophy and religion became commonplaces right through the long Judaeo-Christian tradition that culminated some 1200 years later in Maimonides and Aquinas. Clement, Origen, Augustine, Abelard, Maimonides and Aquinas all repeat in their own way the Philonic principles that govern the relations between philosophy and religion (2).

Philo, along with his Jewish Alexandrian contemporaries, saw the Greek philosophy he knew (a mélange of Stoic ethical ideas, Platonic metaphysics and elements of Aristotelian logic) as hinting obscurely at truths that were more fully and explicitly made known in the Old Testament. It was the Jewish Alexandrians in fact who, to account for this supposed similarity, invented the legend that the Greek sages must have either had contact with Moses or been able to read his writings, an idea that retained currency right up until the Middle Ages (3). At the same time Philo made a sharp distinction between the truths contained in the Law revealed by God through Moses, and the truths attained by human wisdom. And it was the twofold recognition that, first, divine wisdom (revelation) is of a higher order than human wisdom, and second, that nevertheless divine wisdom is in some way continuous and reconcilable with the human wisdom of the philosophers, that lead Philo to develop a tentative view of philosophy as the 'handmaid' of religion. In this view philosophy serves religion by explicating its meaning (for example, in discerning the true meaning of scriptural allegories), and by defending it against sceptical attacks. This latter defensive or apologetical role also involved for Philo the finding of rational proofs of the existence of God and of certain of his basic attributes. The classical Greek tradition had described the liberal arts as the 'handmaid' of philosophy and Philo used the analogy to describe philosophy's function with regard to the revealed wisdom of the Law (4).

Philo presupposes that, since both human and divine wisdom come from the same God, there can be no contradiction between the Mosaic Law and philosophy. And it is this firm *a priori* conviction of the harmony of reason and revelation that causes him to give such a large and decisive role to philosophy in the interpretation of Scripture. Thus, for Philo scriptural texts have both a literal or apparent meaning and an allegorical or underlying meaning (5). And we know that a text is *not* to be taken literally or at its face value, if it would lead one to be 'at variance with the truth', or involve one in anthropomorphic talk about God, or compel one 'to admit anything base or unworthy of the dignity' of the inspired words of God. In all such cases we must interpret the texts 'allegorically' (6). This would seem to imply that the sense of Scripture is to be determined (at least indirectly) by reference to human reason, for how are we to determine what in the meaning of Scripture is at variance with the truth, or what would involve anthropomorphic or unfitting talk about God, if not by extra-scriptural or philosophical means? As Wolfson has put it: 'By his allegorical method Philo found it possible to explain away any narration of incident in Scripture that seemed to him to run counter to reason or expectation or to have some similarity with Greek myths, without necessarily impugning the historicity of the essential basic fact of the story' (7). The true sense of Scripture then is that which does not conflict with the truths of human reason. This test does not, of course, tell us positively what the true sense of any scriptural

47

text actually *is*, but it does at least tell us negatively what the true sense is *not*, and to that extent philosophy or pure reason establishes the negative possibility of revelation.

Here we have the germ of an idea which is to be developed later in a much more sophisticated way by Moses Maimonides and Aquinas. Philo himself, however, does not bother to tease out these implications of his position. He thinks of philosophy and religion as being in harmony, even though distinct, and he sees philosophy as serving theology on the latter's terms. Theology is the mistress and philosophy the handmaid, and the mistress by definition cannot be dependent upon the handmaid.

(c) The Christian Platonists

Although the Christian Gospel is not wholly independent of Hellenic ideas (as witness the 'Logos' of St John's Gospel which is 'the principle of rationality and order in the cosmos and in mankind') (8), it is not, after all, concerned to present a philosophical system. However, a number of factors forced the second- and third-century Christian thinkers to arrange an accommodation between Christian doctrine and Greek philosophy. First, there was the need to defend the Christian Gospel against the pseudo-philosophical mishmash of Gnosticism (9), and from the charges made by anti-Christian critics, such as Origen's antagonist Celsus, that Christianity was incoherent and irrational. Thus, for instance, Celsus claimed that Christians 'do not even want to give or to receive a reason for what they believe, and they say such things as, "Do not ask questions; just believe", and "Thy faith will save thee" ' (10). The only way of meeting these objections based on philosophical argument was to use counter-philosophical arguments.

Second, although the members of the early Christian Church were for the most part simple and unlettered people, there was a sizeable and important class of Christian intellectuals who had been trained in the schools where they gained a deep respect for Greek philosophy before their conversion to Christianity (11). Even those Christian thinkers like Tertullian who rejected philosophy's theological pretensions, could not altogether get rid of this sense of respect for pure reason given them by their Greek education. Thus, Tertullian's famous piece of bravado, 'I believe because it is absurd' (*credo quia absurdum*), needs to be balanced by his remark that there is a natural or innate awareness of God in the soul (*anima naturaliter Christiana*) (12).

Justin Martyr in the second century (d. 164) is a good example of the new Christian intellectual. Educated in Greek philosophy he subsequently became a Christian, while remaining convinced of the fundamental harmony between Platonism and Christianity (13). Justin was so impressed by the similarities between Greek philosophical ideas and the Old Testament that he repeated Philo's fanciful speculation that Socrates and Plato must have read Moses's works and plagiarised them. At the same time he saw Christ as the universal *Logos* or Reason (14), in which human reason in its various modes 'participates'. 'This Logos', it has been said, 'who is the sole source of all man's knowledge of divine things, is also the one who in Christ made himself wholly known to those who will believe. It follows then that in Christ incarnate is available the full and definitive form of that truth which the philosopher can know only in a limited way' (15).

In very much the same vein, the third-century apologist, Clement of Alexandria, views Christianity as fulfilling the dim and partial intuitions of Platonism. Philosophy, Clement says, prepares for theology just as in Plato's system mathematics prepares for philosophy (16). Religion demands faith, for we cannot rationally prove the truths of revelation; but religious faith is not thereby irrational or blind since it is assent to truth on the authority of God who is the primal Truth. Reason is not, as certain Christian anti-intellectuals hold, the creation of the devil; it is rather the creation of God and is the image of God in man (17), and as such is man's highest and most noble attribute. Faith, indeed, is inferior to knowledge in one sense, and it will eventually give way, in the next life, to knowledge or 'true gnosis' (18).

These tentative ideas on the relationship between philosophy and religious faith are brought together and given a more definite shape by the great Christian thinker of the third century, Origen. Origen, apparently educated in the Alexandrian schools, shows a close knowledge of the various strands of Greek philosophy, in particular Platonism and neo-Platonism. Much of his writing consists of scriptural exposition and his views on the relationship between philosophy and religion are worked out in the margin of his biblical exegesis. The rule of faith, Origen says, is laid down by the Apostles and the Church, but neither of these two sources give the rational grounds presupposed by the articles of faith. It is then the task of the theologian to speculate about these rational grounds or presuppositions of faith. However, although reason can in this way prepare for and defend faith, there is nevertheless a clear-cut distinction between the two realms, for God cannot really be known in his nature as God save through the help of divine grace. 'Human nature', Origen says, 'is not sufficient to seek for God and find him in his pure nature unless it is helped by God who is the object of the search' (19). Plato may have gained some knowledge of God but his knowledge was imperfect, as is shown by the fact that he confused with 'the majesty of God, things which ought not to be ascribed to him' (20). Again, Origen's adversary, Celsus, himself admits that the philosophical approach to God is only for the choice few. So citing Plato's 'Timaeus', Celsus says: 'To find the Maker and Father of this universe is difficult and after finding him it is impossible to declare him to all men.' And he adds: 'You see how the way of truth is sought by seers and philosophers, and how Plato knew that it is impossible for all men to travel it' (21). But, so Origen argues, the God of faith is available to *all* mankind, and this shows the superiority of the divine *Logos* of Christianity to the human *logos* of philosophy. 'Consider', Origen says, 'whether there is not more regard for the needs of mankind when the divine word introduces the divine Logos, who was in the beginning with God, as becoming flesh, so that the Logos (of whom Plato says that after finding him it is

50

impossible to declare him to all men) might be able to reach anybody' (22).

Perfect or pure knowledge of God can, for Origen, only be got through theological reflection on Scripture, and this involves a distinction between the literal and allegorical meanings of the scriptural texts. Since the Scriptures 'were composed by the Spirit of God . . . they have not only that meaning which is obvious, but also another which is hidden from the majority of readers. For the contents of Scripture are the outward forms of certain mysteries and the images of divine things' (23). Origen uses very much the same method as Philo in order to distinguish between the apparent and real sense of Scripture. Thus he says that where a text, taken at its face value, would involve impossibilities or anything unworthy of God, it must be interpreted in a non-literal way (24). The bold manner in which Origen applies this method of interpretation in fact leaves very little of the literal sense of the Bible intact. Often in his exegesis the clear sense of Scripture is arbitrarily explained away and interpreted instead in terms of quasi-philosophical and moral truths, although for the most part it is taken as an allegory of Christ or the Church or the spiritual life of the soul (25). Like Philo, Origen does not seem to be aware of the implications of his method, nor, more generally, of the problems raised by his conception of the role of philosophy with respect to religion.

(d) *St Augustine on faith and reason*

Although in many respects St Augustine simply sums up the ideas of the Early Christian Fathers on the relationship of faith and reason, the very powerful strain of neo-Platonic religious intellectualism that was present in his thought (26) gives his position an original twist.

First of all, it is clear that for Augustine reason has a value of its own, independently of its help to faith, for by implanting reason in man God has made him superior to the rest of creation. In fact, we could not believe unless we had rational souls. And again, reason can persuade the mind to rise to faith. This function of reason is anterior to faith and is contrasted with another function of reason, posterior to the act of religious belief, seeking to understand what is believed by faith. As Augustine puts it: 'So, therefore, if it is rational that faith precedes reason in the case of certain great matters which cannot be grasped, there cannot be the least doubt that reason which persuades us on this precept – that faith precedes reason–itself precedes faith' (27). Again, St Augustine concludes one of his sermons with the following words: 'Believe in Him whom you do not see because of the things which you do see. And do not imagine that it is I alone who exhort you thus. Listen to what the Apostle says to you: "The invisible things of God, from the creation of the world are made visible by the works He has made" ' (28).

On the other hand, St Augustine also uses frequently the celebrated formula from Isaiah, 'unless you believe, you will not understand'. So, for example, he remarks at the end of another sermon: 'Understand my word in order to believe it; but believe the word of God in order to understand it' (29). Here Augustine seems to distinguish between the 'word' of human reason approaching God independently of faith, and the 'word' of God revealing truths about himself not accessible to human reason. Understood in this way the principle 'believe so that you may understand' is restricted to the sphere of revealed truth and does not apply to the 'preambles' of faith (the existence and attributes of God), nor, *a fortiori*, to other truths available to human reason.

We must not force St Augustine's ideas on this point too much, for he does not distinguish formally and explicitly between the different functions of 'understanding' in relation to faith. Again, it has been pointed out that Augustine does not make the assumption of Aquinas and the other medieval thinkers, based upon their Aristotelian theory of knowledge, that the human mind cannot of itself attain to direct knowledge of God. Augustine suggests that if the human mind is purified by the action of the will, its latent powers may be brought into exercise, thus enabling it to

52

know God. In fact, the general distinction between the order of nature and the order of supernatural grace has to be made in a different way in the neo-Platonic context of Augustine's thought than in an Aristotelian perspective, for although there is in neo-Platonism a distinction between nature and the supra-sensible world of 'divinity', the former at the same time is held to 'participate' in the latter (30). Thus, it has been said that

> while to an Aristotelian the suggestion that the vision of God is a natural possibility would imply a secret identity between the finite mind and God, Augustine's theory of knowledge proceeds in terms of the vision of luminous objects rather than an identity of knower and known; the centre of gravity is in the object rather than the mind and there is no difficulty if the object is 'above' the mind and 'greater' than the mind – indeed, that is always the case with the timeless objects of thought, which are discovered and acknowledged rather than posited by the mind. The mind, in other words, does not function according to its own *a priori* rules, but can somehow accommodate itself with elasticity to intelligibles which are somehow disclosed to the mind. (31)

Augustine uses philosophy boldly and extensively both in defending the truths of faith against anti-Christian and heretical adversaries, and also in the elaboration of Christian doctrine. For example, his work on the Trinity is permeated with Platonic and neo-Platonic themes. At the same time, as we have already suggested, Augustine is equally anxious to affirm the possibility of rational speculation about God prior to and independent of supernatural faith in God. In his own writing he devotes a great deal of attention to what were later to be called the 'preambles' of faith – the possibility of knowing God as the ground of rational certitude, the nature of the soul, freedom of the will – and it is not too much to say that he sees a 'natural theology' or a philosophical theology as an important propaedeutic to theology proper.

In the 'De Libero Arbitrio', for example, he offers a

proof of the existence of God and clearly admits the possibility of a rational justification of belief in God prior to faith. The proof is of some interest since it contains the elements of the argument that St Anselm was later to outline in the 'Proslogion' and that has become known as the ontological proof of God. In the 'De Libero Arbitrio', Augustine is engaged in a discussion with Evodius and he asks him whether he is certain that God exists? Evodius answers that he does not directly know that God exists, but rather *believes* it, and Augustine remarks:

> If then one of those fools of whom Scripture writes, 'The fool said in his heart: there is no God', should say this to you, and should refuse to believe with you what you believe, but wished to know whether your belief is true, would you have nothing to do with this man, or would you think he ought to be convinced in some way of what you hold firmly – especially if he should seriously wish to know it and not obstinately to oppose it? (32)

Evodius replies that it is sufficient to appeal to the testimony of 'all those writers who have testified that they lived with the Son of God'. Augustine agrees that, in a sense, we must believe in God in order to understand him, but he then proceeds to develop a purely rational and independent proof of the existence of God which is apparently meant to be convincing to the unbeliever. Reason, he argues, is the supreme element in man, but reason apprehends the existence of eternal and unchangeable truth. Now, if there is anything higher than eternal truth it is God; but if there is not, then truth itself is God. Augustine concludes his argument by saying to Evodius:

> If I showed there was something above our minds, you conceded you would confess it to be God, provided there was nothing still higher. Accepting your admission I said it was enough that I should show this. For if there is something more excellent, it is this which is God, but, if there is nothing more excellent, then truth itself is God. Whichever is the case, you cannot deny that God exists. (33)

54

In other words, God is defined as the 'highest' and 'most excellent' thing that we can conceive, so that to prove the existence of a highest and most excellent conceivable thing (eternal truth) is precisely to prove the existence of God. Augustine concludes that, even though we know God only in a very oblique way by rational means, we still do know him. 'God exists, and he exists truly and supremely. We not only hold this, I think, by our undoubted faith, but we also attain to it by a sure, though very tenuous, kind of knowledge' (34).

Augustine's bold use of philosophy in his explication of theological doctrines was imitated by his later follower Boëthius (470–525), at least in his 'Theological Tractates' as distinct from the 'Consolation of Philosophy'. At the same time Boëthius emphasised the limits of reason and viewed his philosophico-theological analyses as giving rational support to what was already believed by faith, not as furnishing the grounds of the doctrines of faith (35).

(e) Philosophy and theology in the Middle Ages

These various elements from Philo, the Early Fathers and St Augustine were taken up by the Christian medieval thinkers in the West and combined with the new Aristotelian ideas about the specification of the various 'sciences' (or systematic and deductively constituted bodies of knowledge) and also with the Aristotelian 'natural theology' developed in the 'Physics' and 'Metaphysics'. Peter Abelard is usually given the credit for being the first to use the word 'theologia' to mean the explication of the data of faith by philosophical means, in contradistinction to the older Aristotelian usage where 'theology' was a special branch of metaphysics (36).

In his 'Tractatus' Abelard makes the traditional distinction about the functions of reason with respect to faith. First, reason helps in the understanding of the meaning of Scripture; second, it helps refute the objections of the philosophers to faith; and third, it gives rational support to what is believed on God's authority (37). Cottiaux has described

55

these ancillary functions of reason as 'the hermeneutical use of *ratio*, the apologetical use and the constructive use' (38), and all three are in evidence in Abelard's 'Christian Theology' (39). Although Abelard's employment of philosophical analysis in his theology gave great scandal to certain of his contemporaries, such as St Bernard of Clairvaux (40), and caused some of his ideas to be condemned by the Council of Sens in 1141, his view on faith and reason is entirely traditional. The God of faith, he emphasises, 'exceeds what can come under human discussion or the powers of human intelligence; it would be a great slight to the faithful if God proclaimed himself as accessible to petty human arguments or as definable in mere mortal words' (41). Again, referring to St Gregory the Great, Abelard says that he did not disdain 'defending the Resurrection against those doubting it, by suitable examples and illustrations from nature. He did not claim that we ought never to reason with regard to faith, but only that faith has no merit in the eyes of God if it rests on human argument rather than on divine authority' (42). Again, Abelard declares that faith has no merit 'if one believes, not the God of whom the Saints speak, but human arguments' (43). It is for this reason that the supportive proofs of what we believe by authority cannot be strictly demonstrative or 'necessary', but merely arguments of 'fittingness' (*convenientia*) and of analogy (44).

These same views on the function of reason with regard to theology are continued in the thought of St Anselm of Bec (1033–1109). At times Anselm seems to tend towards a kind of theological rationalism according to which certain at least of the mysteries of faith could in principle be rationally demonstrated by 'necessary arguments' (*rationes necessariae*). But in his theological practice Anselm always makes the appropriate reservations and implicitly acknowledges the transcendence of the articles of faith with respect to philosophical reason (45).

The originality of St Anselm consists in his adumbration of rational proofs of the existence of God both in the 'Monologion' and the 'Proslogion'. Though St Anselm does not explicitly propose these proofs of the existence of God as

56

the ground of the Christian's faith in God, he does implicitly acknowledge that they could be the logical ground of belief for the non-believer – the fool or atheist of the Psalm to whom the 'Proslogion' is addressed. With St Anselm the problem of the non-believer who shares no presuppositions about God with the Christian believer (as distinct from the Jew and the Moslem) becomes real for the first time and the place of rational proofs of the existence of God becomes correspondingly more important. For Philo and Clement and Origen these proofs merely confirmed what we already knew by faith; but for Anselm (following in this St Augustine's hint) a systematic natural theology logically prior to faith is seen to be at least a possibility.

The traditional view of faith and reason is maintained by most theologians in the twelfth and early thirteenth century after Anselm without anything new being added to it. Thus St Bonaventure (1217–74) describes the method of theology as 'perscrutorius', that is to say, elaborated by rational means and argumentation (46); and he declares this method to be appropriate to theology for 'the refutation of the adversaries of the faith, the support of the faith of those weak in faith, and the satisfaction of those perfect in the faith' (47). Alexander of Hales (1186–1245) and St Albertus Magnus (1206–80) adopt the same view. Alexander, however, introduces a new note by raising the objection that theology cannot be a 'science' in the Aristotelian sense since it is based ultimately on the particular brute historical facts described by the Scriptures, and as Aristotle notes, there cannot be the universal and necessary knowledge proper to 'science' of particular contingent facts. Alexander replies, not altogether convincingly, that in Scripture particular historical facts always have a universal significance; they exemplify general and quasi-necessary truths and so in this way can be the subject of 'scientific' knowledge (48). We have here for the first time a dim awareness of a problem that is to become important later on – how to find a place for the historical dimension of Christianity within a philosophy of religion that is, as philosophy, concerned with the universal and necessary features of religion.

(f) Moses Maimonides

The line of thought about the relationship of faith and philosophy that we have been tracing is also discernible in the medieval Jewish tradition that culminates in Moses Maimonides (1135–1204). For Maimonides, as for Abelard, philosophy *vis-à-vis* the Law that is made known by God through Moses and the Prophets, has a hermeneutical function, an apologetical function and a properly theological function (49). Maimonides also acknowledges the possibility of rational demonstration of the existence of God, for the most part based upon Aristotle's proofs in the 'Physics'. Though he was, also like Abelard, accused by conservative Jewish theologians of rationalising away the content of the Law, it is clear that Maimonides recognised the transcendence of the realm of religious faith with respect to that of philosophical reason.

Maimonides's treatment of Aristotle's philosophical doctrine that the world was not created in time, affords a very good illustration of his view of philosophy's task with respect to faith. Thus, he says, the Aristotelian doctrine is prima facie opposed to the teaching of the Law which clearly states in the Book of Genesis that God created the world in time. How can we resolve this apparent conflict? First, Maimonides argues, we can demonstrate philosophically that the Aristotelian theory is not conclusive; that is, we can show that it does not prove that we must admit, under pain of contradiction, that the world is eternal. To hold that the world was created in time is therefore not impossible. As Maimonides puts it:

> All that Aristotle and his followers have set forth in the way of proof of the eternity of the world does not constitute in my opinion a cogent demonstration, but rather arguments subject to grave doubts, as you shall hear. What I myself desire to make clear is that the world's being created in time, according to the opinion of our Law – an opinion that I have already explained – is not impossible and that all those philosophic proofs from which it seems that the matter is different from what we have

58

stated, all those aruguments have a certain point through which they may be invalidated and the inference drawn from them against us shown to be incorrect. (50)

Now it is an Aristotelian doctrine that 'where no demonstration is possible, the two contrary opinions with regard to the matter in question should be posited as hypotheses' (51), and the only way of deciding between two possible and rival hypotheses is on 'probable' grounds, that is, by analysing the kinds of consequences each hypothesis leads to. 'It should be seen what doubts attach to each of them: the one to which fewer doubts attach should be believed' (52).

When we examine the consequences of Aristotle's hypothesis (that since everything comes to be of necessity, the world is eternal) we see that if it were true then, (i) things would not be able to come into being simply because God willed them to be; (ii) miraculous interventions by God would be impossible; (iii) contingent free acts would be impossible and the rewards and punishments promised by the Law with respect to human acts would have no meaning; (iv) consequently the teachings of the Law (about God's creative power, miracles, etc.) would all have to be interpreted allegorically. As Maimonides says:

> The belief in eternity the way Aristotle sees it – that is, the belief according to which the world exists in virtue of necessity, that no nature changes at all, and that the customary course of events cannot be modified with regard to anything – destroys the Law in its principle, necessarily gives the lie to every miracle, and reduces to inanity all the hopes and threats that the Law has held out, unless – by God! – one interprets the miracles figuratively also, as was done by the Islamic allegorisers; this, however, would result in some sort of crazy imaginings. (53)

On the other hand, if we accept the hypothesis of the creation of the world in time, these various consequences are evaded and the possibility of the Law is established:

> Know that with a belief in the creation of the world in

59

time, all the miracles become possible and the Law becomes possible, and all questions that may be asked on this subject, vanish. Thus it might be said: Why did God give prophetic revelation to this one and not to that? Why did God give this Law to this particular nation, and why did he not legislate to the others? Why did he legislate at this particular time, and why did he not legislate before it or after? Why did he impose these commandments and these prohibitions? Why did he privilege the prophet with the miracles mentioned in relation to him and not with some others? What was God's aim in giving this Law? Why did he not, if such was his purpose, put the accomplishment of the commandments and the non-transgression of the prohibitions into our nature? If this were said, the answer to all these questions would be that it would be said: He wanted it this way; or his wisdom required it this way. And just as he brought the world into existence, having the form it has, when he wanted to, without our knowing his will with regard to this or in what respect there was wisdom in his particularising the forms of the world and the time of its creation – in the same way we do not know his will or the exigency of his wisdom that caused all the matters, about which questions have been posed above, to be particularised. If, however [Maimonides continues], someone says that the world is as it is in virtue of necessity, it would be a necessary obligation to ask all those questions; and there would be no way out of them except through a recourse to unseemly answers in which there would be combined the giving the lie to, and the annulment of, all the external meanings of the Law with regard to which no intelligent man has any doubt that they are to be taken in their external meanings. It is then because of this that this opinion is shunned and that the lives of virtuous men have been and will be spent in investigating this question. For if creation in time were demonstrated – if only as Plato understands creation – all the overhasty claims made to us on this point by the philosophers would become void. In the same way, if the philosophers would succeed in demonstrating eternity as

Aristotle understands it, the Law as a whole would become void, and a shift to other opinions would take place. I have thus explained to you that everything is bound up with this problem. Know this. (54)

It is then for this kind of reason that we can say, 'The Law has given us knowledge of a matter the grasp of which is not within our power' (55).

Maimonides thus ingeniously avoids one of the main difficulties already alluded to, namely, that if reason formally demonstrates the possibility of what we hold by faith, then the articles of faith will by that very fact be shown to be necessarily true (since the articles of faith are in themselves necessarily true, though they are not known in this way *by us*). Here Maimonides makes it clear that philosophy is restricted to showing that what the Law (or revelation) teaches is *not-impossible*. Philosophy is not concerned to establish the positive possibility of the truths of faith (as for example we can establish the possibility of a golden mountain) but rather their negative possibility or non-impossibility. Whether it is reasonable to hold that the negative possibility is actually realised or not in a particular use has to be shown probabilistically or by 'reasons of fittingness'.

(g) Summary

So far we have been tracing the emergence of a new view of the philosophy of religion, a view in which philosophy is seen as the servant or handmaid of religious faith. Philosophy and religion are both concerned with God and the divine, but their 'formal objects' (the aspect under which they consider God) are irreducibly distinct. In other words, the God disclosed by pure reason and the God disclosed by revelation are formally different. Similarly their modes of knowledge and apprehension are distinct, for philosophy relies upon demonstration and rational evidence, while religion relies upon faith, that is to say belief on the authority of God. Further, whereas the God of philosophical reason is accessible only to a few sages, the God of religious faith is accessible to all men.

However, if philosophy and religion, reason and faith, are distinct, they are not wholly discontinuous. For (i) philosophical reason is just as much a part of God's creation as religious faith; in fact it is by virtue of his reason that man is the 'image of God'; (ii) since all truth, both philosophical and revealed, comes from God, and since God cannot contradict himself, philosophical and revealed truth likewise cannot be contradictory. The two orders of truth must be, at least negatively, harmonisable with each other, and faith and reason must complement each other; (iii) faith uses reason to express itself meaningfully and to discern the real, as opposed to the literal or apparent, meaning of Scripture; (iv) faith also uses reason for apologetical or defensive purposes by showing that apparent philosophical objections to the truths of faith are not necessarily conclusive; (v) faith also uses reason to justify its presuppositions; (vi) faith uses reason to explicate the virtualities of the data of faith and to systematise them; (vii) philosophical reason is able to prove the existence of God and certain of his fundamental attributes.

It will be seen from this that the various services of philosophy with regard to faith are reducible to two main functions: the first is *within* the realm of faith, philosophy having here a hermeneutical and systematising function; the second is external to the realm of faith, philosophy in this case playing a defensive and justificatory role with regard to the presuppositions of faith. Within this second function, we have to distinguish between the role of philosophy in negatively defending the articles of faith proper by showing that apparently demonstrative philosophical arguments against them are not in fact conclusive (and thereby at the same time showing the negative possibility or non-impossibility of the truths of faith in question); and on the other hand, the role of reason in proving the existence of God. When we prove the existence of God, we are not merely showing that the concept of God is not self-contradictory or incoherent (as we do, for example, with regard to the revealed truths of faith); rather we are showing positively that the concept is both meaningful and instantiated.

This tradition of philosophico-theological thought represents a very remarkable attempt to reconcile the demands of Greek philosophy with those of the Judaeo-Christian religion without doing violence to either. The requirements of pure reason are met, while at the same time, it is claimed, the revelatory and supernatural and universalist character of the Christian religion is also given its full due.

However, the problems attending this whole conception of the philosophy of religion are hardly noticed by the thinkers we have considered. What is to happen, for example, when there is a prima facie conflict between a philosophical truth and a truth of religious revelation? Which is to be the *final* arbiter – philosophy or faith? The principle of the harmony of all truth (both philosophical and revealed) – itself, by the way, a philosophical principle – espoused by all the thinkers in this tradition, depends on the supposition that we know clearly in each case what the philosophical truth is and what, on the other hand, revelation declares to be the truth. But we do not know the latter without analysis and interpretation, for as both Philo and Origen acknowledge, we can only determine the *real* sense of any revelation-statement by first seeing whether or not it conflicts with truths of reason. Thus with respect to Maimonides's example of the apparent conflict between the Aristotelian thesis of the eternity of the world and the Old Testament's thesis of the creation of the world in time, we can either argue (as Maimonides does) that it can be shown on philosophical grounds that Aristotle's doctrine is not conclusive; or we can remove the apparent contradiction between Aristotle and Moses by holding to Aristotle's philosophical doctrine and interpreting the relevant Old Testament texts in a non-literal or allegorical manner. But, once again, we will only be led to do this if we first recognise that the literal interpretation of the texts would result in philosophically untenable conclusions. If philosophy and faith do not conflict, it is because philosophy so interprets the truths of faith that they cannot conflict.

M. Gilson, following Aquinas, remarks that 'to any believer who is at the same time a true philosopher, the slightest opposition between his faith and his reason is a sure sign that something is the matter with his philosophy. For indeed faith is not a principle of philosophical knowledge, but it is a safe guide to rational truth and an infallible warning against philosophical error' (56). But, as we have said, revelation does not bear its meaning upon its face and the determination of what is and is not of faith inevitably involves indirect recourse to reason.

Again, if philosophy justifies the presuppositions of faith, either negatively as with the defence of the mysteries of faith proper, or positively as with the proof of the existence of God and his basic attributes, then this would seem to make faith logically dependent upon reason, in the sense that the meaning of the truths of faith depends, at least indirectly, upon the meaning of the truths of pure reason. To put the matter crudely, if we can give no meaning to the concept of God at the level of philosophical reason, then equally the concept of God at the level of faith must also be meaningless. God cannot give us the grace to believe in something that is unbelievable.

Philo, Origen, Augustine, Abelard, Anselm and Maimonides all speak of philosophy being the handmaid of theology humbly serving the latter on its own terms. But philosophy finds it hard to keep to its purely ancillary role and tends to usurp the role of mistress of the house. We shall see this process taking place in the thought of St Thomas Aquinas in the thirteenth century, who sums up and crystallises this whole tradition we have been considering.

(h) St Thomas Aquinas

The very first article of Aquinas's 'Summa Theologiae' is concerned with the question, 'Whether, besides philosophy, any further doctrine is necessary?' The fact that Aquinas could pose this question to himself is significant enough, for it indicates that he acknowledged the plausibility of the philosophical religion that had been proposed by his masters,

Aristotle and the neo-Platonists. The contemporary movement of 'Latin Averroism', which translated Ibn Rushd's ideas on the identity of philosophy and religion into the Christian West, had indeed virtually denied that any other doctrine save philosophy was necessary. So, in 1277, just after Aquinas's death, Bishop Étienne Tempier of Paris condemned a number of propositions such as 'there is no higher life than that of the philosophers' and 'there is no wisdom in the world except that of the philosophers' (57).

The two objections Aquinas urges against his own position are both taken from this latter tradition of thought. First, he makes his objector say, we should not seek knowledge that goes 'beyond reason', and since knowledge that does not go beyond reason is coterminous with philosophy, 'any other knowledge is superfluous'. Second, philosophy treats of 'everything that is', including the kind of being that God is. The knowledge of God, 'theology' as Aristotle calls it, is therefore a 'part of philosophy', so that, once again, 'there is no need of further knowledge' (58).

Aquinas, however, rejects this position, for religious doctrine, as expressed in the Scriptures, is 'inspired by God' and thus cannot be part of philosophy which is 'the work of human reason'. There are, he goes on, truths about God which can be discovered by human reason or philosophy, and there are other truths about God which 'surpass the grasp of his reason' and which therefore need to be made known to men by God revealing them. This latter knowledge of God, or 'theology' in the Christian sense of the word, 'differs in kind from that theology which is part of philosophy' in the Aristotelian sense, both with respect to the truths about God which it knows and to the mode of its knowledge. God's revelation discloses truths of a different order from the truths disclosed by pure reason, and again, whereas we know the former by faith – assenting to them because of the authority and trustworthiness of the one (God) who reveals them, and not because we see them to be evidently or demonstrably true – we know the latter by virtue of their intrinsic rational evidence (59).

This clear-cut discussion between religion (dependent on

God's revelation and man's faith in that revelation) and philosophy (dependent upon pure reason and rational evidence) is blurred by Aquinas's further contention that certain philosophical truths about God (for example, that God is one and non-material) (60) can also be made known by revelation and believed by faith. This is because religious salvation depends upon the knowledge of all the basic truths about God, and since philosophical truths about God can be known only by philosophical experts and are also subject to the fallibilities of human reason, it is practically necessary that these truths should be made known to the majority of men by revelation, otherwise 'the truth about God which human reason could discover, would be only known by a few, and that after a long time, and with the admixture of many errors'. Presupposed to Aquinas's argument here is the idea that religious salvation must be accessible to all men, with the consequence that knowledge of the essential truths about God on which salvation depends, must also be universally accessible (61).

It remains true, however, that if I know a truth about God by reason then I do not, *ipso facto*, know it by faith since the motive of my assent in both cases is quite different. 'Rational knowledge and faith cannot be in the same subject and about the same object', although one person may believe by faith what another knows rationally (62). It remains true also that there is a sharp distinction between those truths about God that are *in themselves* rationally *knowable* and those that are merely religiously *credible*.

Philosophy (in so far as it is concerned with God) and theology proper both have God as their 'material object', but they consider God under different 'formal objects' (63). Supernatural theology, or 'sacred doctrine', 'essentially treats of God viewed as the highest cause – not only in so far as he can be known through creatures in the same way the philosopher knows him ... but also in so far as he is known to himself alone and revealed to others' (64). Since it has its own formal object and its own 'principles' (the data of faith) from which 'conclusions' may be deduced, it may therefore be considered in its own right as a systematic body of knowledge or a 'science' in the Aristotelian sense (65).

It is of great importance to note here that Aquinas uses the notion of 'faith' in a technical and exact way that goes far beyond its common-sense connotation of believing on the authority of God. First, for Aquinas faith is primarily a matter of *assent* to truths about God, and for him it is not, as it is for many contemporary theologians, a practical attitude of commitment, or trust, or 'belief in'. However, the assent of faith is not motivated by the evidence of the truths to which it assents, as my assent to the truth 'two plus two equals four' is so motivated by its evidence. No doubt the truths of faith are evident in themselves (God, so to speak, would see *why* they were true and had to be assented to, and we will see and be compelled by their evidence later in the next life when we enjoy the vision of God), but we cannot now in this life appreciate that evidence and see why they are true. Instead we assent to them because they are revealed by God who is the Primal Truth. 'An act of faith', Aquinas says, 'is to believe God since . . . the formal object of faith is the Primal Truth, to which man gives his adherence, so as to assent for its sake to whatever he believes' (66). And this belief in God as the author of revelation is aided by a special grace from God; 'since man, by assenting to matters of faith, is raised above his nature, this must needs be supplied to him from some supernatural source moving him inwardly, and this is God' (67).

It will be seen from this that Aquinas's account of faith is based upon his philosophical analysis of the intellectual act of assent. The intellect is motivated to assent to the truth of a proposition because of the *evidence* of the proposition. The evidence does not strictly *cause* one to assent, since for Aquinas assenting, like all mental acts, is an intentional act; but equally I do not decide or will to assent, for assenting is not a voluntary act. For Aquinas, following Aristotle's deductive model, propositions are either self-evident (*per se nota*) or they derive their evidence from propositions which are self-evident.

In the case of religious faith, the intellect assents to certain propositions as true, but the assent is not motivated by the evidence of the propositions, since this evidence is not available to us – the truths in question belonging to the supra-rational realm of revelation. The assent of faith needs then some other kind of extra-intellectual motivation and this, according to Aquinas, is supplied by the will. Here, in contrast with ordinary assent, I do have to *decide* or *will* to assent. And I decide or will to assent on the authority of someone whom I take as the guarantor of the truth of the propositions I assent to, and whose guarantee in this way supplies for the evidence that is lacking to me.

There are then two distinct moments in faith: first, my assent to God as the guarantor of the truth of the propositions of revelation; and second, my willed assent to the truth of revelation which is motivated by this first assent to God as guarantor of the truth of revelation. The first moment of assent obviously cannot be an assent based upon evidence, for the only evidence I have here is that God, the author of revelation, is negatively possible, and this is insufficient to motivate my assent to an actual God of revelation actually revealing truths (e.g. the Judaeo-Christian God). Again, it cannot itself be a willed assent motivated by assent to the authority of God. It must therefore be a willed assent motivated by a special grace from God.

For Aquinas the grace of faith does not give us any special cognitive 'insight' into the objects of faith, as though by faith we were empowered to know, directly or intuitively, things that we could not know by ordinary reason. Rather, the grace of faith acts upon the will in that it enables me to will to believe propositions (since revealed by God) which I do not see to be true (68), and which therefore do not of themselves command my assent. Aquinas takes St Paul's remarks about faith being a dark and enigmatic way of knowing very seriously (69) and he makes it clear that religious faith is not in any way what Rudolf Otto calls 'a non-rational knowledge of God', or bound up with 'religious experience'. God can, no doubt, miraculously intervene in the normal processes of human knowledge to give certain men special 'prophetic visions', but these miraculous and extraordinary interventions are not to be confused with the

grace of faith. Since the grace of faith perfects and comple-
ments man's rational nature and does not involve a suspension of the ordinary operations of that nature (70), it is
clearly distinct from any miraculously endowed religious
experiences.

It will also be clear from this account of the act of faith
that, although for Aquinas religious faith is primarily a
matter of intellectual assent, and only secondarily a practical
attitude involving the affective side of man, the assent of
faith is at the same time motivated by the will. It is therefore,
in this respect, very different from ordinary evidential assent.
The grace of faith orients me practically to assent to God as
the author of revelation, and so to accept him as guarantor
of the truth of revelation. For Aquinas, then, the modern
debate over whether faith is 'belief that' or 'belief in' is
misconceived, for the act of faith can be seen both as 'belief
that' (propositional assent) and as 'belief in' (practical
attitude or disposition) and we cannot have the one without
the other.

We may also remark the fundamental continuity, for
Aquinas, between the God of philosophy and the God of
revelation and faith. Certainly, as we have seen, revelation
and philosophy are essentially distinct and so are faith and
reason, but they are not thereby discontinuous, for just as
grace perfects nature and does not contradict it, so also the
truths of revelation complement and perfect the truths of
philosophy about God. In a certain sense even, grace cannot
function without nature as its basis nor can faith function
without reason as its basis: 'faith presupposes natural reason,
even as grace presupposes nature . . . and perfection supposes
something that can be perfected' (71).

The great French Catholic thinker, Maurice Blondel, has
complained that Aquinas's account of the relationship
between natural reason and supernatural faith simply
juxtaposes the one against the other and does not show how
they really complement each other. For the Thomist tradition, he says,

the natural and supernatural orders were placed one
above the other, but in touch, in an ascending hierarchy.

There were three zones, as it were, on different levels: on the lowest, reason was in sole charge; on the highest, faith alone revealed to us the mystery of divine life and that of our summons to the feast of God; between the two was a meeting ground where reason discovered in an incomplete way the more important of natural truths, and these were confirmed and later explained by faith. By thus bearing upon certain common *objects*, these two currents, flowing from different sources, mingled their waters without losing their identities. But there was hardly any thought of examining in a critical spirit what might be called the subjective possibility or the formal compatibility of these two orders. (72)

However, as we have said, Aquinas himself sees that the order of nature and the order of the supernatural cannot simply be juxtaposed, for he insists that the supernatural 'perfects' and 'elevates' the natural, so that consequently the natural must be in itself perfectible or elevatable by supernatural grace in a quasi-dispositional way and not just in a merely passive way. What is true in Blondel's objection is that Aquinas did not work out fully the implications of what are, in themselves, very bold ideas (73).

It is at all events this general view of the complementarity of grace and nature that lies behind Aquinas's account of the role of philosophy *vis-à-vis* religious faith. First, philosophy helps faith to express and systematise its truths; second, philosophy justifies the preambles or presuppositions of faith; and third, philosophy defends the truths of faith from sceptical objections. With regard to the first, Aquinas emphasises that philosophy's role is a purely ancillary one and that religious faith does not really depend upon philosophy, at least in this respect. Theology, he says,

can in a sense depend upon the philosophical sciences, not as though it stood in need of them, but only in order to make its teaching clearer . . . . Therefore it does not depend upon other sciences as upon the higher, but makes use of them as of the lesser, and as handmaidens (*ancillae*). That it thus makes use of them is not due to its own defect or insufficiency, but to the defect of our intelligence,

70

which is more easily led by what is known through natural reason . . . . to that which is above reason' (74).

Regarding the external role of philosophy with respect to faith, Aquinas' position is much less clear-cut. At times he appears to suggest that both the justification of the pre-ambles of faith and the defence of the articles of faith are also merely confirmatory of faith and do not involve any kind of dependence of faith upon reason. But at other times he clearly thinks that faith is, at least in these respects, dependent upon reason. Thus, on the one hand, he holds that the merit of faith is diminished if it depends in any way upon rational argument (75); while on the other hand he acknowledges that 'faith presupposes natural knowledge'. So in his discussion of the rational proofs of the existence of God (76), Aquinas proposes the following objection to himself: 'It seems that the existence of God cannot be demonstrated. For it is an article of faith that God exists. But what is of faith cannot be demonstrated, because demonstrations produce scientific (i.e. deductive) knowledge, whereas faith is of the unseen (Heb. 11 : 1). Therefore it cannot be demonstrated that God exists.' Aquinas replies to this as follows: 'The existence of God and other like truths about God, which can be known by natural reason, are not articles of faith, but are preambles to the articles: for faith presupposes natural reason, even as grace presupposes nature, and perfection supposes something that can be perfected.' This seems clearly to make faith dependent upon philosophy in the sense that the concept of God, as used in a specifically religious realm of discourse, only has meaning if we can first show that it is *philosophically* meaningful.

We must distinguish here between the logical dependence of faith on reason, as just described, and the psychological dependence of faith upon reason. It may very well be the case, as a matter of psychological fact, that a man may come to understand the concept God in a context of religious faith, without explicitly adverting to its philosophical presuppositions. But this does not imply that the religious concept of 'God' is not logically dependent upon the philosophical concept of God, in the sense that if no meaning can be given to the latter than no meaning can be given to the former (77).

Much the same considerations apply, *mutatis mutandis*, to the role of philosophy in defending the articles of faith against sceptical attacks, since although Aquinas does not discuss the matter in any detail, the meaning of the articles of faith for him indirectly depends upon the philosophical demonstration of their non-impossibility. Aquinas adopts here the position of Maimonides and argues that, while we cannot demonstrate the truth of the articles of faith (as distinct from the preambles of faith), we can at least show that supposed arguments against them, purporting to prove that they are incoherent or self-contradictory, are themselves inconclusive. As he puts it: 'Since faith rests upon infallible truth, and since the contrary of a truth can never be demonstrated, it is clear that the arguments brought against faith cannot be demonstrated, but are difficulties that can be solved' (78).

Aquinas's position with regard to revelation and philosophy, faith and reason, is in its essentials the same as that we have traced from Philo through the early Christian thinkers and Augustine, to Abelard and Maimonides – though with Aquinas the position is systematised and made more rigorous by his use of the Aristotelian theory of knowledge and his reference to Aristotle's natural theology. With Aquinas's formulation also the difficulties of this position become much more obvious, for Aquinas sees, at least in part, that if philosophy is a handmaid to faith it is a logically indispensable handmaid. Aquinas dimly discerns the price that has to be paid for the reconciliation of philosophy and faith, but he is hesitant in drawing out the full consequences that are implicit in his own position. Let us then look at some of those consequences, and the difficulties that they raise.

We remarked before that, for Aquinas, there are three main functions of philosophical reason with regard to religious faith – one internal to faith, expressing and elaborating the data of faith, and the other two external to faith, justifying the preambles of faith and defending the articles of faith.

72

With regard to the first, Aquinas appears at times to think that we can in some way understand the truths of faith as contained in the Scriptures independently of natural reason, so that reason only comes in later and secondarily when we want to explicate those truths and to see their relations with one another. But, on Aquinas's own premisses, it is difficult to see how this can be so, for, as we have seen, he does not hold that faith is a special kind of knowledge with its own peculiar 'logic'. God's revelation to man must be expressed in ordinary human concepts and propositions that retain their own ordinary use and obey the ordinary logical laws. Unless we can understand at least the meaning of the propositions that we believe by faith, then we cannot believe them, for otherwise we could not say *what* we were believing. It may well be that we do not *fully* or *completely* understand what we believe (Aquinas himself draws a distinction between understanding and 'comprehending') (79), but we must understand at least that what we believe is not gibberish or conceptually incoherent. Again, no doubt the content of revelation inevitably transcends the capacity of any human conceptual system, but it has to be expressed in ordinary concepts, for in what other way could it be expressed? As a recent English writer has put it:

Christian doctrines are said to be *mysteries*. It is necessary to explain in what sense they are such in a way that leaves enough, but not too much room for faith . . . . If faith is a kind of belief, and a virtue because it is exercised in circumstances where knowledge is impossible for us, it seems that on the one hand it is a minimum condition that it should be possible to understand what is believed, and on the other a maximum condition that it should be impossible for us to understand *how* it is true. To take a parallel example from physics, we can attach a sense to, and hence know the truth-conditions of, saying that light is particles, and that light is waves; but we do not (as yet) understand how anything can be both particle and wave. It is in the sense given by this latter condition that Christian doctrines are mysteries, for were it impossible for us to understand what it is we believe, it is difficult to see how we could be said to believe it. To be sure, there are degrees of understanding, and it is enough here to be able to show that the propositions in which we express our beliefs can be given a sense, and that they are not self-contradictory. If we cannot do either of these things, we are as yet unable to explain to non-Christians what Christian doctrine consists in, and they are accordingly not in a position to assess its relevance (80).

In the sense, then, that the propositions expressing our beliefs have to be given a meaning, faith depends on reason. As we saw before, very much the same point comes up apropos Philo's and Origen's theory of the allegorical meaning of Scripture, for we only know that Scripture is to be interpreted allegorically when we see that a literal interpretation would lead to absurdity at the level of philosophy and natural reason.

Similar remarks may be made about the third or defensive function of philosophy with respect to religious faith. Even though philosophy is here restricted to showing that objections against the truths of faith are not cogent, and so to showing that the truths themselves are negatively possible or non-impossible, this is still to admit that the conditions of meaning of the truths of faith are established by philosophy. It is also to admit that, if a given article of faith is to be meaningful, some philosophical positions must implicitly be rejected or denied. For example, if the notion of the supernatural is to have any meaning, then the philosophical position of radical empiricism must be rejected as false, since this latter denies the very possibility of any trans-empirical order of reality. Again, if the notion of personal immortality is meaningful, then the philosophical position of materialism must be denied, since this latter also denies the possibility of any real distinction between the mind (and personality) and the body. Aquinas himself holds, for instance, that belief in the Trinity involves the denial of the philosophical doctrine of nominalism (81); that the doctrine of the Eucharist involves the denial of any

74

quasi-Humean account of things as simply the sum of their accidental properties (so that the notion of 'substance' as distinct from 'accidents' has no meaning); and that the doctrine of the Incarnation involves the rejection of any philosophical position that refuses to distinguish between 'person' and 'nature'. Religious belief or faith therefore involves one willy-nilly in philosophy, at least in this indirect and negative way. It does not, of course, involve one in having positively to espouse a particular philosophical position, but it does require that one deny certain positions as false and that one be able to show their falsity by philosophical argument.

Thus, to believe in the meaningfulness and truth of an article of faith is *ipso facto* to believe, on the authority of God, that no particular argument will ever actually succeed in showing conclusively that the article of faith is necessarily self-contradictory. Or put in another way, to believe in an article of faith is to hold implicitly that we will always be able to counter successfully, *on the philosophical level*, any such arguments by showing that they are not philosophically cogent. Is this position intelligible? Can we have a *general* belief that we will always be able to show *ad hoc* that any *particular* argument against the meaningfulness of an article of faith will not be cogent? Perhaps it might be possible to strike an analogy here with Wittgenstein's conception of philosophy, for Wittgenstein had a general philosophical belief that it is possible to show *ad hoc* that all philosophical problems are as a matter of fact 'dissolvable' and so not substantive problems. Again, another Wittgensteinian, Professor Norman Malcolm, has this to say:

> With respect to any particular reasoning that is offered for holding that the concept of seeing a material thing, for example, is self-contradictory, one may try to show the invalidity of the reasoning and thus free the concept from the charge of being self-contradictory *on that ground*. But I do not understand what it would be to demonstrate *in general* and not in respect to any particular reasoning, that the concept is not self-contradictory. (82)

75

This logical dependence of faith upon reason is seen at its most flagrant in Aquinas's philosophical proofs of the existence of God and of certain of his basic attributes – the 'preambles' of faith as he calls them. Thus the God that emerges from Aquinas's 'Five Ways' (83) is boldly equated by him with the Yahweh of Exodus. Aquinas blandly takes Yahweh's description of himself as 'I am who I am' (84) as equivalent to his own Aristotelian philosophical definition of God as one whose essence and existence are identical (85). Again, the obvious intent of the long and complex philosophical discussion of the attributes of God in the first twenty-six questions of the 'Summa Theologiae' is to provide a rational justification of the God of revelation discussed in the various parts of the rest of the 'Summa'. And Aquinas assumes without question that the God of the Five Ways and of the beginning of the Prima Pars of the 'Summa' coincides perfectly with the God of Judaeo-Christian revelation.

We might ask, however, what right we have to assume that the God of natural reason and the God of Christian faith do so nicely coincide? There are, after all, many profound differences between the Old Testament conception of Yahweh and Aquinas's Aristotelian God. It has, for instance, been remarked that in the prophetic literature in the Old Testament 'the character of Yahweh is more and more intimately revealed, not as the lord of nature, but as the lord of human life, who imposes moral obligations' (86). Thus, instead of seeing God in a cosmological perspective, as Aquinas does, the Old Testament sees him primarily as the ground of the moral life of man (87).

The Old Testament view of God is, in fact, philosophically speaking, a very loose and imprecise one, and it contrasts in this respect with the clear and distinct and highly technical conception of God that Aquinas (relying upon Aristotle's ideas on contingency and necessity and potentiality and actuality) develops (88). Again, it has often been noted that the whole perspective of the Old Testament is an historical one, so that 'the God of the Bible is the God of a people's historical experience' (89). Of course, truths of universal import emerge through the historical record of

Yahweh's dealings with Israel, but the whole atmosphere of the Bible is still predominantly historical, whereas of course Aquinas's approach to God is severely philosophical. Like his Greek mentors, Aquinas has very little sense of history, for it is the universal and necessary and eternal that is of main interest to him and not the particular and contingent facts that constitute 'historia'.

Much the same could be said of the discrepancy between the God of the New Testament on the one hand, and the God of the 'Five Ways' and the Prima Pars of the 'Summa Theologiae' on the other. As Rahner has put it: 'The essential point of view of the New Testament is not that of metaphysical contemplation of the elements that necessarily belong to the concept of God – elements that risk remaining impersonal and abstract. The New Testament is mainly interested in a personal God and in his free and concrete action' (90).

It may well be that Aquinas's philosophical conception of God is reconcilable with the biblical view of God in that it can be shown that the latter presupposes the former; but this in turn would involve subjecting the God of the Bible to philosophical analysis and showing that, as it stands, the biblical concept of God is incomplete. Aquinas himself simply assumes without question that the two concepts of God are complementary because he has already implicitly interpreted the God of revelation in philosophical categories. Philosophy and faith cannot conflict over their respective concepts of God because philosophy has already pre-arranged their harmony.

Aquinas's basic position on faith and reason was given a special and favoured place in the theological teaching of the Roman Catholic Church after the Council of Trent in the sixteenth century, and, at least until the Second Vatican Council, it represented the typical (if by no means the only or exclusive) Roman Catholic view. Thus, in the so-called Thomist tradition that runs through Cajetan in the sixteenth century, and John of St Thomas in the seventeenth century, to twentieth-century Catholic philosophers such as Garrigou-Lagrange, Gilson and Maritain, the essentials of Aquinas's theory on the relations between philosophy and religious revelation are maintained (91). There is also an interesting Thomistic stream within Anglicanism that runs from the great Anglican divines of the seventeenth century to contemporary thinkers such as E. L. Mascall and A. Farrer (92) who also adopt, with modifications, Aquinas's philosophy of religion.

(i) Butler's 'Analogy of Religion'

Bishop Joseph Butler's (1692–1752) celebrated work, 'The Analogy of Religion Natural and Revealed to the Constitution and Course of Nature' (93), is in its essentials very akin to the position already described here, although Butler's thesis is presented in terms of a theory of probability and of probable belief and reasoning, and at first sight seems to claim more than that of Aquinas. It has had so much fame and influence in English philosophical theology that, for the sake of piety, something must be said of it here.

'The Analogy of Religion' is directed mainly against the Deist who accepts on rational grounds the existence of God as 'the author of Nature', but who rejects revealed religion, in particular Christian revelation, as being irrational and improbable. Butler clearly recognises that it is possible to prove the existence of God (for example, by an argument from design (94)), but in 'The Analogy of Religion' he takes such a proof for granted. His aim is rather to show, first, that Christian revelation does not involve anything contrary to reason; and second, that the statements of revelation are in fact more probably true than not. We cannot show that the statements of revelation are demonstrably or necessarily true, but we can show that they are not impossible and even, by analogy with the truths about the natural order discoverable by pure reason, probable. Like Aquinas, Butler thus safeguards the autonomy of revelation which, he says, 'contains an account of a dispensation of things not at all discoverable by reason' (95); while at the same time insisting that the truths of reason and those of

78

revelation are complementary and not wholly discontinuous (96).

Probable truths, for example, that water will probably freeze in England in January next, are based upon knowledge of similar happenings in the past. I have seen water freeze many times in England in January before, so therefore I conclude that it will probably freeze again next January. Butler calls this reasoning by 'analogy', but it is really inductive reasoning for it is based upon similarity in the ordinary sense and not upon analogous similarity. I do not argue that the water will probably freeze next January 'by analogy' with what I have observed about the English climate in the past, but simply on the basis of what I have observed to happen in the past, together with the supposition that future climatic conditions will probably be *similar* in the relevant respects to those of the past.

Butler now considers the order of truths discoverable by reason and the order of truths, or purported truths, found in Christian revelation, and he argues that, although they are of course not similar in the ordinary sense, we can nevertheless show that there are analogous similarities between the two orders – for example, between revelation's account of God punishing the wicked and rewarding the good, and natural reason's account of the connection between virtue and happiness and that between vice and unhappiness. And second, he claims that, given that the order of natural truth is directed by God, this analogy shows that there is a strong probability that the order of revelation equally has God as its author.

Butler also argues that the difficulties about the purported truths of revelation are paralleled by analogously similar difficulties in the order of truths of reason, so that if we can show the latter to be inconclusive, there is a strong probability that the former difficulties are also inconclusive. 'Those objections being supposed and shown not to be conclusive, the things objected against, considered as matters of fact, are further shown to be creditable, from their conformity to the constitution of nature' (97).

The notion of analogous similarity between the truths of

revelation and the truths of reason is nowhere made very clear by Butler. At times he seems to understand by it roughly what Aquinas means by the relationship between faith and the 'presuppositions of faith'. That is to say, any truth of revelation presupposes (albeit indirectly or negatively) a corresponding truth of reason which is, so to speak, its rational or philosophical analogue. But, for the most part, Butler seems to take the notion of analogy in its ordinary sense as meaning a particular kind of similarity between two different orders or kinds of things; for example, the similarity between the operations of seeing and understanding may be said to be analogous, or again, mental and physical health might be said to be analogous. And he assumes that we can extend the notion of analogous similarity from its proper application, as between different kinds of natural things, to an application as between the order of natural things taken as a whole and the supernatural or supra-rational order of revelation. We can, as it were, compare the two orders and remark the similarities between them, and on the basis of these similarities show the probability of the latter, given the truth of the former. However, it is difficult to see exactly how we can infer on the basis of this analogous similarity between the two orders. If they are *really* similar, or similar in an unqualified sense, then we will be able to argue inductively or probabilistically (as in Butler's example the freezing of the water in January) from the natural to the revealed order, but then of course there will be no real distinction of kind between the two orders. On the other hand, if we hold that a truth in the natural order is not really similar to a truth in the order of revelation but only *analogously* similar, how can we argue inductively or probabilistically from the former to the latter? To use one of Butler's examples, why should the natural truth (assuming that it is a truth) that virtue is generally attended by happiness and vice by unhappiness afford any *ground* for arguing that the account of Christian revelation that God rewards the good and punishes the wicked is not just possibly true but *probably* true?

Certainly the revelation account presupposes the rational
80

truth that there is some connection between virtue and reward and vice and punishability, in the sense that if the latter is true then the former is thereby shown to be negatively possible. But it is difficult to go any further than this.

As Aquinas saw very acutely, there are severe difficulties even in establishing analogous similarities between the natural order known by reason and the God that is demonstrated to exist by philosophical reason (98). Thus when we say 'Socrates exists', 'Socrates is good', 'Socrates is a person' and 'God exists', 'God is good', 'God is a person', we are, according to Aquinas, using 'exists', 'is good', 'is a person' in an analogous way in the two cases. But while I know *what* 'exists', 'is good', 'is a person' means in the case of Socrates, I certainly do not know *what* 'exists', 'is good', 'is a person' means as applied to God. All I know is that I am forced by the logic of the demonstration to conclude *that* 'exists', 'is good', 'is a person' must be predicated of God. For Aquinas, then, my analogical knowledge of God is of the most negative and attenuated kind. And so, when it is a matter of establishing analogous similarities between the natural order known by reason and the God disclosed by *revelation* (which by definition goes beyond or transcends the God proved to exist by reason), these similarities must, *a fortiori*, be even weaker still than those just considered, and the knowledge of the God of revelation based upon them must accordingly be even more negative and more attenuated.

Butler's attempt to claim probability for the truths of revelation, on the basis of the analogy between the orders or reason and revelation, seems then to be faced with formidable objections. What is valid in Butler's position, and this is in essence what it comes to, is that the truths of revelation presuppose truths of reason as their 'analogues', and that the demonstration of the truths of the latter is *ipso facto* a demonstration of the negative possibility of the former. This is, no doubt, a much weaker thesis than the one Butler thought he was arguing, but, as Aquinas shows, it is at least a defensible one.

(j) *Critique and conclusion*

The tradition of thought which Aquinas sums up and systematises is a very bold and remarkable attempt to have the best of both the world of Greek philosophical theology and the world of Judaeo-Christian religion. On the one hand, it insists with the Greek religious intellectualism that, if religion is a worth-while human enterprise, it must be within the realm of reason, or at least not contrary to reason. If the realm of divinity is mysterious, that mysteriousness must be due to its excess of intelligibility and not to its irrational unintelligibility. Or again, if religious faith goes beyond reason, it must at the same time build upon and complement reason. As grace perfects nature and does not destroy it, so faith perfects reason and raises it to a higher power and does not contradict or nullify it. As we have seen, for Aquinas faith is not a miraculously given kind of religious insight or intuitive experience which suspends or interrupts the ordinary course of the natural processes of reason; rather it presupposes nature and in a certain sense requires it as its basis. Reason, this whole tradition holds, is just as much God's work as his revelation, and the truths of pure reason about God are just as valid, in their own way, as the truths of revelation. Reason can no more be denied or slighted for the sake of faith than faith can be denigrated for the sake of reason. For, as Augustine says, if man is saved by the truths of revelation it is equally by his reason that he is *imago Dei*.

On the other hand, by restricting philosophy to proving the preambles or presuppositions of faith, and to the negative task of showing the non-impossibility of the articles of faith, this tradition of thought allows room for an order of revelation and faith transcending the order of philosophy and pure reason. It insists, as we have seen, that the truths of revelation are essentially distinct from the truths of philosophy about God, and that religion and philosophy cannot be identified. Religion and philosophical theology both have the same 'material object,' namely God, but they have different 'formal objects' in that the one considers God

82

under the aspect of author of revelation, and the other considers him under the aspect of author of nature or cosmological First Cause. In this context Aquinas emphasises the 'remotive' or 'negative' character of our philosophical thinking about God – we know what God is mainly by knowing what he is not (99). This is, indeed, implicit in his theory of analogical predication which plays a central role in his philosophical theology, for, as we have seen, although we know that predicates such as 'exists', 'is the cause of the world', 'is good', 'is a person', apply properly to God and not merely metaphorically, we do not know *how* they apply to God. All that we know is that such predicates do not mean apropos God what they mean when they are applied to created things within our experience. Their meaning in the two cases is not univocally similar but analogously similar (100).

At the same time, for Aquinas there is no doubt that we can rationally prove the existence of God and, albeit in an analogical way, what basic properties or attributes he has (101). And again, no matter how indirect and negative the role of reason *vis-à-vis* faith may be, reason is in some sense always the final arbiter. This does not mean, as the Reformation theologians were to complain later, that the admission of reason inevitably results in the rationalising away of faith, the violation of the autonomy of faith, and the denial of its gratuitousness in that, so far as belief is made to depend upon man's reason, to that extent it does not depend upon the pure grace of God. The objections of the Reformers in fact neglect the negative role of reason with regard to faith, and they also presuppose a radically different view of grace and nature from that of Aquinas. However, it remains true that both for its own expression and elaboration, as well as for the justification of its preambles and its defence, faith is dependent, in the sense explained, upon reason. Neither Philo, Origen, Augustine, Maimonides nor Aquinas are altogether clear about the nature of this dependence, but it follows nevertheless from the logic of their position and, as we have seen, is especially obvious in Aquinas's formulation.

Although this conception of the philosophy of religion

83

escapes the full force of the objections that we saw could be brought against the position of religious intellectualism which identified philosophy and religion, it is nevertheless subject to those same objections in an oblique form. First, it does involve a predominantly intellectualist or speculative view of religion, the practical side of religion being secondary. Indeed, man's final happiness for Aquinas consists in the contemplative vision of God, the love of God being consequent upon this vision (102). And religious faith is, as we have seen, primarily a matter of *assent*, even if that assent is not of an ordinary kind but has to be willed in lieu of rationally compelling evidence.

For Aquinas, then, religious belief consists essentially in intellectual assent to the truth of certain propositions. Although practical conclusions as to how the believer should live his life follow these acts of assent, they do not constitute religious belief. To put it crudely, one is defined a religious believer if one assents to certain propositions; whereas, it one does not adopt the practical policies or attitudes consequent upon those beliefs, one may be classed as an inconsistent or hypocritical believer, but one will still be a believer. For Aquinas it is therefore at least possible to say without contradiction, 'I believe in God but this belief makes no difference to the way I live my life', and in this sense there is for him a logical gap between religious belief and religious practice. For Kant and the Kantians, of course, this furnishes grounds for a conclusive objection to the whole intellectualist position represented by Aquinas. Religious belief, they claim, is of its very nature practical so that to say, 'I believe in God' is precisely to commit oneself to live in a certain way.

Second, the understanding of the mysteries of faith involves, at least negatively, the use of philosophical reason; for example, I can only take in and believe what is involved in the mystery of the Eucharist if I can understand (at least implicitly) that no formal contradiction is involved in supposing that the 'substance' of the bread and wine can change while the 'accidents' remain the same. And to this extent Aquinas's position does involve some degree of

84

esotericism. Aquinas attempts to evade this objection by arguing that the majority of non-philosophical believers can believe by faith the presuppositions of faith, although the latter are in themselves capable of being known philosophically or by pure reason. But, given his view of the nature of faith, it is difficult to see how we can believe by faith truths that are presupposed by faith. Third, as we have remarked, Aquinas's theological perspective is largely a-historical, in the manner of the whole Greek tradition of philosophical religion (163). It is also an impersonal and 'objective' view that leaves aside altogether the dimension of what Pascal calls 'the heart' and Kierkegaard 'subjectivity'.

Kierkegaard's strictures against St Augustine could also be applied here to Aquinas. 'He resuscitated the Platonic–Aristotelian definition, the whole Greek philosophical pagan definition of faith . . . a concept which belongs to the sphere of the intellect.' 'From the Christian point of view', Kierkegaard continues, 'faith belongs to the existential: God did not appear in the character of a professor who has some doctrines which must first be believed and then understood . . . . Faith expresses a relation from personality to personality' (104). This objection depends, of course, on the philosophical validity of the notion of 'personal knowledge' – a non-intellectual mode of apprehension that, it is claimed, is typical of personal relationships: a 'belief in' that is essentially distinct from 'belief that'.

The fundamental difficulty, however, with Aquinas's whole approach is that it makes religious belief dependent upon the success of particular philosophical arguments, and indeed upon the viability of a specific conception of philosophy, so that the religious believer is, by his belief, exposed to philosophical dispute. This view of the philosophy of religion depends, for instance, upon a 'transcendentalist' conception of the role of philosophy according to which philosophy can go beyond what Kant calls the limits of our immediate experience. It must be admitted that Aquinas's conception of the nature and scope of philosophy is certainly more restricted and more modest than that of the Platonic/

neo-Platonic tradition, since he insists that we can only know God and the other beings outside our experience by *a posteriori* inference. In other words, we do not know God directly or self-evidently and we have no innate knowledge of him; rather the concept of God only emerges after we have reflected upon our experience of the material world and have been led to seek a causal explanation of it. Further, as we have seen, even this indirect and inferential and postulatory knowledge of God is negative and 'analogical' in its mode. We know much more what God is *not* than what God *is*.

However, it remains true that Aquinas does see philosophy as having a 'transcendent' role and that his conception of philosophy is, to speak anachronistically, an anti-Kantian one. And, in turn, this means that his whole view of the philosophy of religion rests upon the validity of this contestable, or at least arguable, conception of the nature and scope of philosophy. For the philosopher who is convinced by Kant's radical criticism of this view of philosophy, this is a conclusive objection to Aquinas's whole position. And for the Reformation theologians also with their insistence upon the pure autonomy of faith, this represents the fatal flaw in Aquinas's philosophy of religion. But for Aquinas, of course, this is the inevitable risk that has to be run by any position that wants to emphasise the continuity and complementarity of the realms of grace and nature, faith and reason – a position of 'both/and' rather than 'either/or'. For him there cannot be an order of pure faith where we can escape making any rational or philosophical commitments and be safe from argument. Unless religious faith has some repercussions in the realm of reason and makes some philosophical demands upon us, it is empty. For Aquinas, if nothing is ventured in philosophy, nothing is won in faith.

3 Philosophy as Making Room for Faith

(a) Agnosticism in the service of fideism

'If we submit everything to reason, our religion will have no mysterious or supernatural element' (1). Pascal's statement very aptly expresses the persistent fear and suspicion of philosophy within the Christian tradition that has existed alongside the religious intellectualism we have just been discussing. Once philosophy is allowed a foothold within the domain of religious faith, it inevitably ends, so it is claimed, by rationalising away the mysterious and supernatural dimension of faith, and by making religion appear as all man's own work and achievement instead of being a free gift and gratuitous disclosure from God. Again, the philosophising of religious faith makes it into a kind of speculative assent, so that the practical or moral or personal dimension of religion becomes secondary; or, put in another way, philosophical religion is necessarily 'objective' in the sense that it is concerned with impersonal truths that are available to all, and the 'subjective' or 'personal' or 'inward' character of religious faith is neglected. The God of the philosophers, as Pascal says again, is not the God of Abraham and Isaac and Jacob (2).

This anti-intellectualist or fideist trend has had a long and complex history, and it has usually been supported by St Paul's dark warnings against philosophy and worldly wisdom, as well as by other scriptural texts. St Paul's denunciation of 'philosophy and vain deceit' (3) was in fact directed against the Gnostics who claimed to have a special kind of knowledge superior to that of faith, but his strictures were exploited in a general and undiscriminating way, and the other Pauline doctrine to the effect that man could come to know God by his reason (4) was conveniently neglected. In the same way, the saying of Jesus that the kingdom of heaven is hidden from the wise and the prudent and revealed to babes (5) came to be generalised into an anti-intellectualist canon. As McTaggart tartly put it: 'Such a principle is sure to be popular, for it enables a man to believe that he is showing meekness and humility by the confident assertion of propositions which he will not investigate and cannot prove' (6).

Among certain of the early Christian thinkers, this fear of philosophy (at least in religion) was coupled with what has been called an 'absolute conviction in the self-sufficiency of Christian Revelation' (7). Tertullian, for instance, rejects the 'foolishness' of philosophy and of 'unhappy Aristotle' since all that the Christian needs to know is in the Gospel'.

> What indeed has Athens to do with Jerusalem? What concord is there between the Academy and the Church? What between heretics and Christians? Our instruction comes from the porch of Solomon who himself taught that the Lord should be sought in simplicity of heart. Away with all attempts to produce a mottled Christianity of Stoic, Platonic and dialectic composition! We want no curious disputation after possessing Christ Jesus, no inquisition after enjoying the Gospel! With our faith, we desire no further belief. For this is our palmary faith, that there is nothing which we ought to believe besides. (8)

Elsewhere Tertullian makes his famous, or notorious, statement: 'I believe because it is absurd' (9), meaning that what is taken (wrongly) to be absurd by philosophy is nevertheless seen to be true by the eyes of faith.

Tertullian's rejection of philosophy, it is important to note, is not inspired by a 'know nothing' obscurantism backed up by a simple-minded religious fundamentalism, for Tertullian makes extensive use of the instruments of reason in order to show the limits of reason in the religious domain. As Pascal will remark later on, there are two kinds of ignorance – 'natural ignorance', and 'learned' or 'educated' ignorance (*docta ignorantia*) (10) – and it is this latter kind of philosophical ignorance which Tertullian argues is proper to the Christian.

In the same way, certain medieval thinkers, such as the eleventh-century St Peter Damian and St Bernard of Clairvaux in the twelfth century, themselves use dialectics to argue against the pretensions of the dialecticians in theology (11). Neither Peter Damian nor St Bernard is an intellectual barbarian, for both make free use of the dialectical and rhetorical arts they condemn so vociferously. Thus in St Bernard's letter to the Pope indicating Abelard's 'errors', he claims that Abelard presumptuously applies dialectics to theology, and he asks, 'what could be more against reason than to attempt to go beyond reason by means of reason?' (12). But he sees nothing paradoxical in his own procedure, for in his view he is using reason in order to delimit reason and to show its incompetence in matters of religion and thus, in turn, to safeguard the autonomy of the realm of faith. Exactly the same position is taken up within the medieval Islamic tradition by the great and remarkable Al Ghazzali who sees it as the task of philosophy to show the 'inconsistency' of the philosophers' views of religion. Philosophy ends inevitably in antinomies if it attempts to touch upon religious issues, and by showing this we make a place for the supernatural religion of the Qur'an and for personal religious experience. As we shall see, Al Ghazzali is the first to attempt to formalise this whole position.

In later medieval philosophy, William of Ockham and the Ockhamist school also emphasise very strongly the limits of philosophy with respect to supernatural faith. Ockham is certainly not in any way a philosophical sceptic, but he is concerned to emphasise the omnipotence of God and this, in turn, leads him to take a fairly agnostic view of philosophy's capacities with regard even to the preambles of faith. Thus, for Ockham, while we can prove by reason that God exists, we cannot prove that there must necessarily be one and only one God. Again, while it can be shown that the intellectual soul is distinct from the body, we can neither prove nor disprove the immortality of the soul. It is through faith alone that we come to know that God is one and that the soul is immortal. God can do anything save what involves self-contradiction, and this means that we can be certain only of those truths guaranteed by the principle of non-contradiction. All other truths are contingent, and that they are as they are is dependent upon the free will of God (13) whose acts of course cannot be known demonstratively or necessarily by reason. One might say that there is much more scope and play for God's free will in Ockham's world than in Aquinas's, so that there is much greater scope for faith and correspondingly less scope for reason in the religious order.

Ockham's agnosticism, as we have called it, is even more pronounced in certain of his followers such as Nicholas of Autrecourt (1300–60). For Nicholas the principle of causality is not an absolutely certain truth since it can be denied without contradiction, and this means of course that all arguments relying upon the principle of causality – such as the arguments for the existence of God and the immortality of the soul – can claim neither certainty nor even probability (14). Once again, Nicholas's intention is not in any way a sceptical one, for what he takes away from philosophy he gives to faith. His agnosticism, like that of Ockham, is very much in the service of faith and is meant to safeguard its independence and autonomy. Ockham and the later Ockhamists, such as Gabriel Biel (Luther's mentor), however, remain within the medieval scholastic tradition, and they do not ever carry their philosophical agnosticism *vis-à-vis* religion to the extreme to which subsequent post-Reformation thinkers will later take it (15).

All these various tendencies receive a powerful addition through the ideas on faith and reason set in train by the Reformation. The interests of the Reformers, Luther and Calvin, are exclusively theological, and they are content to make their theological points about revelation and faith and to leave philosophy to cope with them as best it can. No doubt, they assume implicitly that there cannot be any real conflict between the conclusions of philosophy and the demands of religious faith, and that therefore we must be able to show at the philosophical level that philosophy does in fact allow room for the conception of religious faith they propose. In other words, they tacitly presuppose that some such conception of the scope and limits of philosophy as that put forward later by Kant is philosophically viable. But they do not themselves argue for such a conception and in this sense they do not have a philosophy of religion. However, the ideas of the Reformers have been so influential within the stream of thought we are considering that something must be said about them.

Luther does not deny that reason has a proper place in the ordering of human affairs – law, government, the arts, science – nor even that we can in principle have a general knowledge of God and of his moral law. However, after the Fall, man's reason has a fatal tendency to pride; it refuses to accept its creaturely status and sets itself up as the final judge of everything, including God's Word. 'This is the vice of human nature,' Luther says, 'it does not consider these things to be creatures and gifts but rather says, "This I have made". Instead it should rather say: "I have received and the Lord has given", not "man has made" ' (16). Luther apparently thinks that this Pelagian tendency of human reason is inevitable and that, although theoretically reason and philosophy can come to a knowledge of God, in the actual state in which man finds himself this is practically impossible. A natural theology would have been possible for Adam, but it is no longer possible for us. Our only knowledge of God comes through God-given faith which we cannot merit by our own human efforts in any way. 'Reason is a whore', Luther says, for it seduces the believer from his trusting acceptance of God's Word and leads him to think himself self-sufficient (17). Luther's rejection of reason in matters of faith is thus principally motivated by his theological stress on the wholly gratuitous nature of God's grace, including the grace of faith, and his corresponding view of the inevitable Pelagian tendencies of human reason. Reason always tends to set itself up over-weeningly as the arbiter of God's revelation so that the creature becomes the judge of the Creator. For Luther, grace does not build on nature and perfect and complete it, as it does for Aquinas; rather grace stands in for corrupt nature and supplies for its deficiencies. In the same way, faith supplies for the deficiencies of reason and does not presuppose it or complement it (18).

Calvin likewise emphasises the theoretical possibility of human reason coming to know God. Indeed, in the first part of the 'Institutes of the Christian Religion', he argues that 'the knowledge of God has been naturally implanted in the minds of men' (19). If this were not so then men would be able to claim that they were ignorant of God and they would not be culpable for refusing to acknowledge him. However, 'since men one and all perceive that there is a God and that he is their Maker, they are condemned by their own testimony because they have failed to honour him and to consecrate their lives to his will' (20). Men are then capable of knowing God, but in actual fact they refuse to know him because of their 'proud vanity and obstinacy'. 'They do not therefore apprehend God as he offers himself, but imagine him as they have fashioned him in their own presumption' (21). The God of reason is thus 'a figment and dream' of man's own making; it is in fact a 'dead and empty idol' that has nothing to do with the true God (22), a 'shadow deity' that displaces the true God 'whom we should fear and adore' (23).

It is therefore in vain [Calvin concludes] that so many burning lamps shine for us in the workmanship of the universe to show forth the glory of its Author. Although they bathe us wholly in their radiance, yet they can of themselves in no way lead us into the right path. Surely they strike some sparks, but before their fuller light shines forth these are smothered. For this reason, the apostle, in that very passage where he calls the worlds the images of things invisible, adds that through faith we understand that they have been fashioned by God's word (24). He means by this that the invisible divinity is made manifest in such spectacles, but that we have not the ideas to see this unless they be illumined by the inner revelation of God through faith. And where Paul teaches that what is

92

to be made known of God is made plain from the creation of the universe (25), he does not signify such a manifestation as men's discernment can comprehend; but rather, shows it not to go farther than to render them inexcusable. (26)

It is interesting in this passage to see Calvin's interpretation of the Pauline texts which, prima facie, seem to suggest the possibility of a natural knowledge of God. For Aquinas, these texts were direct support of his thesis that faith presupposed such a natural theology; but for Calvin, Romans 1:19 simply means that man is culpable if he rejects God, since he is capable of knowing him at least in a minimal way.

For Calvin the only real way of knowing God is through his revelation in the Scriptures. And we know in this way both what Aquinas calls the preambles of faith – God as creator and 'sole Author and Ruler of all that is made' (27) – and the articles of faith about God as Mediator and Redeemer: 'Seeing that it is impossible for us men ever to come to the true knowledge of God, God has revealed himself to us in his Word. The incarnate Word attested in Scripture, the Son of God himself, has entered into the breach between God and ourselves' (28).

For both Luther and Calvin therefore philosophy is, for theological reasons, forbidden to enter into the domain of faith. To admit the possibility of a natural theology, through which man's reason could come to know God merely as the author of nature, would be to impugn the doctrine of God's transcendence with respect to his creatures as well as the doctrine of the pure gratuitousness of his dealings with men. It would also be to impugn the theological doctrine of man's sinfulness and corruption, manifested above all in his overweening pride which even causes him to fashion God in his own image. To the extent that a natural theology is possible man can save himself by his own efforts, and to that extent he is independent of God and does not need God's grace. But, Luther and Calvin claim, no Christian can believe that man can save himself (even partially) by his own efforts – that is the heresy of Pelagianism – nor that man can be independent of God's grace. 'All is a gift of God, even the faith by which we appropriate the gift' (29). Therefore we must deny the possibility of a natural theology.

It is within this theological context that both Kant and Kierkegaard attempt, in their different ways, to work out a new conception of philosophy's role with regard to religion. It is too facile to call Kant 'the philosopher of Protestantism', for Kant's own conception of religion is highly complex and not simply reducible to the basic Protestant position. Nevertheless his view of the philosophy of religion, like that of his great sceptical mentor David Hume, chimes in with Luther and Calvin's theological position. Thus, in the 'Critique of Pure Reason', philosophy demonstrates its own limits with respect to the objects of religion, and so makes room for faith. And then in the 'Critique of Practical Reason' religion is shown to be a phenomenon that belongs to, or is solely approachable through, the practical or moral or 'subjective' realm. For Kierkegaard also, reason makes room for faith by showing its own limitations. The whole tendency of Kierkegaard's thought is to destroy the pretensions of the 'objective' thinking that is typical of philosophy (or at least of one kind of philosophy), and thereby to show that religion belongs to the realm of 'subjectivity'. As it has been said, for Kierkegaard 'God cannot be proved, because what can be proved, if it could be proved, cannot be God' (30). And of course this same position is maintained in modern Protestant philosophy of religion, profoundly influenced as it has been by both Kant and Kierkegaard.

Outside the Protestant theological context, the position we have been characterising is represented also (though with its own highly original twist) in the thought of the great French Catholic thinker Pascal (1623–62). 'The last proceeding of reason', Pascal says, 'is to recognise that there is an infinity of things which are beyond it' (31). God is approachable only through 'the heart' and not through Cartesian reason; the personal God of authentic religion has nothing to do with the abstract and impersonal God of the philosophers.

We have here a distinct view of the philosophy of religion.

Even though in this view philosophy is excluded from the religious realm, it is philosophy itself which effects this exclusion by a kind of self-denying ordinance. As in the other two traditions we have already considered, this position involves its own conception of the scope and nature of philosophy, and its own conception of religion. Again, as a specific form of the philosophy of religion it has its own credits and its own debits, its own insights and its own deficiencies. Let us then attempt to analyse the structure and 'logic' of this position by looking at some typical formulations of it.

(b) Al Ghazzali: The inconsistency of the philosophers

Although the tradition of philosophical agnosticism in respect of religion had, as we have seen, very ancient origins, the first attempt in Western thought to formalise this position is to be found in the philosophical theology of the remarkable Islamic thinker Al Ghazzali (1058–1111). Al Ghazzali in his own way anticipates most of the moves that Kant was to make later in the 'Critique of Pure Reason' concerning the antinomies of speculative reason with respect to the subjects of 'God, freedom and immortality', and it is worthwhile looking briefly at his ideas (32).

In his autobiography of his intellectual and spiritual career, 'The Deliverance from Error' (33), Al Ghazzali recounts the story of his conversion to philosophy and of his subsequent disillusionment in that, first, it did not lead him to the knowledge of God, and second, it came to conclusions that were directly contrary to the religious teachings of the Qur'an, particularly concerning the resurrection of the body, God's providential knowledge of particular events, and the beginning of the world in time (34). However, instead of totally rejecting philosophy like the Islamic fundamentalists, 'loyal to Islam but ignorant, who think that religion must be defended by rejecting every science connected with the philosophers' (35), Al Ghazzali attempts to show the religious limitations of philosophy from within philosophy itself and

95

by using philosophical means. Al Ghazzali's purpose is not a sceptical one, for he clearly acknowledges that philosophy has its rightful place; but in respect of the religious order generally, his aim is to show the necessary agnosticism of philosophy. It has been said that the import of his teaching is that 'intellect should only be used to destroy trust in itself' (36), and this is true if it is understood with respect to the intellect's attempt to intervene in the religious domain. It is the task of philosophy to show that religious truths can neither be proved nor disproved, and thus to clear the way for faith.

This is, in effect, the thesis of Al Ghazzali's great work 'The Inconsistency of the Philosophers' ('Tafahut al-Falasifa') (37). In this work Al Ghazzali attempts to show that the philosophico-theological speculations of Al Farabi and Ibn Sina either end inevitably in antinomies or involve false philosophical assumptions. Thus, for example, he attacks the view of Ibn Sina, that since the universe is governed by causal laws, therefore everything takes place by deterministic necessity so that, in turn, God's free will can have no exercise in the world and miracles are impossible. But, argues Al Ghazzali, we can show by a philosophical analysis of the notion of causality that it does not entail necessity. 'In our view,' he says, 'the connection between what are believed to be cause and effect is not necessary' (38). No self-contradiction is involved in denying the truth of a causal proposition and this shows that it is not logically necessary. In fact, causal connections are based upon observation of the succession or conjunction of events. Thus the fire is not the cause of the effect of burning; rather 'observation shows only that one is *with* the other and not that it is *by* it'. In other words, the burning happens *with* the fire and not *by* it or because of it (39). Al Ghazzali further anticipates Hume by arguing that the apparent necessity of causal connections derives from our psychological expectations. 'It is only when something possible is repeated over and over again (so as to form the norm) that its pursuance of a uniform course in accordance with the norm in the past is indelibly impressed upon our minds' (40). Given this idea

96

of causality, we can see that miracles are not impossible, for there is nothing self-contradictory involved in supposing that God might suspend the natural order of so-called cause and effect. God may then by his free will bring about the resurrection of the body in the next life and effect all the other things that are promised in the Qur'an and which 'elude the discernment of human sensibility'. As with William of Ockham later on, the only restriction on God's omnipotence is the law of contradiction, for God cannot of course effect what is logically impossible. Apart from that we cannot set any limits to the power of God.

For Al Ghazzali, the space that philosophy clears for religion is to be filled by a direct and immediate kind of religious experience. Al Ghazzali adopted the religion of Sufi mysticism which emphasises direct experience of God – the 'sinking of the heart completely in the recollection of God and . . . complete absorption in God' (41). This is accompanied by revelations and visions, and it culminates in an ecstatic state which is 'hard to describe in language'. As he says:

> What is most distinctive of mysticism is something which cannot be apprehended by study, but only by immediate experience or tasting, by ecstasy and by a moral change. What a difference there is between *knowing* the definition of health and satiety, together with their causes and pre-suppositions, and *being* healthy and satisfied . . . . Similarly there is a difference between knowing the true nature and causes of the ascetic life and actually leading such a life and forsaking the world. (42)

It is the personal or subjective dimension of religion that is all-important for Al Ghazzali and that necessarily escapes the grasp of reason and philosophy, inevitably concerned as the latter is with knowing *about* things in an 'objective 'way. As we shall see, this combination of philosophical agnosticism with a personalistic or 'subjectivistic' view of religion is a constant feature of the strain of philosophy of religion of which Al Ghazzali is the first systematiser.

(c) Pascal: The reasons of the heart

Pascal's 'Pensées' are merely the rough notes for a projected apologetical work on the Christian religion, so that his ideas are expressed in a fragmentary and aphoristic style without much argument or detailed development. We can, however, discern in this religious classic a well-defined position on the relations of philosophical reason to religious faith.

Pascal admits that it is theoretically possible to prove the existence of God by reason (43), and for all his suspicions of philosophy and philosophers he is not in any sense an irrationalist. Thus he says that man's dignity consists in the fact that he is capable of thinking (he is a 'thinking reed') (44), and he holds firmly that religion cannot flout the principles of reason: 'If we offend the principles of reason our religion will be absurd and ridiculous' (45). But, these admissions having been made, the main drift of Pascal's thought in the 'Pensées' is to expose the limitations and impotence, even dangers, of philosophy and reason in the domain of religion. This is shown in a number of different ways and from different points of view, which we can set out summarily as follows: (i) Man is a finite creature and is therefore a 'Nothing in comparison with the Infinite' (46). And since he is finite he can only comprehend what is finite and cannot comprehend the Infinite: 'the end of things and their beginning are hopelessly hidden from him in an impenetrable secret; he is equally incapable of seeing the Nothing from which he was made, and the Infinite in which he is swallowed up' (47). In fact, 'there is an unconquerable opposition between us and God' which cannot be overcome by human reason (48). In this view man's inability to have any natural rational knowledge of God derives from his ontological finitude. And it would seem that not only is knowledge of the actual existence of the supernatural order excluded by the argument, but also knowledge of the *possibility* of the supernatural. (ii) Pascal, however, also offers another argument to show that, while reason can admit the *possibility* of a supra-rational order, and so of a supernatural order, it cannot in any way demonstrate

98

whether that possibility is in fact realised or not. Such a demonstration would presuppose that there is some common ground or 'affinity' between the rational and supra-rational, or between the natural and supernatural orders. But of course there cannot be any such affinity or likeness. 'If there is a God,' Pascal says, 'he is infinitely incomprehensible, since, having neither parts nor limits, he has no affinity to us. We are then incapable of knowing what he is or if he is. This being so, who will dare to undertake the decision of the question. Not we, who have no affinity to him' (49). And he goes on, 'God is, or he is not. But to what side shall we incline? Reason can decide nothing here. There is an infinite chaos which separates us' (50).

It is this situation which is the basis of Pascal's famous 'wager', for given that we cannot decide certainly about the actuality of God's existence, the best we can do is to calculate the advantages and disadvantages of adopting one or the other of the two possibilities. According to Pascal's very dubious 'games strategy' argument, it is a better bet to believe that the possibility that there is a God is actually realised, rather than to believe the opposite (51). But he admits that the purpose of the wager is not so much to convince the non-believer as to shake his religious indifference. (iii) Apart from these *a priori* arguments purporting to show the necessary agnosticism of the human mind with respect to the supernatural order, Pascal employs a number of subsidiary arguments which are meant to prove the practical inability of human reason to understand anything about God. Thus human knowledge, he says, is subject to error and deception of all kinds with regard to mundane objects (52), the implication being that *a fortiori* we can hardly have any certain knowledge of religious realities since they are so much more remote than mundane realities. And again, he remarks that the evidences in Nature of the existence of God are all of them ambiguous. Nature does not unequivocally testify to the existence of God, nor does it unequivocally testify against the existence of God (53). 'It is incomprehensible that God should exist, and it is incomprehensible that he should not exist' (54). (iv) Pascal also

99

uses an argument based upon the theological doctrine of the
Fall. In the actual existential state in which man finds
himself, his knowledge is so distorted by his pride and
vanity that he finds it difficult to see and accept the truth.
Rather he tends to see what he wants to see and to invent
the kind of God he wants. This is exactly what the deists do,
and it is because of this that, so Pascal claims, the God of
deism (a 'great, powerful and eternal being') has nothing
to do with the God of religion. Indeed, deism is "almost as
far removed from the Christian religion as atheism' (55).
(v) In any case, even if the proofs for the existence of God
were cogent, they are of their very nature remote and
abstract and impersonal, so that the God they produce is
likewise remote and impersonal. But 'it is the heart which
experiences God, and not the reason', and faith is 'God felt
by the heart, not by the reason' (56). In other words,
religious faith is a personal commitment to God involving a
direct experiential contact with God: 'The heart has its
reasons, which reason does not know' (57). By 'the heart'
Pascal means the capacity for direct, intuitive, affective,
personal knowledge ('spiritual insight') (58), as contrasted
with the inferential, abstract, objective and impersonal
knowledge of philosophy. And there is no doubt that when he
speaks of God being felt by the heart Pascal always has in
mind his own overwhelming experience of God on 23
November, 1654 (59). Again – an important point – whereas
we are not free to refuse assent to the necessary truths of
philosophy, faith is of its nature a free acceptance of God
(60).

Pascal insists that it is reason itself which shows us these
limits of reason, and so demonstrates its necessary agnosticism with regard to the supernatural order. In this sense
reason is indispensable to faith, even if its sole function is a
self-abnegating one. It is worth while citing Pascal at length
on this point, since he himself views it as of central importance.

The last proceeding of reason [he says] is to recognise
that there is an infinity of things which are beyond it. It
100

is but feeble if it does not see so far as to know this. But if natural things are beyond it, what will be said of supernatural? . . . We must know where to doubt, where to feel certain, where to submit. He who does not do so, understands not the force of reason . . . . Submission is the use of reason in which consists true Christianity . . . . Reason would never submit, if it did not judge that there are some occasions on which it ought to submit. It is then right for it to submit, when it judges that it ought to submit . . . . Wisdom sends us to childhood. *Nisi efficiamini sicut parvuli.* There is nothing so conformable to reason as this disavowal of reason. (61)

Pascal unfortunately does not develop this position in any detail. Above all he does not explain what he means by the knowledge of 'the heart', by which alone, according to him, we can apprehend the God of Abraham and Isaac and Jacob. Is there a distinctive mode of knowledge proper to 'the heart'? Does it have its own logic? How is this 'subjective' or experiential knowledge of God related to philosophical and 'objective' knowledge of God? Is it really the case that there is nothing in common between the God of religion apprehended by 'the heart' and the God of the philosophers? Is this subjective knowledge communicable in any way? Is it 'self-authenticating' or infallible, or does it admit the possibility of error? If the latter, what tests are there for distinguishing between veridical and non-veridical experiences or intuitions of 'the heart'? Nevertheless, although Pascal does not argue for his position, he does sketch its outline in firm strokes: reason showing its own agnosticism with regard to the religious order, and so allowing space for revelation and faith; the relation of religious faith to the knowledge of 'the heart' as against the remote and abstract character of philosophical religion; and the necessary freedom of religious faith which is incompatible with the 'necessitarianism' of philosophy logically exacting the mind's assent.

101

(d) David Hume: Scepticism and faith

In the Preface to his 'Prologomena to Any Future Metaphysics', Kant testifies that it was David Hume's 'Philosophical Essays' that first interrupted his 'dogmatic slumbers' and
set him on a new path that led to his 'critical philosophy'.
Hume's influence also seems to have been of central importance in the profound change that came over Kant's
philosophy of religion in its development from its 'pre-
critical' to its 'critical' phase. Kant's early essays in the philosophy of religion were for the most part in the standard
Wolffian mould. In his thesis of 1735, for instance, he
admitted the possibility of proving the existence of a being
which exists with 'absolute necessity', and in the short work
'The Only Possible Proof of the Being of God', written in
1763, he set out a proof of an 'unconditionally necessary
being' and of its basic attributes (62). In all these proofs
Kant assumes that 'the world as given is an object for which
we are bound by the principle of causality to seek an
explanation' (63). It was, however, both these assumptions
– that the world as a whole is an 'object' needing an explanation of its existence, and that we can extrapolate the
principle of causality 'outside' the world of our experience –
that Hume was concerned to attack both in the 'Enquiry
Concerning Human Understanding' (1751) and in the later
'Dialogues Concerning Natural Religion' (1779), and there
seems little doubt that Kant's philosophy of religion was
radically changed as a result of his reading of Hume. We
know, in fact, that Kant read the 'Dialogues' in translation
in 1780, the year before the publication of the 'Critique of
Pure Reason', and that Hume's powerful criticism of the
teleological argument for the existence of God caused him
to revise his ideas on philosophical theology in the forth-
coming 'Critique' (64). But Hume's influence on Kant's
philosophy of religion shows in other more fundamental
ways. First, Hume rejects any use of the principle of causality
'beyond the reach of human experience' (65). Second,
Hume attempts to show that irresolvable problems arise
when reason tries to grapple with religious topics: 'All

religious systems ... are subject to great and insuperable difficulties' (66). Third, the notion of God as 'a necessarily existent Being' is dismissed by Hume as meaningless on the ground that 'whatever we conceive as existent, we can also conceive as non-existent' (67). Fourth, Hume allows the possibility that philosophical scepticism about religious matters may encourage men to 'fly to revealed truth with the greatest avidity' (68), although it is clear enough that this is not Hume's personal position or the intention behind his own scepticism. Fifth, Hume emphasises the persistence and quasi-inevitability of religious belief, despite its irrationality. For Hume, it has been said, 'neither the experience of evil nor the lesson of scepticism entirely eliminates a post-critical residual belief in a divine mind beyond nature' (69).

All of these points are taken up by Kant in the 'Critique of Pure Reason' and become essential features of the philosophy of religion developed in the latter part of that work. To understand Kant on religion, then, we have to look briefly at Hume's own philosophy of religion, even though, no doubt, Hume would be very amused to see his radical religious scepticism dignified as a 'philosophy of religion' (70).

At the conclusion of the 'Dialogues', Philo (Hume's *alter ego*), after showing the sterility of 'natural theology', comes to the following ironic conclusion:

> Believe me ... the most natural sentiment which a well-disposed mind will feel on this occasion, is a longing desire and expectation, that Heaven would be pleased to dissipate, at least alleviate, this profound ignorance, by affording some more particular revelation to mankind, and making discoveries of the nature, attributes, and operations of the divine object of our Faith. A person, seasoned with a just sense of the imperfections of natural reason, will fly to revealed truth with the greatest avidity: while the haughty dogmatist, persuaded that he can erect a complete system of theology by the mere help of philosophy, disdains any further aid, and rejects this adventitious instructor. To be a philosophical sceptic is, in a man

103

of letters, the first and most essential step towards being a sound, believing Christian. (71)

This pretended alliance of philosophical scepticism with revelation and faith was, in fact, a constant feature of Hume's philosophy of religion. Thus, in his conclusion to the essay 'Of Miracles' Hume has this to say: 'I am the better pleased with the method of reasoning here delivered, as I think it may serve to confound those dangerous friends or disguised enemies to the Christian Religion, who have undertaken to defend it by the principles of human reason. Our most holy religion is founded on Faith, not on reason; and it is a sure method of exposing it to such a trial as it is, by no means, fitted to endure' (72). Again in the essay 'Of the Immortality of the Soul' which is, as Kemp Smith nicely says, 'quite definitely negative of any such belief', Hume writes: 'By the mere light of reason it seems difficult to prove the immortality of the Soul .... But in reality, it is the gospel, and the gospel alone, that has brought life and immortality to light' (73). And, finally, there is the celebrated passage in the 'Enquiry Concerning Human Understanding' where Hume couples his own scepticism with the Calvinist view of faith as a miraculous supplanting of reason:

We may conclude [says Hume with malice aforethought] that the Christian religion not only was at first attended with miracles, but even at this day cannot be believed by any reasonable person without one. Mere reason is insufficient to convince us of its veracity. And whoever is moved by Faith to assent to it, is conscious of a continued miracle in his own person, which subverts all the principles of his understanding, and gives him a determination to believe what is most contrary to custom and experience. (74)

Hume's general position here is primarily a tactic, which he learned from Pierre Bayle, of cutting the rational ground from under religion while pretending to be concerned with preserving its autonomy. But it is also a direct expression of his view of the scope and limits of philosophy, and of its

104

necessary agnosticism with regard to questions that are 'beyond the reach of human experience'. Thomas Huxley invented the word 'agnosticism' to describe Hume's position, and it does so very exactly. In the realm of religion, Hume says, we are 'quite beyond the reach of our faculties' (75). 'We are', he goes on, 'like foreigners in a strange country, to whom everything must seem suspicious, and who are in danger every moment of transgressing against the laws and customs of the people with whom they live and converse' (76). And later he concludes: 'A total suspense of judgement is here our only reasonable resource' (77). It is also this conviction that led Hume to adopt the dialogue form for his main work on religion, for, as he puts it, 'any question of philosophy . . . which is so obscure and uncertain, that human reason can reach no fixed determination with regard to it; if it should be treated at all, seems to lead us naturally into the style of dialogue and conversation' (78).

Whether or not this philosophical agnosticism, despite its plausible air, is really possible, is a question that will have to be discussed later. How can philosophical reason draw its own limits without being able to stand outside the limits? How, in other words, can we *know* that there is a possible order of things that we cannot in principle know? This, as we shall see, is a problem that Hume bequeathes to Kant.

However, Hume admits at least the possibility that religious faith may be erected on philosophical scepticism. Certainly Hume himself does not think that this possibility is actually realised, and he would not have wanted religious believers to have used his position in this way so as to guarantee the autonomy of faith by making it invulnerable to rational criticism. He is, indeed, very sarcastic about those 'sagacious divines' who use reason or deny reason as it suits them: 'Thus, sceptics in one age, dogmatists in another; whichever system best suits the purpose of these reverend gentlemen, in giving them an ascendant over mankind, they are sure to make it their favourite principle, and established tenet' (79). But it remains true that his position is able to be exploited by the fideist wishing to deny reason

105

in order to make room for faith. It is a final irony (that the great master of irony would perhaps not have altogether appreciated) that Hume is thus the precursor of Kant and Kierkegaard (80).

(e) Kant: Religion and practical reason

Everything turns to complexity in Kant's hands and his philosophy of religion is no exception to this rule. At first sight, perhaps, Kant's views on the relationship of philosophy and religion seem to be simple enough; but when we probe more deeply his position is seen to be much more intricate and, it might be said, much more ambiguous. To help us to thread our way through the Kantian maze it may be useful to set out in a very general way the main theses of Kant's philosophy of religion.

1. Speculative or theoretical reason – reason in so far as it is concerned to know what is true and false about the world of our experience, and about the conditions of possibility of such knowledge – cannot either prove or disprove that there is a God, or indeed establish anything at all positively about the religious order. Of its very nature speculative reason is agnostic about God, and for that matter any other realities that transcend our ordinary experience. This is a purely philosophical thesis derived from a 'critical' analysis of the scope and limits of speculative reason.

2. Religion is in any case not a speculative phenomenon but a practical or moral one. To be religious, for Kant, is not to assent to certain truths, but rather to direct or orient one's life in a certain way. Religion, in other words, is a matter of the will – it being understood that for Kant the will is identified with practical reason, that is to say, reason in so far as it is concerned with recognising that certain acts ought to be done or that certain attitudes ought to be adopted. Religion, one might say, is one of the practical conditions of morality, or at least an important dimension of morality, and the concept of God becomes meaningful to us only through morality, that is to say through the lived

106

experience of the moral life. Rousseau's ideas on religion had a very great influence on Kant in this respect.

3. An analysis of practical reason – reason in so far as it is concerned with prescribing how we ought to act, and not with describing what is the case – allows us to conclude to the existence of God (along with the immortality of the soul) as a 'postulate' or presupposition of its own adequate exercise. We do not *know*, speculatively or theoretically, that there *is* a God; but our analysis of practical reason shows the real possibility of God, and then the reality of God becomes clear to us in the living out of the moral life. God is that which justifies our hope of attaining the highest moral good and of becoming morally perfect and happy. Or, put in another way, which Kant sometimes suggests, to believe that moral perfection is ultimately attainable and that virtue and happiness will finally coincide, is in effect to believe in God.

4. Kant speaks on occasion as though the essence of religion is identical with morality, in the sense just mentioned. To believe in God just is to take up certain fundamental moral attitudes. This involves, of course, the denial of any supernatural or revelatory dimension to religion and the de-emphasising of the particular and historical aspects of Christianity. At other times, however, Kant speaks as though God exists in a 'transcendent' way quite independently of any moral attitudes we may have. And in this vein he allows some place for the supernatural dimension of Christianity and also for its historical and particular aspects.

It will be seen from this brief summary that there are two quite distinct strands in Kant's philosophy of religion. If we see religion within the context of speculative reason, then philosophy's task *vis-à-vis* religion is a purely negative or agnostic one. Its function is simply to make room for faith by delimiting the scope of speculative reason in such a way that both speculative proofs and disproofs of God come to be seen as illusory. If we cannot prove the existence of God, equally we cannot disprove it. On the other hand, within the perspective of practical reason, both the possibility and reality of God become manifest to us, and philosophy, in so

107

far as it is concerned with the presuppositions or postulates of practical reason, has therefore a positive task with respect to religion. In fact, if we adopt one of the alternative readings of Kant's position here, philosophy (in the sense just described) does not simply prepare the way for religion but is, in effect, identical with religion. To acknowledge certain of the postulates of practical reason – those conditions without which the operations of practical or moral reason would be 'unjustified' – is *ipso facto* to acknowledge the existence of God and to be a religious person.

With this general plan before us, let us look in more detail at Kant's position.

In one of his letters, Kant tells us that the 'Critique of Pure Reason' was written in order to resolve the antinomies that confront reason as soon as it tries to engage in any 'transcendent' speculation: 'That is what first aroused me from my dogmatic slumber and drove me to the critique of reason itself, in order to resolve the scandal of ostensible contradiction of reason with itself' (81).

Kant's answer to this problem in the 'Critique of Pure Reason' rests upon what has been called 'the principle of significance', namely, that

> there can be no legitimate, or even meaningful, employment of ideas or concepts which does not relate them to empirical or experiential conditions of their application. If we wish to use a concept in a certain way, but are unable to specify the kind of experience-situation to which the concept, used in that way, would apply, then we are not really envisaging any legitimate use of that concept at all. In so using it, we shall not merely be saying what we do not know; we shall not really know what we are saying. (82)

For knowledge, both sense perception and understanding are necessary, and we can no more have understanding without sensibility than we can get knowledge from sensibility without understanding. 'Without sensibility no object would be given to us, without understanding no object would be thought. Thoughts without content are empty, intuitions without concepts are blind . . . . The understanding can intuit nothing, the senses can think nothing. Only through their union can knowledge arise' (83). It follows from this that any attempt to use understanding in a 'transcendent' way outside the bounds of sensibility, or beyond our experience, is doomed to futility since in such a situation understanding would have no object; there would be nothing to understand. Nevertheless we are led, almost irresistibly, to attempt to use reason in this way. Thus, it is a natural tendency of the mind to see the world of experience in a unified and connected way, as a 'systematic unity', and to this end we suppose that it originated 'from an all-sufficient necessary cause' or God. This is innocent enough if it is seen for what it is – a methodological supposition or heuristic device, or as Kant calls it, 'a regulative principle of reason'. But if it becomes hypostatised and taken for a real objective entity, then we fall into illusion (84).

All attempts to prove the existence of God, either 'cosmologically' by way of the principle of causality, or 'ontologically' by analysis of the concept of God, are therefore rejected by Kant since they inevitably involve either the fallacy of taking the world as a totality or whole which requires explanation for its existence (85), or they involve an illicit extension of the principle of causality beyond the world of experience (86), or they involve an illicit transition from the conceptual to the real order. Kant shows with great brilliance how we are fatally tempted to use understanding beyond all possible experience, and how plausible this 'transcendent' use of reason can seem, particularly with respect to the concept of God. He is not solely concerned to expose the illusory character of this kind of reasoning, but he also wishes to show the pathological structure of the illusion and so of all attempts at speculative religion where, it is claimed, God is attained by speculative reason. One might say indeed that Kant is trying to answer Hume's mystified query as to how belief in God persists despite all the evidence to the contrary (87).

At the end of his discussion of the speculative proofs of the existence of God, Kant sums up his 'critique of all theology based upon speculative principles of reason'. 'All attempts', he says, 'to construct a theology through purely speculative reason, by means of a transcendental procedure, are without result' (88). And he goes on: 'Through concepts alone, it is quite impossible to advance to the discovery of new objects and supernatural beings; and it is useless to appeal to experience, which in all cases yields only appearances' (89). As far as speculative reason is concerned, God cannot be known, and necessarily cannot be known, and 'there is not one shred of evidence for believing in the existence of God or in a future life' (90). If, however, it is impossible for us – given the constitution of the human mind – ever to know God speculatively or ever to be able to affirm the proposition 'God exists' as true, Kant certainly does not want to say that the concept of God is *in itself* meaningless. If it were meaningless, then of course we could neither affirm it nor deny it; but this is not what Kant means when he says that we can neither affirm nor deny the existence of God by speculative reason. We can neither affirm nor deny the existence of God because God is beyond the reach of speculative reason; but for Kant what is beyond the reach of speculative reason is not thereby beyond the reach of *all* reason and so meaningless. How does speculative reason know that there is another realm of reason in which objects of thought may be meaningful, even if they are not meaningful (though this does not mean that they are therefore meaningless) for speculative reason? Or, put in another way, how does speculative reason see both sides of the limits that circumscribe it, so that it is able to know that there is a sphere that it cannot know? This, as we shall see presently, is a difficulty which Kant never satisfactorily resolves.

Kant supposes that, by showing the limits of speculative reason, we also show that all purported *dis*proofs of the existence of God are equally illusory, and in addition that deistic and anthropomorphic conceptions of the nature of God are without foundation. We can thus purify the idea of God, so to speak.

110

Such critical treatment [Kant says] is, indeed, far from being difficult inasmuch as the same grounds which have enabled us to demonstrate the inability of human reason to maintain the existence of such a being must also suffice to prove the invalidity of all counter-assertions. For from what source could we, through a purely speculative employment of reason, derive the knowledge that there is *no* supreme being as ultimate ground of all things, or that it has none of the attributes which, arguing from their consequences we represent to ourselves as analogical with the dynamical realities of a thinking being, or (as the anthropomorphists contend) that it must be subject to all the limitations which sensibility inevitably imposes on those intelligences which are known to us through experience. Thus, while for the merely speculative employment of reason the supreme being remains a mere *ideal*, it is yet an *ideal without a flaw*, a concept which completes and crowns the whole of human knowledge. Its objective reality cannot indeed be proved, but also cannot be disproved, by merely speculative reason. (91)

The benefit of Kant's agnosticism is that religion is removed from any dependence upon philosophy and so is not exposed to philosophical doubt and refutation in the way in which all forms of religious intellectualism are.

In the case of Maimonides and Aquinas we saw that they distinguished sharply between the functions of philosophical reason with respect to the existence and attributes of God on the one hand, and with respect to the 'revealed' articles of faith on the other hand. Philosophical reason could prove the former, but it could only show the negative possibility or non-impossibility of the latter. Kant, however, denies any positive demonstrative function to philosophy apropos God and his attributes, and holds that its only function is the negative one of showing the non-impossibility of God and of any other objects of religious faith. In other words, he extends the negative or defensive role of philosophy with regard to religion even to what Aquinas calls 'the preambles of faith'. But, as we have seen, it is not at all clear

111

how speculative reason can be aware that even this negative possibility of the existence of God obtains, since in order for it to know that it is limited (so that there is thus 'room for faith') it must, so to speak, be able to stand outside the limits. As we remarked before, although agnosticism appears to be a plausible position, it is in fact difficult to make sense of it. 'I have found it necessary', Kant says in the famous passage in the 'Critique of Pure Reason' 'to deny knowledge, in order to make room for faith' (92), meaning by this that speculative knowledge of God (and of freedom and immortality) is to be denied in order to allow us to become aware of his reality (not to 'know' him in the strict sense) through practical reason and morality (93). But how can we deny that we do have knowledge of a realm of objects, and at the same time know that they are apprehensible in another non-speculative way? We can know that our sense knowledge is limited by the nature of our sense organs and that there are sensible objects that *we* are unable to sense; but it is paradoxical to hold that our intellectual knowledge is limited in an analogous way by 'the constitution of the mind' and that there are objects which are in principle unknowable (94).

These questions will come up anew when we examine Kant's theory of practical reason and its implications for religion. But before we go into that topic we must say something of Kant's own personal view of religion. Though it boggles the imagination to think of the stern sage of Königsberg avidly reading the fervent prose of Jean-Jacques, Kant was in fact an enthusiastic admirer of Rousseau and there is little doubt that the latter's ideas about religion made a deep impression on him. Thus in the remarkable 'Confession de foi d'un vicaire savoyard' that forms the latter part of Book IV of 'Émile', Rousseau advanced a view of religious belief that radically changed Kant's early Wolffian rationalism. For Rousseau the essence of religion consists in its moral dimension and not in 'subtle dogmas'. Religious belief is not a matter of speculation but an affair of 'the heart'. 'Consult your heart while I speak', says the Savoyard priest to Émile, 'that is all I ask' (95). The idea of revelation and of the Church as custodian of the truths of revelation are both rejected, and the relevance of miracles is likewise denied. The Gospel, Jean-Jacques says through his simple priest,

> is full of incredible things, things repugnant to reason, things which no natural man can understand or accept .... This is the unwilling scepticism in which I rest; but this scepticism is in no way painful to me, for it does not extend to matters of practice, and I am well assured as to the principles underlying all my duties. [And he concludes:] I serve God in the simplicity of my heart. I only seek to know what affects my conduct. As to those dogmas which have no effect upon my actions or morality, dogmas about which so many people torment themselves, I give no heed to them. (96)

For Rousseau it is through the conscience above all that we become aware of God, and since the voice of conscience is innate in every man learned and unlearned, whether they be philosophers or non-philosophers, both morality and religion are available to all men and not just to a few scholars:

> Conscience! Conscience! Divine instinct; immortal voice from heaven; sure guide for a creature ignorant and finite indeed, yet intelligent and free; infallible judge of good and evil, making man like to God. In thee consists the excellence of man's nature and the morality of his actions; apart from thee I find nothing in myself to raise me above the beasts, nothing but the sad privilege of wandering from one error to another, by the help of an unbridled understanding and a reason which knows no principle. Thank heaven we have now got rid of that alarming show of philosophy; we may be men without being scholars. (97)

Again, Rousseau's parish priest warns of the dangers of philosophy regarding religion:

> The abuse of knowledge causes incredulity. The learned always despise the opinions of the crowd and each of

113

them must have his own opinion. A haughty philosophy leads to atheism just as much as blind devotion leads to fanaticism. (98)

Rousseau's point here about the universal accessibility of moral and religious truth, as contrasted with the exclusivism of philosophy, greatly impressed Kant, as he himself testified: 'I am a seeker by nature,' Kant wrote in 1764, two years after the publication of 'Émile',

> avid for knowledge. I sincerely thought that the greatness of man lies there and that in this way the cultivated man is to be distinguished from the plebs. Rousseau put me back on the right road. Rousseau is another Newton. Newton completed the science of external nature, Rousseau that of the internal universe or of man. Just as Newton laid bare the order and regularity of the external world, so Rousseau discovered the hidden nature of man. It was imperative to recover a true conception of the nature of man. Philosophy is nothing but the practical knowledge of man. (99)

Rousseau, it might be noted, had in 'Émile' proposed a striking anticipation of Kant's argument for the immortality of the soul in the 'Critique of Practical Reason'. God is supremely just and therefore supremely good. He would not be good if people lived just lives and were not made happy as a consequence. In the present condition of things, however, this conjunction of justice and happiness does not obtain, so that if man's life ended with the death of the body God would be guilty of deception and injustice and so not good. Therefore man must survive the death of his body in order that justice and happiness may coincide. 'If the soul is immaterial, it may survive the body; and if it so survives, Providence is justified' (100).

Kant's personal views on religion are expressed in their clearest and frankest form in a letter written in 1775. This is such an important confession of faith that it is worth while citing it at some length:

> I distinguish the *teachings of* Christ [he writes] from the

114

report we have of those teachings. In order that the former may be seen in their purity, I seek above all to separate out the moral teachings from all the dogmas of the New Testament. These moral teachings are certainly the fundamental doctrine of the Gospels, and the remainder can only serve as an auxiliary to them. Dogmas tell us only what God has done to help us see our frailty in seeking justification before him, whereas the moral law tells us what we must do to make ourselves worthy of justification . . . . Our trust in God is unconditional, that is, it is not accompanied by any inquisitive desire to know how his purposes will be achieved or, still less, by any presumptuous confidence that the soul's salvation will follow from our acceptance of certain Gospel disclosures. That is the meaning of the moral faith that I find in the Gospels, when I seek out the pure, fundamental teachings that underlie the mixture of facts and revelations there. Perhaps, in view of the opposition of Judaism, miracles and revelations were needed, in those days, to promulgate and disseminate a pure religion, one that would do away with all the world's dogmas. And perhaps it was necessary to have many *ad hominem* arguments, which would have great force in those times. But once the doctrine of the purity of conscience in faith and of the good transformation of our lives has been sufficiently propagated as the only true religion for man's salvation (the faith that God, in a manner we need not at all understand, will provide what our frail natures lack, without our seeking his aid by means of the so-called worship that religious fanaticism always demands) – when this true religious structure has been built up so that it can maintain itself in the world – then the scaffolding must be taken down. I respect the reports of the evangelists and apostles [Kant continues] and I put my humble trust in that means of reconciliation with God of which they have given us historical tidings–or in any other means that God, in his secret counsels, may have concealed. For I do not become in the least bit a better man if I know this, since it concerns only what God does; and I dare not be so presumptuous as to declare before God that this is the real means, the only means whereby I can attain my salvation and, so to speak, swear my soul and my salvation on it. For what those men give us are only their reports. I am not close enough to their times to be able to make such dangerous and audacious decisions. Moreover, even if I could be sure, it would not make me in any way more worthy of the good, were I to confess it, swear it, and fill up my soul with it, though that may be of help to some people. On the contrary, nothing is needed for my union with this divine force except my using my natural God-given powers in such a way as not to be unworthy of his aid or, if you prefer, unfit for it.

Kant goes on to emphasise that it is 'moral faith' that is of the essence of religion, all else – confessions of faith, appeals to holy names, rituals and observances, veneration of the person of Jesus, the Gospel stories – being secondary and dispensable. 'I seek in the Gospels not the ground of my faith but its fortification', he says; and again, 'the essential and most excellent part of the teachings of Christ is this: that righteousness is the sum of all religion and that we ought to seek it with all our might' (101).

From this it is clear that for Kant, as for Rousseau, the essence of religion lies in 'moral faith', the 'unconditional trust in divine aid', 'the striving for purity of conscience and the conscientious conversion of our lives toward the good'. The Judaeo-Christian revelation, the gospels, miracles, religious observances and rituals, prayer, theological dogmas, historical reports about Jesus, are all adventitious and dispensable devices, though they may be of some help in bringing simple people to see 'the necessity of moral faith'. Again, even if the latter are not the 'ground' of religious faith they may nevertheless fortify it. At the same time, while rejecting religious revelation in any speculative or theoretical sense – that is, as the disclosure of certain truths about the divine order – Kant seems to admit that there is a place for God's grace supporting and fortifying man's will in the pursuit of the good: 'God, in a manner we need not at all understand, will provide what our frail natures lack'; 'God will supplement our efforts and supply the good that is in our power'. We could then speak of a 'practical' revelation, a supernatural supplement to the will. However, we cannot merit this divine help through specifically religious means – prayers, religious ceremonies, rituals, belief in miracles and revelations: 'No confession of faith, no appeal to holy names nor any observance of religious ceremonies can help – though the consoling hope is offered that, if we do as much good as is in our power, trusting in the unknown and mysterious help of God (without meritorious "works" of any sort) we may partake of this divine supplement' (102).

The task of the 'Critique of Pure Reason' is, as we have seen, to display the limits of pure reason. But for Kant this negative task was simply the preparation for the more positive one of making room for practical reason, or showing the negative possibility of the whole order of morality. 'On a cursory view of the present work,' Kant says, 'it may seem that its results are merely *negative*, warning us that we must never venture in speculative reason beyond the limits of experience'. But, he goes on, the 'Critique of Pure Reason' also shows by the same stroke that these limits are estab- lished by the nature of sensibility and not by reason, so that the scope of speculative reason is not coterminous with reason as such, nor are 'the bounds of sensibility co-extensive with the real'. There can possibly be another kind of em- ployment of reason, and there can possibly be other kinds of 'realities'. This other kind of exercise of reason is what Kant calls practical reason and these other kinds of 'realities' are disclosed within the sphere of practical reason. The argument of the 'Critique of Pure Reason', Kant says, 'removes an obstacle which stands in the way of the employ- ment of practical reason, nay threatens to destroy it', and in this way has a 'positive and very important use'. 'At least this is so', Kant goes on, 'immediately we are convinced that there is an absolutely necessary *practical* employment of pure reason – the *moral* – in which it inevitably goes beyond the limits of sensibility. Though practical reason, in thus proceeding, requires no assistance from speculative

117

reason, it must yet be assured against its opposition that reason may not be brought into conflict with itself' (103). In order fully to understand Kant's doctrine here, we have to take account of his distinction between things as they appear to us in experience and things as they are in themselves. 'All possible speculative knowledge of reason', he says, 'is limited to mere objects of experience' (104). But at the same time the objects of our experience also exist as things in themselves ('otherwise we should be landed in the absurd conclusion that there can be appearances without anything that appears'). We cannot, of course, *know* speculatively things as they are in themselves, but we can *think* them in the sense that we can see that they are not self-contradictory, or are logically possible. Kant's argument here is very difficult to follow, for he seems to imply that although we cannot know things in themselves or even their 'real possibility', we can nevertheless have some kind of cognitive apprehension of them in that we see them to be logically possible. But even to think something as logically possible presupposes that I know it in some minimal sense; I must at least have a *concept* of it, even if I do not know that it is instantiated or has what Kant calls 'objective validity'.

At all events, Kant seems to think that speculative reason leaves the way open for practical reason without in any way delimiting or specifying what is really possible within the latter realm. All that we know speculatively is that the law of causality applies only to the phenomenal world of our experience, so that there would be nothing self-contradictory in supposing some kind of noumenal agency (e.g. the will) that was not subject to causality but was free. But we do not as yet *know*, prior to an analysis of practical reason, that the human will is *in fact* free. In the same way, we apprehend that there would be nothing self-contradictory in supposing the existence of God, but we do not *know* that the concept of God has objective validity until we follow out the implications of practical reason or morality. It is only within the sphere of morality that the concept of God comes to have 'real possibility' for us, and not merely logical possibility, though Kant does not explain how the category of possibility,

118

which belongs to the sphere of speculative reason, can also apply within the sphere of practical reason.

It is here that we must turn to the 'Critique of Practical Reason' (105). The idea of God, Kant argues, arises when we analyse what is implied in man's moral willing of the highest good. All men cannot but desire perfect happiness, and they equally cannot but hope that if they fulfil their moral obligations they will attain happiness. But, Kant argues, the existence of God is a condition of this hope being justified, for it is only God who can secure an 'exact coincidence of happiness with morality'. As he puts it:

> The postulate of the possibility of a highest derived good (the best world) is at the same time the postulate of the reality of a highest original good; and it is not merely our privilege but a necessity connected with duty as a requisite to presuppose the possibility of this highest good. This presupposition is made only under the condition of the existence of God, and this condition inseparably connects this supposition with duty. Therefore it is morally necessary to assume the existence of God. (106)

Kant emphasises that the existence of God is not the condition of morality or obligation as such, but of morality in so far as it is concerned with bringing about the highest good (107): 'Through the concept of the highest good as the object and final end of pure practical reason, the moral law leads to religion' (108).

What kind of assumption is involved in postulating the existence of God as the condition of achieving the highest moral good? Or, put in another way, what is the 'moral necessity' of which Kant speaks as attaching to the existence of God? At times Kant speaks as though the assumption is of a speculative kind, and that the necessity that belongs to the postulation of the existence of God is the same as that which belongs to any explanatory hypothesis. The final end of morality would not be attainable unless God exists; but the final end of morality must be attainable; therefore God must exist. As Kant puts it in the 'Critique of Pure Reason': 'Reason finds itself constrained to assume' the existence of

119

God, 'otherwise it would have to regard the moral laws as empty figments of the brain, since without this postulate the necessary consequence which is itself connected with these laws could not follow' (109). This is a piece of speculative reasoning, even though the 'facts' it is attempting to explain or save are facts about morality. Instead of arguing to the existence of God from facts about the world (God being postulated as an explanatory hypothesis to account for the mutability or contingency of things in the world), we argue here to the existence of God from facts about our moral life (God being postulated to explain the fact that we have an obligation to seek to further the highest good) (110).

At other times, however, Kant argues that the 'inference' that leads us to assume the existence of God is wholly practical in mode. We find ourselves under an obligation to promote the highest good, and we adopt the practical attitude that this can be effectively realised, and that, despite appearances, it will coincide with happiness. If God is a postulate of the practical reason, then our knowledge of God must be couched in terms of practical reason – not in terms of 'is' but in terms of 'ought'; not in indicatives but in imperatives. As Kant notes, practical reason cannot be concerned with postulating the existence of hypothetical entities, 'since such a supposition concerns only the theoretical use of reason' (111). 'God exists' therefore would have to be rendered in practical terms as follows: 'Act with confidence or firm hope that the highest good may be secured, that happiness and morality will coincide, and that nature and morality come into harmony'. From this point of view, to believe in God is to take up a fundamental moral attitude, an attitude presupposed to other moral attitudes. What this involves may be seen, Kant suggests, by looking at other forms of morality that do not make this presupposition, or adopt this attitude about the ultimate coincidence of virtue and happiness. Thus the Epicureans had based their morality upon happiness, without expecting any coincidence between happiness and obligation, while on the other hand the Stoics based their morality on obligation without expecting any coincidence between obligation and happiness. In both

120

cases morality was distorted, for in the one case it became sub-human (arbitrary inclination taking the place of duty), and in the other it became supra-human '(something which is contradicted by all our knowledge of men' (112)). To believe in God, then, is to adopt an attitude that helps us to avoid these distortions and to make a truly human morality possible. Put in another way, it is the practical conviction that the apparent diseconomy between nature and morality is not final or absolute. This is in fact the gist of Christianity:

> The moral law does not of itself promise happiness, for the latter is not, according to the concepts of any order of nature, necessarily connected with obedience to the law. Christian ethics supplies this defect ... by presenting a world wherein reasonable beings single-mindedly devote themselves to the moral law; this is the Kingdom of God, in which nature and morality come into a harmony, which is foreign to each as such, through a holy Author of the world, who makes possible the derived highest good. (113)

If we were to follow out this vein of Kant's reasoning we would have to say that all talk about God would have to be translated into the practical mode, that is in terms of obligations and imperatives; or, in other words, that the existence of God has to be translated into terms of human needs, attitudes, actions. And in this sense religion would be co-terminous with a truly human morality which respects the conditions of the moral will. Kant almost says this in a number of passages:

> Religion [he says] is the recognition of all duties as divine commands, not as sanctions, i.e. arbitrary and contingent ordinances of a foreign will, but as essential laws of any free will as such' (114). [And again:] Granted that the pure moral law inexorably binds every man as a command (not as a rule of prudence) the righteous man may say: I will that there be a God, that my existence in this world be also an existence in a pure world of the understanding outside the system of natural connections

. . . . I stand by this and will not give up this belief, for this is the only case where my interest inevitably determines my judgement because I will not yield anything of this interest. (115)

In other words, my practical interest in promoting the highest moral good 'determines' my judgement that there is a God.

The consequence of this, however, is that we cannot in any way know that God exists, nor indeed can we speak of God existing apart from human needs and attitudes and action. If God is a postulate of the practical reason, then we cannot make any truth claims about him, nor about the religious sphere at all. As we have already said, to believe in God will not be to assent to the existence of an entity, but rather to adopt a certain fundamental moral attitude or to make an act of practical faith about the ultimate attainability of moral perfection and the coincidence of happiness and virtue (116). Kant, however, sees the difficulties that attend this position and he tries to argue that, although God is a postulate of the practical reason, we can nevertheless speak about the existence of God and make truth claims about the religious order in general. We can, that is, *know* through practical reason that God exists, and further that he exists apart from human practical interests.

But this is surely a case of wanting to have your cake and eat it. For either this knowledge of God's existence is speculative in mode, that is inferred by speculative reason as an explanatory hypothesis to account for the 'facts' of morality (117); or it is in the practical mode and so expressible only in terms of moral imperatives. The first alternative falls foul of the same objections that Kant urges against the cosmological proofs for the existence of God, for even if the moral 'facts' are not the same as sensible facts from which the cosmological proofs start, we still have to extrapolate the principle of causality beyond the world of sense experience in order to account for them, and this of course for Kant is quite illicit. More generally, as H. L. Mansel says, if Kant is right,

122

it follows indeed that the infinite is beyond the reach of man's arguments, but only as it is also beyond the reach of his feelings or volitions. We cannot indeed reason to the existence of an infinite Cause from the presence of finite effects, nor contemplate the infinite as a finite mode of knowledge; but neither can we feel the infinite in the form of a finite affection, nor discern it as the law of finite action (118).

The second alternative, as we have seen, has the consequence that we cannot make any truth claims about God or the religious order, and if this is so then it is difficult to see how we can in any sense 'know' God or have any religious knowledge. Practical reason, on Kant's own account, cannot tell us what is or what exists, or make truth claims; it can only formulate imperatives commanding us to do certain things, what attitudes to take up, what we ought to do. Its whole purpose is not to describe what is the case but to prescribe what ought to be done and in this sense it cannot give us any knowledge about reality. We can, however, by *speculative* reflection on practical reason and morality attempt to show its presuppositions – what reality must be like in order for there to be the phenomenon of morality and all that it implies – and in this sense we can (if we allow that Kant's argument is valid) gain a *speculative* knowledge of God as an explanatory hypothesis. We cannot, however, as Kant suggests, have a *practical knowledge* of God even in the minimal sense he gives to such a 'knowledge' (119).

We shall make no progress [a recent Kantian scholar writes] in our understanding of Kant's conception of practical reason unless we recognise the basic paradox which lies at the heart of any discussion of practical reason. Practical reason is reason at work in the field of action. A *discussion* of practical reason is an example of speculative reason at work . . . . Knowing or proving freedom would be an activity of theoretical reason and in making freedom an object of knowledge we should have converted it into something other than itself; in fact, as Kant seems to be fully aware, we should have converted it into the only

123

category of knowledge which could be relevant, namely, natural causality.... Freedom is not and cannot be known. Freedom is acted or directly experienced in action or, to put the point paradoxically, freedom is known in action. (120)

Precisely the same point could be made about the other 'postulates of practical reason', God and immortality. If God is a postulate of practical reason then God is not and cannot be known. Knowing God would be an activity of theoretical reason and in making God an object of knowledge we would convert him into something other than himself, for the concept of God only has meaning in and through moral action.

We are therefore forced to conclude that Kant's strenuous attempt to provide a systematic basis for Pascal's and Rousseau's appeal to the 'heart' in matters of religion as against theoretical reason, does not succeed. The heart cannot have 'reasons' that reason knows nothing of; and practical reason cannot 'know' things that are inaccessible to speculative reason.

The ambivalence in Kant's thought that has been already remarked, continues in his later philosophy of religion. Thus in his work 'Religion within the Limits of Reason Alone' (1791) Kant appears to identify religion with morality and he offers a very bold and comprehensive reductionist account of religious doctrines as disguised moral prescriptions (121). As it has been put: 'Kant sees in religion neither an enlargement of our speculative knowledge, nor yet a collection of special duties towards God distinct from those to our neighbour, but a peculiar way of regarding the latter' (122). Similarly in 'The Dispute of the Faculties' (1798) Kant defines true religion as 'that faith which finds the essential feature of all honour paid to God in human morality' (123). Again he says in the same work that 'the God who speaks through our own Practical Reason is an infallible and universal interpreter of this work of his and there can indeed be no other, since religion is a matter of pure reason' (124). This apparent identification of religion with morality is expressed in even more extreme terms in Kant's last writings, the so-called 'Opus Postumum' (1800–3). 'God is not', he says, 'a Being outside of me, but merely a thought within me. God is the morally practical reason giving laws to itself'. And again, 'The proposition, "There is a God", means no more than: "There is in human reason, determining itself according to morality, a supreme principle which perceives itself determined and necessitated to act without cessation in accordance with such a principle" ' (125). God therefore is not a transcendent being distinct from our practical reason confronting us with moral duties. 'There is a God,' Kant says, 'for there is a categorical imperative of duty, before which all knees do bow, whether they be in heaven or in the earth or under the earth; and whose Name is holy, without our having to suppose a substance which represents this Being to the senses' (126).

Kant, however, did not follow out this train of thought to its final conclusion so as to deny absolutely the existence of God conceived apart from morality. Thus, alongside the passages just cited from the 'Opus Postumum' there are others that speak of God as an actual entity existing externally to man (127), and in the famous letter to Friedrich Wilhelm II (1794) after the official censure of 'Religion within the Limits of Reason Alone', Kant claims that his philosophy of religion is perfectly in accord with the traditional doctrines of Christianity (128). Again, in 'The Dispute of the Faculties' Kant admits that there is a modest place for theology, narrowly conceived as the study of the historical representation of God in the Bible (as distinct from the God revealed through 'moral faith' or practical reason), and he says 'the biblical theologian proves that God exists by means of the fact that he has spoken in the Bible' (129).

There is no doubt, however, that Kant's dominant view is that propositions about God, and indeed all religious propositions, are only fully meaningful if they are translated into the practical mode, that is, into the form of moral imperatives or prescriptions. But Kant shrinks from the consequences of this view, namely that we can no longer

125

speak of God or other religious realities existing apart from morality or make any truth claims about them, nor can we *know* God in any adequate sense. The best we can say is that God is experienced in moral action in its highest and most complete form; or rather, more exactly, we should have to say that God is experienced as a dimension of moral action. In this context to believe in God and to be a religious person *just is* to act in the confident hope that the pursuit of the highest moral good is not vain and that the apparent disharmony between the world of nature and the world of human morality is apparent only. To evade these consequences Kant tries to show that practical reason discloses the existence of God as a presupposition of its own exercise with respect to its pursuit of the highest moral good. But, as we have seen, this leads Kant into paradox, for to know the existence of God as a presupposition of practical reason is an exercise of *speculative* reason, and for Kant God can never be known by speculative reason.

Kant's monumental attempt to combine philosophical agnosticism with religion defined in terms of the 'heart' or morality or the practical reason, is thus beset by fatal difficulties. For, first, it is hard to see how a position of pure agnosticism with regard to the existence of God is philosophically viable. The concept of God must either be logically possible or meaningful, or logically impossible or meaningless, and if it is known to be logically possible (in whatever way this might be done) then, to that extent, we must have some speculative knowledge of it. Whether or not the concept of God is actually instantiated or not is of course a further question, though, as St Anselm in his 'Proslogion' saw very acutely, the question as to the logical possibility of the concept God and that of the instantiation or non-instantiation of the concept cannot really be separated in the same way as with ordinary concepts. I may very well have the concept of a unicorn and yet remain agnostic about whether that concept is instantiated or not; but I cannot in the same sense have the concept of *God* and remain agnostic about whether there is an actual instance of that concept or not. The debate between the theist and non-theist is not

126

really over whether or not there is actually an instance of the concept of God, but rather over whether the very concept of God is logically possible or meaningful. In this sense God either necessarily exists or necessarily does not exist and there is no place left for agnosticism, at least of the Kantian kind. Second, as we have seen, Kant's ingenious attempt to define God and religion in practical or moral terms leads him into deep waters. We cannot have a practical knowledge of God, for the notion of 'practical knowledge' is, on Kant's own premises, a paradoxical one. Again, the faith for which philosophy makes room is no longer religious faith in any recognisable sense, for it is identified (albeit tentatively) with morality itself (130).

(f) *Kierkegaard: Speculation and subjectivity*

Kierkegaard (1813–55) was above all a theologian, or rather a religious prophet attempting to awaken men to the need for unconditional religious commitment. And it is mainly for this reason that his typical style was that of rhetorical exaggeration and paradox and irony. Kierkegaard used any dialectical means that would jolt the reader out of his complacency and self-conceit and conventional behaviour, and into a realisation of the need for opting vitally for himself and for making the 'leap' of faith. Again, Kierkegaard's thought was elaborated largely by way of exasperated reaction against the 'System' of his arch-enemy Hegel (131). In countering the extravagances of Hegel's religious rationalism ('there is no philosophy so harmful to Christianity as the Hegelian') (132), Kierkegaard was led into equal and opposite anti-rational extravagances, so that he appears to exalt the irrational and absurd and paradoxical at the expense of the rational and intelligible. If we took Kierkegaard's thought on the relationship between philosophy and religion at its own face value, we would be tempted to dismiss it as sheer and wilful obscurantism – a deliberate denial of reason and a perverse glorying in the irrationality and absurdity of religious faith, as though

127

Kierkegaard held that it was precisely *because* religious faith was paradoxical and flouted reason that it was thereby believable.

Both Kierkegaards' friends and enemies have indeed often interpreted his thought in this way – as though for him irrationality were the *ground* of religious faith. However, if we take the trouble to look beneath the surface of his rhetoric and his prophetic exaggerations, and if we make allowance for the fact that for him Reason is equated with Hegel, we can no longer see Kierkegaard as an obscurantist. We can, in fact, discern the outlines of a philosophy of religion of a Pascalian and Kantian type, even if its metaphysical and epistemological underpinnings are not fully developed.

All honour to philosophy [Kierkegaard says in the 'Concluding Unscientific Postscript'], all praise to everyone who brings a genuine devotion to its service. To deny the value of speculation (though one might wish that the money-changers in the forecourts of the temple could be banished as profane) would be, in my opinion, to prostitute oneself. It would be particularly stupid in one whose energies are for the most part, and in proportion to aptitude and opportunity, consecrated to its service; especially stupid in one who admires the Greeks. For he must know that Aristotle, in treating of what happiness is, identifies the highest happiness with the joys of thought, recalling in this connection the blessed pastime of the eternal gods in speculation. And he must furthermore have some conception of, and respect for, the fearless enthusiasm of the philosophical scholar, his persistent devotion to the service of the Idea. (133)

It is only when philosophy, and reason in general, attempt to play a positive role in the religious sphere – pretending to explain and prove and justify the objects of religious faith – that it is to be rejected, though even this rejection is in part the work of philosophy itself. Philosophy itself sees that faith has an object and mode of exercise other than and beyond its own. The Christian 'believes against the understanding', and 'also uses understanding to make sure that he believes against the understanding' (134).

128

Kierkegaard's basic position is in fact very similar to that of Kant. But Kierkegaard is more consistent than Kant in that he pushes his philosophical agnosticism *vis-à-vis* faith and the religious order to its logical conclusion – a conclusion that Kant himself baulked at. By reason, Kierkegaard argues, we understand that there is a limit to reason and that there is at least the possibility of objects existing that we do not and cannot know – the 'Unknown' as he calls it (135). But for reason, this 'Unknown' remains strictly unknown and unknowable and it cannot be specified or determined in any way. Kant held that speculative reason could at least apprehend the logical possibility of God and to that extent specify or determine what was beyond the reach of speculative reason. And he also held that this logical possibility could be shown through practical reason to be a real possibility. Kierkegaard, however, argues that if there is an 'Unknown', then we cannot know it in any positive or determinate way. 'What then is the Unknown? It is the limit to which the Reason repeatedly comes, and in so far ... it is the different, the absolutely different. But because it is the absolutely different, there is no mark by which it could be distinguished' (136). In particular, we certainly have no right to identify the Unknown with God. Dr Johnson once remarked of Jacob Boehme that if had really experienced the Unutterable he ought not to have tried to utter it; the Unutterable is not something that can be uttered by some special or extraordinary means of expression, but it is that which is precisely beyond the limits of intelligible utterance. In the same way, for Kierkegaard the Unknown is that which lies beyond the limits of knowledge of any kind – though even this way of putting it is misleading in that it suggests that the Unknown is a determinate realm of (knowable) objects.

Philosophical reason, therefore, knows that there is the possibility of objects existing that we do not and cannot know by philosophical reason. And reason also knows that there is a difference between its own 'objective' and speculative mode of apprehension and what Kierkegaard calls 'subjectivity' – a special mode of non-speculative, 'personal'

129

apprehension (if indeed we can call it apprehension, since it is not a form of cognition but rather a form of willed commitment).

It is in this way that philosophy allows room for religious faith, for religious faith is concerned with objects that are beyond the range of reason, and its mode of apprehension also differs from that of philosophy in that it is a species of 'subjectivity'. The first point is obvious enough, for God is infinite, whereas the reason can know only what is finite: 'The understanding is related to the dialectic of finitude' (137). Again, the objects of faith are 'paradoxical', for Christianity claims that God (the infinite) became man (the finite) in the person of Christ so as to do away with the 'absolute unlikeness (between God and sinful man) in absolute likeness' (138). Further, the objects of religious faith are such that they demand a vital and personal response and commitment from us, and not merely speculative assent: 'Faith belongs to and has its home in the existential, and in all eternity it has nothing to do with knowledge . . . . Faith expresses a relation from personality to personality' (139). God is not an object we assent to, or contemplate; he is a person who invites a personal interest and response from us. To the extent that we speculatively contemplate God we cannot be interested in him, for speculation means that we put the object at a distance from us and judge it in an impersonal way, whereas my interest in God implies that I, this individual person, see him and respond to him as the source of my own eternal happiness (140). For Kierkegaard this is a strict either/or; *either* we are infinitely interested in God, *or* we are convinced speculatively of his truth.

The inquiring subject [he says] must be in one or the other of two situations. Either he is in faith convinced of the truth of Christianity, and in faith assured of his own relationship to it; in which case he cannot be infinitely interested in all the rest, since faith itself is the infinite interest in Christianity . . . . Or the inquirer is, on the other hand, not in an attitude of faith, but objectively in an attitude of contemplation and hence not infinitely interested in the determination of the question. (141)

130

The object of religious faith, we have said, is such that it demands a practical commitment from us, not speculative assent. But how are these objects proposed to us in the first place? They are, Kierkegaard says, proposed by God's grace. However, before we consider this point we must examine Kierkegaard's difficult and ambiguous notion of 'subjectivity' in more detail, since religious faith is a species of subjectivity. Kierkegaard says a number of quite different things about subjectivity and it is not easy to reconcile all of them; however, we may try to systematise his ideas by considering the mode of subjectivity, its object and its ground. As to its mode, it goes without saying that for Kierkegaard subjectivity has nothing to do with subjectivism in the sense that belief is equated with feeling or emotion or pure psychological experience. Rather it denotes personal appropriation of an object, as against impersonal assent to, or contemplation of, it. As such, it implies that I have personal interest in or 'passion' towards the object; that I value it as being important for me and my life; that I make a practical commitment to, or choice or option of, the object. This last is an important point for Kierkegaard, for whereas the objects of reason necessitate our assent by their evidence, the objects of subjectivity require that we freely choose them, that we take a 'risk', that we make a 'leap'. As with Pascal, the freedom of the act of faith is of its essence for Kierkegaard. An object of faith that necessitated our response to it would precisely not be an object of faith, any more than a personal relationship that was imposed on us or exacted from us would be an authentic personal relationship. 'Freedom is the true wonderful lamp; when a man rubs it with ethical passion, God comes into being for him' (142).

As to its object, subjectivity is concerned with the individual existent, as against the general and universal and ideal and systematic, since it is only the individual existent that can invite practical interest and 'passion' from us. Existence is always individual existence, whereas reason is always concerned with the universal or the ideal, and that is why we cannot reason systematically about existence.

I always reason from existence, not toward existence, whether I move in the sphere of palpable sensible fact or in the realm of thought. I do not for example prove that a stone exists, but that some existing thing is a stone. The procedure in a court of justice does not prove that a criminal exists, but that the accused, whose existence is given, is a criminal. Whether we call existence an *accessorium* or the eternal *prius*, it is never subject to demonstration. (143)

Again, the object of subjectivity is typically 'paradoxical'; 'it is a sign, an enigma faced with which reason can only say: "I cannot resolve it; for me that is not intelligible". But it does not follow therefrom that the paradox is in fact nonsense' (144).

Finally, as to the ground of subjectivity, for Kierkegaard it is ultimately the will that posits any act of subjectivity. In Kantian terms, it is an act of the practical reason. To the extent that my assent is necessitated by evidence, Kierkegaard seems to suggest, *I* do not believe, it is not *my* act any more than an act of the will is *my* act (or even an *act* in any real sense) if it is necessitated (145).

This, then, is subjectivity, a mode of 'apprehension' that is at every point contrasted with speculative knowledge. And religious faith is subjectivity at its highest and most intense. In religious faith the interest at stake is an 'infinite interest', for my relationship with God concerns my eternal welfare, and for this reason it demands the greatest degree of personal response and commitment from me. At the same time, both the existential and 'paradoxical' features of the object of subjectivity are, in religious faith, intensified to the maximum, for God is both the supreme existent and the absolute paradox. And for the same reason, the role of the will is, in religious faith, at its most pronounced. The 'risk' and the 'leap' involved are of the most dramatic kind, and the introduction of reason and of any kind of rational proof or justification here is correspondingly at its most irrelevant or, as Kierkegaard likes to say, at its most comical (146).

It is God's grace that ultimately moves the will to believe

in God and that sustains us in a relationship of subjectivity towards him. 'God gave to his disciple the condition that enables him to see Him, opening for him the eyes of faith' (147). We can, of course, prepare ourselves for the grace of faith. In fact, faith would be impossible for one who had not entered upon what Kierkegaard calls the 'ethical' plane of living and realised the importance of subjectivity and its irreducibility to the speculative. As Kierkegaard puts it: 'One does not prepare oneself to become attentive to Christianity by reading books, or by world-historical surveys, but by immersing oneself deeper in existence' (148). Again, the consciousness of guilt and willingness to engage in 'self-annihilation' are necessary conditions of religious faith (149). But, in the last resort, it is God's grace that motivates the will to believe, even if that grace works through man's freedom and is not to be conceived of as a quasi-miraculous suspension of man's 'natural' powers. 'To be a Christian means to accept thankfully this infinite grace of having to be a follower of Jesus Christ here in this life and thus being eternally saved by grace' (150).

For Kierkegaard, therefore, religious faith is defined by its opposition at every point to philosophy, and it might be thought that, for this reason, it is nonsense to speak of him having a philosophy of religion. But despite this, and despite Kierkegaard's continual and savage denigration of philosophy and all its works, he does nevertheless have an implicit philosophy of religion. For him it is through philosophy that we know that there is the logical possibility of a realm that cannot be apprehended by philosophy or speculative reason. And again, it is through reason that we appreciate the difference between its own 'objective' mode of exercise and that of subjectivity. One might say, indeed, that Kierkegaard *depends* upon the contrast with philosophy in order to make his points about 'subjectivity' and religious faith. If we did not know first what the object and mode of philosophy was, we would not know what subjectivity and faith were. Or put in another way, a man will only realise fully the true meaning of subjectivity if he has first been seriously tempted by the attractions of philosophy and 'the speculative view',

133

as indeed Kierkegaard himself undoubtedly was. Thus, even though the functions of philosophy with respect to religion are all of them quite negative, they are nevertheless in a certain sense necessary to a right understanding of religious faith, and we can in this sense speak of Kierkegaard's philosophy of religion.

In 'The Works of Love', Kierkegaard indeed speaks of philosophical reflection as having a quasi-apologetical function in that it shows the impossibility of any rational justification of faith. Reflection helps us to understand that we cannot understand Christianity:

> People have always thought that reflection would destroy Christianity, and is its natural enemy. I hope I have shown, with God's aid, that religious reflection can retie the knot which a superficial reflection has unravelled for so many years. The authority of the Bible, and all that belongs to it, have been abolished, and it looks as if one were only waiting for the ultimate stage of reflection to clear up everything. But see how, on the contrary, reflection is going to render service by putting springs under Christianity again, and in such a way that it is able to hold out against reflection. Christianity of course remains completely unchanged; not a jot has been altered. But the struggle has become different: previously it was only between reflection and immediate simple Christianity; now it is between reflection and simplicity armed by reflection .... The real task is not to understand Christianity but *to understand that one cannot understand it*. That is the sacred cause of faith, and reflection is sanctified by being used for it. (151)

The advantages of this view of philosophy's relations with religion are obvious enough. First, the autonomy of religious faith is guaranteed in that it has no kind of dependence upon philosophy or reason at all, so that its certainty cannot be affected by changes in philosophy. As a recent commentator has put it apropos Kierkegaard: 'The point that he grasped so surely was that faith begins when its certainty is inward. If it were a certainty that resulted from a metaphysical

134

scheme then it could be held only as long as that metaphysics is held. Now this is patently not true of faith' (152). In fact, Kierkegaard transposes on to the religious plane Kant's fundamental position about the autonomy of morals. Just as for Kant any attempted justification or explanation of the moral order necessarily meant that it was explained away and reduced to other, non-moral, terms, so for Kierkegaard any 'explanation' or justification of the religious order would mean that it was being explained away in non-religious terms. The only kind of explanation that is in place here is that of showing that religious faith is religious faith and not another thing. It is the 'function of an explanation to render it evident that the something in question was this definite thing, so that the explanation took the obscurity away but not the object. Otherwise the explanation would not be an explanation but something quite different, namely, a correction' (153).

The second advantage of this position is that it does full justice to the 'practical' character of religious belief. For Kierkegaard, to believe religiously is not to give assent to doctrines but to act in a certain way, to orient one's life in a certain way. 'Christianity is not a doctrine but an existential communication expressing an existential contradiction. If Christianity were a doctrine it would *eo ipso* not be an opposite to speculative thought, but rather a phase within it. Christianity has to do with existence, with the act of existing; but existence and existing constitute precisely the opposite of speculation' (154).

The price that has to be paid for these advantages is, however, prohibitively high. For first, by placing faith beyond reason this position severs the religious order completely from philosophy and history and science and the entire realm of human culture – in fact from the whole of God's natural creation. Kierkegaard accepts this consequence. 'If it were God's aim to make a splendid world out of this world, then mankind would be without a guide. For the New Testament, the message of Christ, is based upon the principle that this is an evil world' (155). But it is clear that it is a very drastic consequence. In any case, the severance

135

between faith and reason cannot be complete, for, as Kierkegaard admits, there are rational limits to what is believable by faith. Faith cannot believe the nonsensical or the purely irrational (156) and to this extent at least it is subject to reason, for we must have some criteria for distinguishing between the 'paradoxical'—which is the object of faith – and the nonsensical or contradictory (157).

Second, although Kierkegaard accounts for the practicality of faith, the dichotomy he set up between speculation and 'subjectivity' make it difficult to see how we can specify the object of faith. If to have faith is to be interested, to act in a certain way, to adopt a particular, 'existential' and personal point of view; and if to speculate is precisely to be disinterested, to disengage oneself from the particularity of existence and to adopt a general or universal or impersonal point of view – then by definition there can be no speculation within the realm of faith. We cannot, that is, know the object of faith or specify it in any way; all that we can do is to act with 'infinite passion' without knowing to what we are committing ourselves (158). Thus it would seem that merely to act in a certain way or to have certain fundamental attitudes to life (e.g. to act in imitation of Christ), would constitute faith. Kierkegaard himself almost suggests this when he says that what is important in subjectivity and faith is the 'how' and not the 'what': 'The objective accent falls on WHAT is said, the subjective accent on HOW it is said . . . . It is in the passion of the infinite that is the decisive factor, and not its content, for its content is precisely itself. In this manner subjectivity and the subjective "how" constitute the truth' (159). Kierkegaard goes on to say that a heathen who prays in spirit and in truth, even though the object of his prayer is a false god, in fact believes in the true God; while on the other hand the Christian who prays to the true God, but does not pray truly, is in reality believing in an idol! (160) However, we cannot really make even this distinction, for we cannot adopt one attitude to life rather than another without some principle of discernment; we cannot say *how* we ought to act without specifying *what* the object of our action or attitudes. We cannot just *believe* in

136

something without knowing anything about *what* we are believing in.

If we were to take Kierkegaard's account at its face value, faith would be completely blind and objectless and inexpressible not just to others but even to the believer himself. 'As soon as I speak I express the universal, and when I remain silent, no one can understand me.' In fact, I cannot even understand myself. Again, if Kierkegaard is right in his commendation of the sincere idolator over the insincere Christian, then, as a recent writer has put it, 'truth is being estimated by the standards of sincerity'.

> It might well be said [the same critic goes on] that the fervent idolator is the better man; he makes the utmost of what he has, while the self-deceiving Christian has everything and lets it slip. But is it nothing to have a *true* conception of God? If so, intensity of devotion is the whole of religion, and intensity of devotion may be shown in the pursuit of what is false and even wicked. If we reject this consequence, there must be *some* place in religion for an *objectively* true conception of God (161).

On the other hand, if subjectivity and faith have a cognitively specifiable object – as indeed Kierkegaard seems at times to suggest – then the hard-and-fast distinction between speculative knowledge and subjectivity will have to be abandoned and some kind of philosophical justification of religion will be in order (162).

(g) *Summary and conclusion*

The particular philosophy of religion delineated here can be given very different expressions both in so far as the ground of the philosophical agnosticism, which is an essential part of this position, is susceptible of being established in different ways, and in so far as the 'faith', for which room is made through this agnosticism, is susceptible of different interpretations.

Kierkegaard's Anglican contemporary H. L. Mansel, for

137

example, used Sir William Hamilton's 'philosophy of the Unconditioned' to establish the possibility of a sphere of existence beyond the reach of our finite and determinate knowledge. If there are realities that are finite or conditioned, Mansel argues, then there must be an Infinite or Unconditioned. But human thought is limited to the determinate and finite, and so the Infinite or Unconditioned is 'incognisable and inconceivable', and 'we are thus taught the salutary lesson that the capacity of thought is not to be constituted into the measure of existence, and are warned from recognising the domain of our knowledge as necessarily co-extensive with the horizon of our faith' (163). We must postulate *that* there is an Infinite, but we cannot in any way *know* this Infinite, for an infinite object of consciousness would be a contradiction in terms. 'The condition of consciousness is distinction; and the condition of distinction is limitation. We can have no consciousness of Being in general which is not some Being in particular: a *thing*, in consciousness, is one thing out of many. In assuming the possibility of an infinite object of consciousness, I assume, therefore, that it is at the same time limited and unlimited' (164). For Mansel the identification of the Unconditioned with God, and with the Christian God, is effected by faith. 'In this impotence of Reason', he says, 'we are compelled to take refuge in Faith, and to believe that an Infinite Being exists, though we know not how' (165), although Mansel also admits the relevance of 'evidences' or probable 'presumptions' to the determining of the truth of Christianity.

It is, however, within twentieth-century Protestant thought that the Kantian–Kierkegaardian account of philosophy's relations with religion has had its most important expression. Within this tradition the transcendence and 'otherness' of God, and of the whole order of revelation, is dramatically stressed, while the finiteness of man and his knowledge, and the effects of his sinfulness upon him, are correspondingly emphasised. Calvin's saying, *finitum non capax infiniti*, the finite is not capable of comprehending the infinite, exactly expresses this position. In this perspective religious belief is possible only as a freely given grace from

138

God, and any attempt by philosophy or human reason to prepare positively for faith is seen as an attempt by the creature to judge the Creator – a means 'whereby the rational creature may reverse the order of being and advance towards God in terms not first provided by the Creator' (166).

This whole conception of religion chimes in perfectly with the Kantian and Kierkegaardian philosophy of religion – philosophy demonstrating its own limits and thus its powerlessness in any supra-rational sphere, and thus in turn allowing room for a 'practical' faith that is not subject to rational justification or criticism in any way. Indeed this philosophy of religion harmonises so nicely with radical Protestantism that it is commonly taken for granted by contemporary Protestant thinkers and no need is felt to justify it in any systematic way.

Rudolf Otto's celebrated and influential work 'The Idea of the Holy', for example, limits the sphere of rational and conceptual thought very drastically so as to make room for non-rational modes of awareness. Otto places the primary religious object, the numinous, in the sphere of the 'non-rational', and this means of course that it is 'inexpressible'. We can, however, have a quasi-intuitive 'experience' of the numinous; indeed, Otto suggests that there is a special mode of consciousness – quite apart from speculative rationality and moral consciousness – proper to religion. Just as for Kant we have a special moral consciousness which cannot be 'justified' (since justification could only be in non-moral terms), so for Otto there is a distinct mode of religious consciousness which cannot be justified in other, non-religious, terms. The religious mode of consciousness, or the 'faculty of divination', is 'an original and underivable capacity of the mind' (167).

At the same time Otto claims that reason can in various ways provide helpful analogies or 'ideograms' (168) of the inexpressible numinous, though he does not explain how we are able to judge which 'ideograms' are more revealing and enlightening than others. Again, if the numinous is, as Otto claims, so wholly 'other', how can mere reason even indicate

139

or suggest analogies of it? As Paul Tillich has put it: 'It must be shown in what essential relationship this 'wholly Other' stands to the other forms of consciousness. For if it stands in no relation, or even in a supplementary relation, it splits the unity of consciousness and it would not be *we* who experience the holy' (169).

Again, with the great twentieth-century Protestant thinker Karl Barth, Kant's philosophical agnosticism is welcomed (170), as is Kierkegaard's dichotomy between the speculative and the 'subjective' (171). Barth was deeply influenced by Kierkegaard and like the latter is concerned to show the 'abyss' between the sphere of philosophical reason and that of religious faith. His attack on all kinds of 'natural theology' and on every attempt to justify religion rationally, is so vehement and uncompromising that at times he seems, like Kierkegaard, to be embracing irrationalism of the wildest kind and making virtue out of obscurantism (172).

However, despite his rhetorical exaggerations, Barth does have an implicit philosophical position of a quasi-Kantian kind on the limits of reason; and, moreover, he admits that reason can play a part in the theological elaboration of the Word of God (173). So long as philosophy does not pretend to prove or justify the objects of faith (and so violate the autonomy of the order of faith), it can be used for theological purposes. Rudolf Bultmann, who differs from Barth in many ways, also allows philosophy a role in the theological explication of the data of faith. But although Bultmann has used Heidegger's early philosophical thought in the service of his own theology, he insists that his theology does not thereby become 'dependent upon a philosophical system by . . . seeking to make fruitful use of the concepts of the so-called philosophy of existence, particularly of Heidegger's analysis of existence in "Being and Time".' 'I learned from him', Bultmann continues, 'not *what* theology has to say, but *how* to say it, in order to speak to the thinking man of today in a way he can understand' (174). Despite Barth's fear that Bultmann might be leading theology back into 'an Egyptian bondage in which a philosophy lays down what the Holy Spirit is permitted to say', Bultmann denies that

140

his use of philosophy injures the autonomy of faith. 'Philosophy', he says 'leaves fundamentally free the possibility of a word spoken to man from beyond. It offers, however, the possibility of speaking of Christian existence in a language which is comprehensible today' (175). Philosophy, he argues elsewhere, cannot either determine the meaningfulness or the meaninglessness of human existence and it cannot lead to 'absolute knowledge'. Questions about the meaning of existence can only be answered by 'the concrete man' or by what Kierkegaard would call 'subjectivity' (176), and this is the realm in which faith has its proper place. For Bultmann, as for Barth, the Word of God is presented directly to man by God, and it is only by the faith that God also provides that we can apprehend the religious meaning and import of that Word. God provides both the object of belief and also the motivation of the act of belief itself.

The complex thought of Paul Tillich also in its own way implicitly relies upon a Kantian–Kierkegaardian philosophy of religion. Though Tillich is very much concerned, as against Barth, to bring faith and philosophy into contact and dialectical relationship, he accepts that Kant has shown once and for all the impossibility of demonstrating the idea of God in 'positive rational terms' (177). We can, according to Tillich, apprehend the reality of the 'Unconditioned' (which is not an entity, but the 'ground' of the being and value of everything, a little like Plato's Form of the Good), but the Unconditioned is not comprehensible by theoretical reason, save 'symbolically'. Once again, the main task of philosophy is to know what we cannot know by philosophical reason and so to allow a place for an 'original decision' of the individual person in response to God's grace (178).

As we have seen, the strong points which this tradition of the philosophy of religion emphasises and exploits are, first, that religious faith is made autonomous and so independent of any direct reliance upon disputable philosophical premisses; second, the transcendence of the religious order is guaranteed; and third, the 'practical' mode of religious faith and its personal and 'inward' character ('the reasons of the heart') are given primacy. In other words, all the disadvantages of the intellectualist position are compensated for in the Kantian–Kierkegaardian position. Indeed, this latter view of the philosophy of religion depends for a good deal of its plausibility upon its exposure of the difficulties of the intellectualist position, and its own claims to have overcome them.

However, as we have already remarked, this philosophy of religion faces formidable difficulties of its own. First, in order to draw the limits of reason, so as to make room for faith, we have to rely upon philosophical argument. Thus Kant's criticism, in the latter part of the 'Critique of Pure Reason', of any attempt at philosophical proof or disproof of the existence of God, involves the highly disputable philosophical doctrine of the rest of the 'Critique of Pure Reason'; and Kierkegaard's theory of subjectivity likewise involves the assumption of a particular and very contentious epistemological doctrine. In this way then Kant's and Kierkegaard's philosophical agnosticism with respect to the order of faith, is just as much dependent upon philosophical premises as is the intellectualist position of Aquinas, and it is just as vulnerable and open to philosophical dispute as the latter. Philosophy, both Kant and Kierkegaard say, can neither prove nor disprove the objects of religious faith; but this view of philosophy's limits itself depends upon philosophical argument and cannot merely be taken for granted because it happens to harmonise conveniently with a certain view of religion.

Second, it is difficult to see how reason can establish the limits of reason and so show the possibility of a transcendent 'supra-rational' order. Kant and Kierkegaard both want to claim that what is beyond the reach of speculative reason may nevertheless be meaningful for 'practical reason' or 'subjectivity', so that, as Pascal says, the heart may have its own reasons beyond the reach of ordinary reason. For them, that which is beyond the limits of reason is not thereby strictly irrational or unintelligible or meaningless.

This conception of the limits of reason derives its plausibility from its apparent analogy with the limits of sense perception, for in the case of the latter we can quite meaningfully know that our senses are limited and that there are sensible objects that we cannot sense because of the structure or constitution of our sensory equipment. Given the kind of eyes we have, for example, there are many visible things that cannot be seen by us. Kant supposes that, in the same way, the mind is limited by its structure or constitution. As Mansel puts it: 'My conclusions . . . are not deduced from any necessary axiom concerning the condition of the finite in all possible states of existence, but from certain facts of human consciousness in the present life' (179). But this view of the limits of the mind is clearly incoherent, for to draw the limits of the mind we would, so to speak, have to be able to see both sides of the limits and so to be able to transcend the limits. We would, that is, have to know by our minds what it is that we are precluded from knowing by virtue of the constitution of our minds. Certainly, there are many things that we cannot *in fact* know; but it is paradoxical to argue that we can know that there are things we cannot *in principle* know.

It follows from this that there cannot really be any kind of non-rational or non-conceptual form of knowledge or cognition with its own peculiar 'logic', other than ordinary rational knowledge. Kierkegaard virtually admits this when he says that 'subjectivity' cannot have for its object that which is formally self-contradictory or nonsensical for speculative reason. Something cannot be meaningless for speculative reason and yet meaningful for practical reason, or 'subjectivity', or 'the heart', or for 'faith'. If there are reasons of the heart, they must nevertheless be judged by the reason of the head.

The objects of religious faith therefore cannot be wholly transcendent, wholly 'other', without any kind of relation to reason. If they were without any such relation then, as Tillich himself says, we could not be aware of them at all.

Finally, although this philosophy of religion stresses the practical character of religious faith, so that to believe means not to assent to truths but rather to engage oneself or to commit oneself to certain fundamental attitudes, the

143

separation of the practical realm and of the realm of faith from the speculative means that it is impossible to specify the *object* of faith. The faith that philosophical agnosticism makes room for is necessarily a blind faith. Faith then, as with Kierkegaard, tends to become a matter of purely practical attitude and the object of faith ceases to be important. As Kierkegaard says, it is *how* and not the *what* of faith that is of its essence. To believe means that you adopt an attitude of ultimate concern, or an agapeistic attitude, or an attitude of confidence in the coincidence of virtue and happiness. In this way, the philosophical agnosticism which was supposed to guarantee the autonomy and transcendence of faith, leads eventually to a reductionist position where that autonomy and transcendence is effectively denied.

4 Philosophy and the Analysis of Religious Language

(a) Introduction

In the three varieties of the philosophy of religion so far considered, the part of philosophy has become progressively attenuated, and its function with regard to religion more and more 'negative'. In the fourth and final variety of the philosophy of religion we have now to discuss, this attenuation of philosophy's role is carried to its ultimate extreme in that the task of philosophy with respect to religion is merely that of a 'second-order' or 'meta-' analysis of the 'logic' or 'grammar' of religious language. In this view, it has been said, philosophy cannot relevantly criticise religion; it can only display for us the workings, the style of functioning of religious discourse (1). No doubt this meta-inquiry does have some repercussions within the religious realm proper in that it attempts to give an account of how religious locutions may function meaningfully, and at the same time removes confusions about their logical status and their mode of verification. But if philosophical analysis thus makes a place for religion, this is so only in the most negative sense. For, so it is said, a philosophical account of the function of religious locutions has no more to do with religion in the concrete than a phenomenalist account of material objects in terms of statements about sense-data has to do with our ordinary beliefs about the existence of material objects, or than an account of the logic of moral discourse has to do with the formulation of particular moral rules (2). Two men may very well be in agreement about the existence of chairs and tables, or about specific moral issues, and yet they may differ with respect to the account or analysis of what it is to believe in the existence of chairs and tables, or with respect to the analysis of the

145

meaning of moral judgements (3). In the same way, so it is said, two men may agree upon 'first-order' theological issues and yet differ in their meta-theological accounts or analyses of these issues.

Put in another way, just as we can examine the logical properties of formal systems quite apart from any study of the 'content' that may be given to those systems, so also we can examine the logic of religious language quite apart from any *use* that may be given to that language, for example, by Christian believers. Thus, the philosophy of religion is to religion as meta-ethics is to ethics, or as the philosophy of science is to science, or as the meta-language of a formal system is to the language used within the system itself, or as the talking about or 'mention' of the use of an expression is to the actual use of that expression, or as the study of the grammar of a language is to the language itself, or as a map is to the geographical features that are mapped. All these analogies have in fact been used by those who see philosophy's task with regard to religion to be a purely analytical one.

It is of course within the contemporary movement of linguistic analysis that this variety of the philosophy of religion has been mainly developed, and we must begin with a brief account of this philosophical tradition (4). As we shall see, the main figures in this tradition have taken up such widely different positions that it is perhaps misleading to use the term 'linguistic analysis' at all, since it suggests a unified philosophical movement. Linguistic analysis, however, is not so much a school of philosophy, as a general trend or direction in English philosophical thinking from 1900 onwards and, since the 1940s, in some sections of American philosophy. What those philosophers who may loosely be called linguistic analysts have in common is not a philosophical *doctrine* but rather a common *method* of dealing with philosophical problems. The task of the philosopher, so they claim, is not to invent speculative systems, or syntheses, or 'world-views', in the fashion of the classical metaphysicians, but rather to clarify what we *mean* and how we *mean* by the locutions we use. Many, if not all, of the traditional philosophical problems have arisen, so the analysts say, from

146

logico-linguistic confusions about meaning, and when we analyse the conditions which various kinds of locutions must satisfy in order to have meaning, then these problems or puzzles simply evaporate. Philosophical problems are solved by being 'dissolved'. The function of philosophy is thus predominantly (if not wholly) negative or critical or 'therapeutic' in character. On the other hand, analysis does have epistemological and metaphysical repercussions in that, by delimiting the sphere of meaningful propositions, it enables us to see what can and cannot be meaningfully said, and so, indirectly and negatively, enables us to see what there is in the world and what there is not. And it does this without involving us in any metaphysical or epistemological presuppositions such as had been made by the traditional philosophers. A criterion of meaningfulness can be formulated then in purely *logical* (metaphysically and epistemologically *neutral*) terms and, by using this criterion, we can 'dissolve' many traditional metaphysical and epistemological problems.

For the analyst, therefore, the philosopher does not provide us with supra-scientific 'explanations' by postulating 'transcendental' entities such as God, the mind, the soul, substance, etc. Philosophy is rather a 'second-order' activity, that is to say, it is mainly concerned with thinking about how we think (by common sense and science) about things. This applies also, as we have said, to ethics or moral philosophy. The moral philosopher can, by 'meta-ethical' analysis of the 'logic' of ethical propositions and ethical reasoning, clarify the conditions of meaningful ethical discourse, but he cannot help us (at least by philosophical means) to make a positive and specific option of a moral 'way of life'.

It is important to emphasise, however, that the various English and American philosophers who share this general view of the nature and function of philosophy do so for very different reasons and motives and with all kinds of reservations. For instance, the two pioneers of analysis in England, G. E. Moore and Bertrand Russell, both have significantly different conceptions of the bases of analysis and of its function and scope. Again, Wittgenstein's whole conception of analysis differs radically from that elaborated by the Logical Positivists of the 'Vienna Circle' and their followers, such as A. J. Ayer in England and the American 'Logical Empiricists' (5). One can, indeed, distinguish between the conception of analysis which Wittgenstein, who is the central figure in the movement of linguistic analysis, put forward in his early work, the 'Tractatus Logico-Philosophicus' (1921), and that put forward in the later work, 'The Philosophical Investigations' (1953). Among contemporary analysts also there are those who, like J. L. Austin, view 'ordinary language' or 'ordinary use' as in some way a criterion of 'meaning' – a proposition is meaningful in so far as it has a use in ordinary language, and philosophical puzzles are dissolved by describing the way concepts and propositions are used in ordinary language. On the other hand, as against this conception of analysis as being concerned with the 'therapeutic' description of linguistic use in ordinary language, others claim that analysis involves reference to some kind of 'ideal language', and that it is the task of the philosopher to construct such a language, on the model of the formal calculi in mathematical logic, in which logico-linguistic ambiguity and confusion, and so philosophical puzzlement, cannot arise. Then again, for some, analysis is the sole task of philosophy, while for others analysis is seen rather as an indispensable propaedeutic but by no means the be-all and end-all of philosophy. For the latter the possibility of philosophy having a positive supra-analytic or meta-linguistic role (in formulating some kind of 'descriptive metaphysics', as Strawson has called it) is left open.

The movement of analysis is thus a complex philosophical tradition with diverse and even conflicting tendencies within it. And, from this point of view, there is among the analysts no one definitive or typical position regarding religion and philosophy's relationship with it. All that they have in common is the conviction that the proper task of philosophy with regard to religion is the analysis of the 'logic' or 'grammar' of religious language.

148

(b) Wittgenstein and religion

The central figure in the movement of linguistic analysis is undoubtedly Ludwig Wittgenstein (1889–1951). Wittgenstein develops the tentative and informal ideas of Moore and Russell on the function of analysis into a systematic position so that with him it is possible to speak, for the first time, of a *philosophy* of Analysis. His early work, the 'Tractatus Logico-Philosophicus' (1921), reaches very much the same conclusions as the Logical Positivists of the Vienna Circle, namely, that only the propositions of the natural sciences are meaningful – all other propositions (metaphysical and otherwise, including the propositions contained in the 'Tractatus' itself) being meaningless or 'without sense'. Nevertheless, the whole basis of Wittgenstein's philosophical method in the 'Tractatus' is radically different from that of the Logical Positivists. For whereas the method of the Logical Positivists rests upon an arbitrary (and metaphysical) assumption that only empirically verifiable propositions fulfil the logical conditions for meaningfulness, Wittgenstein claims that his criterion of meaning rested upon a purely formal or logical examination of the structure of language. 'Nonsense', so he claims, arises through attempting to think 'outside' the 'limits of language' and to say what cannot be said in language. This means that philosophy in the traditional sense – the investigation of the ultimate principles of thought and reality – is 'nonsense'. The sole task of philosophy is a negative or critical one – 'the logical clarification of thoughts'.

It follows from this that the whole enterprise of philosophical theology is doomed to failure, for any attempt to express philosophically *that* God is, or *what* God is, must inevitably involve attempting to think outside the 'limits of language' and to say what cannot be said. However, Wittgenstein does not in the 'Tractatus' exclude the concept of God as being meaningless in the strict sense, or in the sense in which the Logical Positivists were to exclude any talk about God and the religious order as 'nonsense'. Thus, in some obscure and ambiguous remarks in the latter part of

149

the 'Tractatus', he says 'God does not reveal himself in the world' (6) – so, it would seem, precluding any possibility of a 'proof' of a transcendent God based upon a consideration of the properties of the things in the world. And yet he seems to admit at the same time that it is licit to ask in some sense why the world exists rather than not – 'Not how the world is, is the mystical; but that it is' – even though one cannot give a philosophical answer to this question (7). So, one of his disciples recounts that Wittgenstein once wrote about the experience of moral excellence, that the 'best way of describing it is to say that when I have it I wonder at the existence of the world. And I am then inclined to use such phrases as "How extraordinary that anything should exist" or, "How extraordinary that the world should exist" ' (8). For all this, as we have said, Wittgenstein does not admit that this sense of the contingency of things can be exploited as a datum in a rational demonstration of the existence of God.

If, however, Wittgenstein denied the possibility of a speculative natural theology, it seems that he thought that the possibility of God and of religion could perhaps best be shown through certain moral experiences such as the awareness of sin and guilt and personal insufficiency (9).

Again, it has been argued that for Wittgenstein in the 'Tractatus' God is identified both with the *limit* of the world of facts and with the subject of ethical willing which is also another 'limit'. To say that there is a God is thus to recognise that there is a world of facts independent of my will, for which no reason or justification can be given, and it is also to recognise that there is an ethical point of view wholly dependent upon the will of the ethical subject and independent of the facts (10).

It seems clear then that Wittgenstein did not exclude God and the religious order as being literally meaningless or 'nonsensical'. Rather, as we have seen, his attitude seems to be that the religious order is in some way ineffable and so does not lend itself to philosophical investigation. Thus, of his later work it is reported that he once said: 'Its advantage is that if you believe, say, Spinoza or Kant, this interferes

150

with what you believe in religion, but if you believe me, nothing of the sort' (11).

In his later work, 'Philosophical Investigations' (12), Wittgenstein develops what might be called a 'pluralist' theory of meaning. Thus, instead of speaking about the structure of 'language' as a unitary whole, as he had done in the 'Tractatus', Wittgenstein now speaks of particular 'language-games', that is to say the sets or groups of concepts which we use in talking about, for example, mental states, or about pleasure and pain, or about perception, etc. The meaning of a word is now defined in terms of its *use* in a particular 'language-game', and the task of analysis is to remind us of the context in ordinary language (and of the whole 'form of life' with which it is involved) in which it is used, for there, by definition, it is used meaningfully. This pluralist theory of meaning has been exploited by certain of the later analysts who have argued that religious utterances have their own peculiar meaning and that religious discourse has its own *sui generis* logic. 'Religious language', it has been claimed, 'is a long-established *fait accompli*, and something which does a job which . . . no other segment of language can do' (13). However, we shall examine this development later.

(c) Verificationism and religious language

Wittgenstein's conception of analysis has been crossed with another strain of philosophical thought, that of Logical Positivism or Logical Empiricism introduced into England in the late 1930s by A. J. Ayer's celebrated book, 'Language, Truth and Logic' (14). Wittgenstein and his followers rejected any attempt any attempt to identify their view of philosophical analysis with that espoused by the Logical Positivists of the Vienna Circle, and it is now clear, some thirty years later, that the Logical Positivist episode in contemporary English philosophy was an interruption of what we might call the native Moore–Russell–Wittgenstein tradition. However, in the 1930s and 1940s Ayer's Logical

Positivism did have a great deal of influence in England and was often confused with the tradition we have just mentioned. Indeed, in philosophical circles outside England the doctrine of Ayer's 'Language, Truth and Logic' is still often taken to be what the linguistic analysts are getting at, the view of the world which analysis would lead to in the long run if it were consistent with itself (15). For Ayer, the very possibility of any philosophy of religion is denied since, according to him, analysis shows that religious locutions violate the logical conditions required for any locution to be meaningful. It is not just that the basic religious claims are false; rather they are so conceptually incoherent that they offer us nothing to believe at all. However, even though for Ayer and his followers analysis shows the meaningless of religious utterances, it is important to say something of their views since a good deal of subsequent thinking about religious language has had them in view. As we shall see, one type of philosophy of religion developed by certain analysts takes Ayer's basic position for granted and attempts to make a virtue out of this necessity.

The heart and soul of Ayer's version of the doctrines of the Vienna Circle is the so-called 'Verification Principle', which states that a proposition is only factually meaningful if it is verifiable. The propositions of logic and mathematics may be meaningful as conventional rules which we lay down for our own purposes, but they do not tell us anything about the real world. All other metaphysical propositions about God, the soul, etc. are 'nonsense', that is, they lack sense or meaning (16). For Ayer, then, analysis consists in using the verification principle to discern between empirical and non-empirical propositions and, from these latter, to eliminate the metaphysical ones as 'nonsense'. Second, apart from the elimination of metaphysics, there is a positive task for philosophy in the analysis and clarification of scientific concepts.

For Ayer, as we have said, propositions about the existence of God and, indeed, all religious propositions of whatever kind, are condemned as 'nonsense' by appeal to the verification principle. In other words, Ayer pretends that religious propositions are to be rejected because they fail to satisfy
152

certain purely formal or logical conditions which every proposition must satisfy if it is to have sense or meaning, quite irrespective of whether it is true or false. However, it is obvious enough that the verification principle, as exploited by Ayer in 'Language, Truth and Logic', is not a purely formal principle but depends upon the surreptitious assumption that the *only* kind of verification is that used in the physical sciences. Ethical propositions constitute an embarrassment for Ayer's theory since they seem to be meaningful and yet are not scientifically verifiable. Ayer's answer to this is that these propositions do not describe any 'facts' of any kind but are rather 'emotive' utterances, that is, utterances by means of which we evince certain emotions and attitudes towards given acts or lines of behaviour. Since they do not describe any 'facts', they are neither true nor false, though they may nevertheless be quite meaningful (17). A consequence of this, of course, is that, as Ayer puts it, 'there can be no way of determining the validity of any ethical system, and, indeed, no sense in asking whether any such system is true. All that one may legitimately enquire in this connection is, what are the moral habits of a given person or group of people, and what causes them to have precisely those habits and feelings?' (18) Faced with such conclusions, one may well wonder whether the emotive theory of ethics does not lead to a complete moral nihilism, for if no reasons at all can be given for the adoption of one attitude in preference to another, then moral conduct, based as it is upon these attitudes, must be completely irrational, completely a matter of arbitrary taste. Ayer, however, has repudiated such charges by claiming that his theory does not mean that

> morals are trivial or unimportant, or that people ought not to bother with them. For this would be itself a judgement of values which I have not made and do not wish to make. And even if I did wish to make it, it would have no logical connection with my theory. For the theory is entirely on the level of analysis; it is an attempt to show what people are doing when they make moral judgements;

153

it is not a set of suggestions as to what moral judgements they are to make. (19)

Whether it is in fact possible to make such a clear-cut distinction between the 'analysis' of moral judgements and the formulation of actual concrete moral judgements, as Ayer claims, is open to question (20). However, the important point for our purpose here is that Ayer implicitly admits that ethical utterances may be meaningful without being verifiable. This concession, as we shall see, will be exploited to the full by later analysts who argue that even if religious locutions are not verifiable, they may none the less be meaningful, on the ground that they are not descriptive in function.

A later and more sophisticated version of Ayer's position has been put forward by those who exclude religious statements as meaningless on the grounds that we do not know what would falsify them, that is to say, what would count against them being true. For an assertion to be meaningful, so the argument goes, one must know what would count against its being true; but with typical religious statements such as 'God exists', 'God is good', 'God is loving', the possibility of them not being true is not (indeed cannot be) admitted by the believer; therefore such statements are shown, on purely logical grounds, to be meaningless. Thus, Professor A. Flew, who has been the main proponent of this view, claims that there is 'no conceivable event or series of events the occurrence of which would be admitted by sophisticated religious people to be a sufficient reason for conceding "There wasn't a God after all" or "God does not really love us then" ' (21). And he concludes that religious propositions must therefore be rejected as meaningless. Flew claims that religious propositions are therefore excluded on purely logical grounds, so that their rejection does not involve one in any prior metaphysical commitment, whether that of positivism or empiricism or materialism or any other.

It is obvious, however, that Flew's 'falsifiability principle' is simply a thinly disguised version of the Logical Positivists' verification principle, for it is only if we understand the

154

principle as signifying that an assertion is meaningful if it is known what would count against its truth *in the way in which it is known what could count against the truth of an empirical assertion*, that it becomes something more than a logical truism and enables us to exclude non-empirical truths (among them religious propositions) as meaningless (22).

(d) Reductionist accounts of religious language

Against this general background we may now consider some attempts at the analysis of the 'logic' or 'grammar' of religious language. There are, first, those philosophers who in essence accept Ayer's and Flew's contention that the verification principle excludes religious locutions from having descriptive meaning of any kind. Religious locutions, they agree, do not describe any 'facts', do not make any truth claims, and are neither verifiable nor falsifiable. However, they point out that both Ayer and Flew allow moral utterances to be meaningful even though they are neither verifiable nor falsifiable, and they argue that religious locutions may similarly be meaningful even though non-descriptive. Religious locutions appear to be making factual or descriptive assertions about trans-empirical realities (God, the Persons of the Trinity, etc.), or about historical events (Christ was born of the Virgin Mary, suffered and died, rose from the dead, etc.). But, it is claimed, this way of looking at religious locutions misinterprets their proper function which is that of declaring a certain attitude to life and to the world. When we see them in this light all the difficulties about the verification and falsification of religious propositions simply vanish, for as declarations of intention or attitude they are perfectly meaningful even though they are not verifiable or falsifiable in the strict sense.

The most uncompromising version of this position is that put forward by Professor R. B. Braithwaite in his essay 'An Empiricist's View of the Nature of Religious Belief' (23). Religious locutions, Braithwaite says, are neither statements about empirical facts, nor scientific hypotheses, nor necessary propositions. However, this does not mean that they are

155

therefore meaningless, any more than the fact that moral utterances are not about empirical facts means that they are meaningless. In fact, religious utterances are similar to moral statements in that they declare an intention to act in a certain way; they are, Braithwaite says, 'primarily declarations of adherence to a policy of action, declarations of commitment to a way of life' (24), – an 'agapeistic' way of life as he calls it, that is to say, the way of life St Paul proposes in the First Epistle to the Corinthians, chapter 13. But what, then, of the doctrines of Christianity? They are not, Braithwaite answers, to be taken as literally true, but rather as 'stories' which will help us to live the agapeistic life (25). For Braithwaite, the whole sense of Christian doctrine is that it is a declaration of intention on the part of the believer to behave in a certain way. Thus, 'God is love' is simply a way of declaring 'I intend to follow an agapeistic way of life', and when I recite the Creed and say that Christ suffered and died and rose from the dead, I am not referring to any historical facts, but I am in effect simply telling myself 'stories' to encourage myself to carry through the agapeistic way of life I have chosen (26).

In terms of Braithwaite's position, then, it is possible to hold not only that the proposition 'God exists', taken as a factual statement, is meaningless, but also that the whole corpus of Christian doctrine, together with all the historical statements that go with it, are false if taken literally – and yet claim that one is a Christian believer using religious language in a meaningful way. If it is possible to be accounted a religious believer in these conditions, how, one might ask, is it possible to be an atheist? For Braithwaite, presumably, an atheist would be one who did not choose to live agapeistically and who did not find it necessary to tell himself the Christian 'stories'. But whether it would be possible to justify the choice of the agapeistic way of life as the right one, as against the atheist, Braithwaite does not say (27).

A more nuanced version of Braithwaite's position has been put forward by R. M. Hare (28). Hare begins by admitting that religious statements cannot be assertions, for if they were we would have to admit the possibility of evidence counting against their truth, that is to say, we would have to admit that it was logically possible that God does not exist or does not have the attributes which he is held to have.

Nevertheless, if religious utterances do not function as factual assertions, they do function quite meaningfully as 'bliks'. Hare invents the term 'blik' to describe certain basic metaphysical attitudes towards the world:

> As Hume saw, without a blik there can be no explanation; for it is only by our bliks that we decide what is and what is not an explanation. Suppose we believed that everything that happened, happened by pure chance. This would not of course be an assertion, for it is compatible with anything happening or not happening, and so, incidentally, is its contradictory. But if we had this belief, we should not be able to explain or predict or plan anything. Thus, although we should not be *asserting* anything different from that of a more normal belief, there would be a great difference between us; and this is the sort of difference that there is between those who believe in God and those who really disbelieve in him (29).

If, then, religious utterances function as 'bliks', this means (i) that they do not assert anything about any facts and as such are neither verifiable nor falsifiable; (ii) that they do nevertheless entail a certain kind of behaviour: that is to say, just as one who has a 'blik' about everything happening by pure chance would tend not to bother to plan and tend not to trust predictions, so one who had a religious and a Christian 'blik' would, presumably, tend to behave in a certain way; (iii) that they are justifiable in that it is, apparently, possible to decide which is the *right* 'blik' to have. (Hare, however, does not show clearly how this justification of the religious and Christian 'blik' as the right one is to be effected.)

In a later essay, Hare admits that religious belief involves 'belief in the truth of certain factual statements', but he says that these facts that religious discourse deals with are 'perfectly ordinary empirical facts'. What makes them

157

'religious' is the fact that 'our whole way of living is organised round them; they have for us value, relevance, importance, which they would not have if we were atheists' (30). It is then our *attitude* to the empirical facts which is expressed in religious utterances. However, Hare goes on to argue that the distinction between facts and attitudes is certainly not a clear-cut one, for even our belief that there are objective facts independent of our dispositions is itself the result of an attitude. As Hare puts it: 'There is no distinction between fact and illusion for a person who does not take up a certain attitude to the world' (31). Then, curiously, Hare suggests that, in part at least, Christian belief is a way of expressing those 'metaphysical' attitudes on the basis of which our cognitive commerce with the world is alone possible. Thus, he says:

> Christians believe that God created the world out of chaos, or out of nothing, in the sense of no *thing*. What I am now going to say I say very tentatively. Is it possible that this is our way of expressing the truth that without belief in a divine order – a belief expressed in other terms by means of worshipping assent to principles for discriminating between fact and illusion – there could be no belief in matters of fact or in real objects? Certainly it is salutary to recognise that *even* our belief in so-called hard facts rests in the end on a faith, a commitment, which is not in or to facts, but in that without which there would not be any facts. Plato, it will be remembered, said of the Idea of the Good, which was his name for God, that it was not itself a being, but the source or cause of being (32).

Hare does not explain how a similar translation might be made for Christian doctrines other than that of creation, nor whether the same kind of translation could be made of both the quasi-metaphysical statements ('God is good', 'God cares for his creation', etc.) and the historical statements ('Christ died and then rose from the dead', etc.), which are involved in Christian belief.

A view similar in some respects to those put forward by Braithwaite and Hare has been proposed by Professor Norman Malcolm in an essay entitled 'Is it a Religious Belief that "God Exists"?' (32) Malcolm criticises the assumption that we must first of all decide whether God exists, and then by a separate act take up an attitude towards him, so that, in other words, 'the belief that he exists would not logically imply any affective attitude toward him, but an affective attitude toward him would logically imply the belief that he exists' (33). However, Malcolm questions whether such a separation between a belief in God's existence and taking up an attitude towards him can be made: 'If one conceived of God as the almighty creator of the world and judge of mankind how could one believe that he exists, but not be touched *at all* by awe or dismay or fear? . . . . Would a belief that he exists, if it were completely non-affective, really be a belief that he exists?' (34) It is not clear whether Malcolm wishes to conclude, with Braithwaite, that there is no distinction at all between belief in God's existence and certain attitudes we assume, so that belief in God simply is nothing more than the taking up of certain attitudes to life and the world.

Malcolm also discusses whether belief in God has any discernible consequences or makes any difference to our 'expectations', for if it does not, then it would seem to be completely vacuous. Religious belief does not, he argues, involve empirical consequences (as, say, a scientific belief does) which would serve to verify or falsify the belief; all the same, religious belief can make a difference to a person's outlook upon life, and in so far as it does, it escapes the charge of vacuity. As Malcolm puts it, 'the man who believes that his sins will be forgiven if he is truly repentant, might thereby be saved from despair. What he believes has, for him, no verification or falsification; yet the belief makes a great deal of difference to his action and feeling' (35). Religious utterances, then, are neither verifiable nor falsifiable; nevertheless they are meaningful in so far as they make a difference to the way a person acts and feels, that is, to his behaviour.

These attempts to analyse religious language take it for granted that religious locutions cannot have a descriptive function, and so cannot be either true or false. For Braithwaite this means not just that they are analogous to moral locutions, but that they perform essentially the same function as the latter and are in fact a species of moral locution. For Hare, on the other hand, they perform the same function as quasi-metaphysical principles and are a species of the latter (36). Thus, for both of them, the meaningfulness of religious language is 'saved' only by reducing it to ethical or metaphysical language, so that it does not have any distinctive and irreducible meaning-function of its own.

It has been claimed that Braithwaite is not in fact reducing religious beliefs to ethical attitudes but is simply offering an account of what it is to have a religious belief, very much in the same sense that Ayer denies that he is a moral nihilist since his emotive theory of ethics is simply presenting a philosophical analysis of moral beliefs without attempting to specify which moral rules we ought to adopt (37). But it is difficult to maintain this distinction here, for the whole gist of Braithwaite's analytical account of the function of religious language is to show that it is a species of ethical language in that it functions in essentially the same way as the latter. It would surely be odd to claim that 'I believe in God' at the 'first-order' level means exactly the same for Braithwaite and for St Thomas Aquinas, and that the only difference between the two is that they offer different 'second-order' philosophical analyses of that 'first-order' statement. For if Braithwaite's analysis is correct, it is simply conceptual confusion to claim, as Aquinas does, that 'God' refers to a special kind of entity.

As against this reductionist analysis of religious language, an attempt has been made to show that religious locutions have their own *sui generis* meaning, by developing Wittgenstein's later ideas about 'language games' and 'forms of life'. In his 'Philosophical Investigations' Wittgenstein proposes a theory of meaning according to which the meaning of any locution can only be determined by the use or function or role it has within the context of a given 'language game' – the whole set of interrelated concepts that are involved in science, for example, or in morality, or in aesthetic appreciation, or – in a more particular sense – in talking about persons, telling a joke, reporting an event, describing an object, giving an account of a dream, etc. (38). And these language-games are themselves involved with what Wittgenstein calls 'forms of life' (39). Thus Wittgenstein says: 'If a lion could talk, we could not understand him' (40), meaning by this that, although a lion might make suitable speech-sounds, it could not be said to have made an intelligible utterance. For the whole context in which those sounds might be made differs too radically from that in which human beings use those sounds to make intelligible utterances. It is these general contexts that Wittgenstein calls 'forms of life' (41).

There is then no such thing as language *tout court* but rather particular 'language games', and similarly there is no general criterion of the meaningfulness of language, but each language-game has its own criterion of meaningfulness proper to it which can only be discovered by looking at the 'form of life' in which it is involved. These forms of life, for Wittgenstein, cannot themselves be justified in any way – they are given, and there is a sense in which one has simply to choose to accept or to reject them. Thus Wittgenstein says: 'What has to be accepted, the given, is – so one could say – forms of life' (42). It is not at all clear how we are to determine which language-games are played and which forms of life obtain. At times Wittgenstein almost suggests that this is to be ascertained by some kind of sociological investigation; at other times, he seems to suggest that analysis can show *a priori* that there is a distinctive 'job' to be done by a specific 'language' that is not done by other languages.

Although Wittgenstein himself says very little systematically about religion and the status of religious locutions, it is obvious that this theory of meaning is applicable to the latter. Thus, it could be said that there was a religious form

161

of life and that it was only within the context of this distinctive form of life that the meaningfulness of religious locutions could be assessed. Any attempt to show that religious locutions are meaningless because they fail to satisfy some supposed general criterion of meaning, such as the verification principle or the falsifiability principle, could then be dismissed, for there cannot be any such general criterion. What we must do rather, it might be argued, is to situate religious locutions in the form of life of which they are a part, and then we will be able to see exactly what function they have.

Wittgenstein suggests tentatively that religious belief typically involves using a 'picture', or a way of looking at the world and at life, in such a manner that it is constantly before the mind, and so that it influences the way in which we live. Believing in the Last Judgement, for example, is a particular way of looking at history and human life, and regulating one's life accordingly:

> Suppose somebody made this guidance for life: believing in the Last Judgement. Whenever he does anything, this is before this mind. In a way, how are we to know whether to say he believes this will happen or not? Asking him is not enough. He will probably say he has (no) proof. But he has what you might call an unshakable belief. It will show, not by reasoning or by appeal to ordinary grounds for belief, but rather by regulating for in all his life. (43)

These fragmentary suggestions have been taken up and developed by certain religiously-minded Wittgensteinians who argue that there is a distinctive religious 'language game' with its own criteria of meaningfulness and that the task of philosophical analysis is to bring out the peculiar significance and intelligibility of religious language, and in general to show that 'religious statements at their rock bottom are in order – i.e. in their own kind of order' (44). Thus, for example, Norman Malcolm has defended St Anselm's definition of God as a necessary existent by claiming that the notion of necessary existence plays a part in the Judaeo-Christian 'language game'. It has, Malcolm says, 'a

162

place in the thinking and the lives of human beings', and as such is meaningful:

> In the Ninetieth Psalm it is said: 'Before the mountains were brought forth, or ever thou hadst formed the earth and the world even from everlasting to everlasting, thou art God.' Here is expressed the idea of the necessary existence and eternity of God, an idea that is essential to the Jewish and Christian religions. In those complex systems of thought, those 'language-games', God has the status of a necessary being. Who can doubt that? Here we must say with Wittgenstein, 'This language-game is played'. I believe we may rightly take the existence of those religious systems of thought in which God figures as a necessary being to be a disproof of the dogma, affirmed by Hume and others, that no existential proposition can be necessary. (45)

Thus, when we examine the religious 'form of life' within which this 'language-game' is played, or when we see the 'human phenomena' behind the use of the concept of 'necessary being', we see something of its meaning. The experience of guilt, for example, can give meaning to the concept of a mercy that is limitless and beyond all measure (46).

Again, G. E. Hughes has criticised attempts to show that religious language is conceptually confused by arguing that all such attempts involve forcing an 'alien logic' upon religious language.

> What are our criteria here for conceptual confusion? [he asks]. I should guess that it is possible to show any category or categories of statements or expressions to be conceptually confused if one is allowed to insist that they must conform to the logic of some other category or categories of statements or expressions if they are to be said to make sense. Such arguments [he goes on] ... can be made to look very different in their upshot if we adopt an alternative programme for meta-theology. This alternative programme can be indicated roughly by saying that it consists

163

in allowing the actual use of religious terms and statements to determine their logic, rather than trying to force an alien logic upon them. If we adopt this basis, we can then regard arguments which show how religious statements generate contradictions when they are construed on the model of other types of statements, not as demonstrating that they are conceptually confused, but as showing by contrast some of the peculiarities of their own logic. (47)

In much the same way, W. D. Hudson has argued that, 'in the case of theism, we must decide whether or not to deal in questions and answers that have to do with God. This decision is logically like deciding whether or not to do science, think morally, or take up some branch of mathematics. It is the decision to give, or not to give, a certain frame to experience' (48). However, Hudson says, the decision is not entirely arbitrary since the religious form of life is one of those forms of life that 'seem to be definitive of humanity in the sense that it is essential to our concept of man, as man, that he should engage in them' (49).

This whole view has received its fullest elaboration in a remarkable essay by Peter Winch entitled 'Understanding a Primitive Society' (50). Winch is mainly concerned with the question of meaning in the social sciences, but he indicates how his view could be applied to religious discourse as well. Winch considers the findings of the English anthropologist E. E. Evans-Pritchard in his work 'Witchcraft, Oracles and Magic among the Azande'. The African Azande believe that some of their members are witches capable of exercising occult influences, and they engage in elaborate rituals and consultation of oracles in order to protect themselves. Given their belief that there are witches, then the kinds of things the Azande do and believe follow quite logically. The Azande do not therefore reason in some kind of 'non-logical' way; they simply reason unscientifically, for they are not concerned to check the truth of the premiss that there are witches in a scientific way (i.e. seeing whether this belief is in accord with objective reality), nor the truth of the conclusions that follow from this premiss.

164

The thought of the Azande is then, so Evans-Pritchard concludes, logical but unscientific, that is, not in accord with objective reality.

Winch objects to this conclusion in that it assumes that the Azande's belief in witches must be a scientific belief, and further that the notion of being 'in accord with objective reality' (at least in the sense Evans-Pritchard gives to it) is intelligible *outside* the context of scientific reasoning. But in fact Evans-Pritchard's notions of 'reality' and 'accordance with reality' mean 'that which is verified by observation and experiment', and it is only within this context that this is intelligible:

> Evans-Pritchard [Winch says] is trying to work with a conception of reality which is *not* determined by its actual use in language. He wants something against which that use can itself be appraised. But this is not possible; and no more possible in the case of scientific discourse than it is in any other. We may ask whether a particular scientific hypothesis agrees with reality and test this by observation and experiment. Given the experimental methods, and the established use of the theoretical terms entering into the hypothesis, then the question whether it holds or not is settled by reference to something independent of what I, or anybody else, care to think. But the general nature of the data revealed by the experiment can only be specified in terms of criteria built into the methods of experiment employed and these, in turn, make sense only to someone who is conversant with the kind of scientific activity within which they are employed. (51)

There are, in fact, Winch goes on, other contexts where 'reality' and 'accordance with reality' are also meaningful, though not in a scientific way:

> The check of the independently real is not peculiar to science. The trouble is that the fascination science has for us makes it easy for us to adopt its scientific form as a paradigm against which to measure the intellectual respectability of other modes of discourse. Consider what

165

God says to Job out of the whirlwind: 'Who is this that darkeneth counsel by words without knowledge? . . . Where wast thou when I laid the foundations of the earth? declare, if thou hast understanding. Who hath laid the measures thereof, if thou knowest? or who hath stretched the line upon it . . . ? Shall he that contendeth with the Almighty instruct him? he that reproveth God, let him answer it.' Job is taken to task for having gone astray by having lost sight of the reality of God; this does not, of course, mean that Job has made any sort of theoretical mistake, which could be put right, perhaps, by means of an experiment. God's reality is certainly independent of what any man may care to think, but what that reality amounts to can only be seen from the religious tradition in which the concept of God is used, and this use is very unlike the use of scientific concepts, say of theoretical entities. The point is that it is within the religious use of language that the conception of God's reality has its place, though, I repeat, this does not mean that it is at the mercy of what anyone cares to say; if this were so, God would have no reality. (52)

Winch stresses that he is not proposing any kind of relativism, but is simply developing Wittgenstein's point that we cannot determine the meaning of a concept apart from an investigation of its use within a given language-game (53). The notion of 'reality' itself, and of 'accordance with reality', of 'truth', and of 'rationality', and 'intelligibility', also have meaning only *within* particular language-games. Thus, in an earlier work Winch says that there is no 'norm for intelligibility in general'. 'Criteria of logic', he goes on, 'are not a direct gift of God, but arise out of, and are only intelligible in the context of, ways of living or modes of social life as such. For instance, science is one such mode and religion is another; and each has criteria of intelligibility peculiar to itself' (54).

For Winch, then, whether and how religious language is meaningful and intelligible can only be determined from *within* the religious language game, or more generally by looking at the complex tissue of activities, attitudes, procedures, beliefs, institutions, that make up the religious form of life, and seeing how religious locutions function within this context. Presumably, for Winch, the only way of being an atheist would be to hold that one does not accept the religious form of life, or more radically, that this latter makes no sense and is not a genuine form of life, though Winch does not clearly say on what grounds one might reject the religious form of life, or how a purported form of life might be shown not to be genuinely one (55). Winch does not discuss in any detail what the characteristics of the religious form of life are, although it is clear that for him it will *not* be a quasi-scientific form of life where belief in God functions as an experimental hypothesis which empirical evidence may falsify or verify. As he says: What God's reality amounts to 'can only be seen from the religious tradition in which the concept of God is used, and this use is very unlike the use of scientific concepts, say of theoretical entities' (56). Some suggestions in this direction have, however, been made by D. Z. Phillips, who takes up a position very like that of Winch's (57). A typical religious belief such as the Last Judgement is not, Phillips claims, an hypothesis or scientific conjecture but rather a 'framework . . . within which [the believer] meets fortune, misfortune, and the evil that he finds in his own life and in life about him' (58). Or again, in Wittgenstein's description, believing in the Last Judgement is to have a picture before one's mind so that it regulates one's actions. This picture is not invented by the believer and he does not stand in judgement on it. 'The believer does not want to say that he measures these pictures and finds that they are all right or finds that they are wanting. On the contrary, the believers wish to claim that it is not they who measure the pictures, since in a sense, the pictures measure them; they are the measure in terms of which they judge themselves' (59). These pictures are not merely symbolic or metaphorical devices as though, independently of the pictures, we could have a notion of divinity. 'The picture is not a metaphorical way of saying something else. It says what it says' (60). Elsewhere Phillips has argued

167

that the concept of the eternal is central to the religious form of life and that this is disclosed in the experience of what he calls 'unconditional love'. 'Coming to see the possibility of such love amounts to the same thing as coming to see the possibility of belief in God' (61).

Fairly obviously, a number of difficulties arise over this whole conception of the meaning of religious language. First, there is the general problem of what is to count as a form of life and how we are to determine it? Is it simply a matter of sociological looking and seeing that groups of people say prayers, perform rituals, entertain certain 'pictures', claim to see the possibility of unconditional love, just as in Winch's example we observe that the Azande believe in witches and consult oracles? If this were the way to determine what was a form of life, then there is nothing that might not be a form of life. There might well be, for example, an atheistic form of life organised around the rejection of God and *within* that form of life the notion of God would be meaningless and the religious language-game simply could not be played. We could then retort to Malcolm, this language-game is *not* played! Can we instead then define a form of life in terms of a distinctive and irreducible set of activities or functions, so that we would admit that there was a religious form of life if there were certain functions that religion fulfilled that were not fulfilled by science or morality or aesthetics, etc.? G. E. Hughes conflates these two modes of determining forms of life by saying, 'the actual usage of religious terms within religious language is taken as normative for the logical type and the kind of meaning they have ... because religious language is a long established *fait accompli*, and something which does a job which, as far as I have been able to discover, no other segment of language can do' (62). However, the fact that religious language is a *fait accompli* (that it has in fact been used for a long time by large numbers of people), and that it does a distinctive and irreducible job, are two quite distinct things (63). If it is the latter that justifies us talking about a distinctive religious language-game and a distinctive religious form of life, then of course we will have to be able to specify

168

what it is that makes it distinctive, or what is the peculiar job that religious language alone can do, over and above scientific language and moral language and aesthetic language and metaphysical language.

If we *are* able to specify a distinctive religious job for religious language, then this will be a good reason for accepting it and entering into the religious form of life. The atheist would then, by rejecting the religious form of life, be cutting himself off from a whole range of experience, very much as a person who rejected any aesthetic dimension to life would be cutting himself off from a dimension of human experience, or one who refused to adopt a moral point of view would be diminishing himself as a man (64). In this sense, the atheist would be analogous to the philistine and amoralist. But the difficulty is how to show that religious language does serve a distinctive function of its own. The mere fact that it is used by numbers of people proves nothing, for what we have to show is that it is being used *in a distinctive way* and is not, for example, just a confused way of making scientific or moral or metaphysical points. Winch claims, for example, that the Azande's belief in witches is not meant by the Azande as a scientific belief that could be tested by observation and experiment, even though perhaps to an outsider their talk about witches may seem to be descriptive in mode and quasi-scientific in intent. But all that this means is that the Azande are using what appears to be descriptive language for non-descriptive purposes. For the Azande 'There are witches' has a non-descriptive meaning, and this means in turn that it cannot be verified or falsified in the way in which descriptive locutions are. This is not a very remarkable conclusion, and it does not imply that the Azande have a special kind of logic, with special concepts of 'accordance with reality' and truth and rationality. Winch's extension of Wittgenstein's doctrine that the meaning of a concept must be determined within a language game, to the fundamental concepts of reality, intelligibility, truth, rationality, etc. (concepts which are presupposed to *all* language-games in that it would be impossible to have a language without reference to them), leads him in fact, despite his protests, to a radical form of relativism. For on his premises there can be no real dispute as to the truth or falsity of religion between one who accepts a religious form of life and one who rejects it; and equally it would be impossible for those within the religious form of life to question it and to 'criticise the standards of intelligibility and rationality which they have held hitherto' (65).

Analysis of religious language is supposed to disclose, as we have said, that it has a *sui generis* function of its own, just as scientific language has its own distinctive function, and moral language its own function. But when we examine what are proposed as central characteristics of the religious form of life, none of them appears to be really distinctive. Thus, if 'I believe in the Last Judgement' is not meant to be a conjecture about a future happening but rather a declaration that one is entertaining a certain picture that has implications for the way in which one lives, this appears to be both a quasi-metaphysical point ('I believe in the Last Judgement' is to be construed as 'I see the world and life in a certain perspective') and a quasi-ethical point ('I believe in the Last Judgement' is to be construed as 'I intend to act in a certain way'). Again, if 'God exists' means 'There is the possibility of unconditional love', then this is to reduce religious language to moral language, very much as Braithwaite does when he says that 'I believe in God' means 'I intend to live agapeistically'. In fact, most of the attempts to characterise religious language end up by making it into a species of moral language or metaphysical language in the manner of the reductionists, though, rather like Kant, they disguise their reductionism by oscillating between the descriptive and non-descriptive (or as Kant would say, between the speculative and practical) functions of religious language. Thus on the one hand it is claimed that religious locutions are not descriptive (and so not subject to verification and falsification), their point being rather to bring out (through 'pictures') certain features of the world or of human life, and to influence one to live in a certain way. And yet, on the other hand, the descriptive grammatical form of religious locutions is retained and exploited, so that, for instance, it seems as though there is after all an entity described by the term 'God', for example, and a future historical happening described by the 'Last Judgement'.

(f) Conclusion

This whole approach to the philosophy of religion rests upon a special view of the nature and scope of philosophy itself and of the role that conceptual analysis plays with respect to 'first-order' realms of discourse. Philosophy for the analyst is essentially clarificatory or therapeutic; it is not concerned to explain but simply to describe. Again, by analogy with the distinction we can make between the meta-language and the object-language of formal systems, the analysts suppose that we can likewise distinguish sharply between meta-ethics and normative ethics and between meta-theology and theology proper. Further, the analysts take for granted Wittgenstein's theory that meaning can only be determined by reference to specific language-games and forms of life, and they also suppose that the theory can be extended without difficulty to the religious sphere, so that we can speak of the religious language-game and the religious form of life within which religious locutions have their own peculiar meaning.

All of these suppositions, it goes without saying, are highly contentious on the purely philosophical level, and they need to be argued for philosophically and not merely taken for granted, as they often are by the Wittgensteinian fideists (66). Thus, as Wittgenstein himself admitted in the 'Tractatus', the idea of a purely therapeutic philosophy that does not itself make any positive philosophical statements, is a paradoxical one (for the 'Tractatus' itself is full of philosophical statements), and nothing he says in his later work helps him to overcome this paradox.

Again, the application of the distinction between first-order and second-order discourse, obvious enough in formal systems, to religious language, is open to grave objections. First, whereas in arithmetic or algebra, say, we can all be

171

in agreement at the 'first-order' level, while differing profoundly about the correct meta-mathematical account of arithmetic and algebra, it is precisely the conceptual coherence of 'first-order' religious talk that is subject to controversy. In a very real sense there is no general agreement on religious data in the same way in which there is agreement upon basic arithmetical truths, or upon the existence of material objects, or even upon the central moral rules. We can question the very possibility of religion in a way in which we cannot really question arithmetic, or the existence of the material world, or the possibility of morality. As it has been put: 'At all times and at all places, even among the most primitive tribes, there have been sceptics and scoffers, people who though perfectly familiar with the religious language-game played in their culture would not play the religious language-game, not because they could not, but because, even though they were perfectly familiar with it, even though they had an insiders' understanding of it, they found it incoherent' (67). Second, if meta-theology has no repercussions at all on 'first-order' religious language, or if 'first-order' religious language does not have any meta-theological implications, then it is difficult to see what the point of meta-theology is. If a 'second-order' analysis is compatible with *any* 'first-order' phenomena, then almost anything goes in the sphere of meta-theological analysis.

There are further difficulties, as we have seen, about the Wittgensteinian theory of meaning being exploited here, for it seems to admit any language-game that is 'played' as *ipso facto* meaningful. Thus, if the fact that numbers of people engage in religious talk implies that religious language is meaningful, then equally we would have to admit that the fact that numbers of people engage in atheistic talk implies that religious language is meaningless. If, to escape this conclusion, it is said that we need to look not just at quasi-sociological facts about linguistic usage, but rather at the distinctive function or job that religious language alone can do, then we must be able to specify what this unique function or job is. We must, that is, be able to show that there is a real and irreducible place for religious language and that it

172

is not just serving as a disguised form of ethical or meta-physical or poetical language. And of course we will not be able to do this simply by inspecting the way in which people actually do use religious language.

Put in another way, the difficulty is how to characterise the religious form of life within which religious locutions have their meaning. If we were allowed to say that a religious form of life is one that is organised around the concept of God, this latter having been proved to be meaningful independently, then of course we could show the distinctiveness of the religious form of life. But, according to the Wittgensteinian theory, we can only determine the meaning of the concept of God *within* the religious form of life, and we are in addition forbidden to use the concept as though it were descriptive of some entity, since this would be to confuse the function of religious language with that of scientific language. As we have seen, none of the characterisations so far offered by the Wittgensteinian fideists show the religious form of life to be *sui generis*, for neither Malcolm's experience of sin and guilt, nor Phillips's experience of unconditional love, nor Wittgenstein's eschatological 'pictures', are so peculiar to religion that they can be used to define it.

If there are these difficulties about characterising the religious form of life – indeed, difficulties as to whether it is characterisable at all – the whole view of the philosophy of religion we are here considering becomes very problematic. For if there is no clear way of determining whether there is a genuine realm of religious discourse, and an irreducibly distinctive religious form of life, then the view that the sole task of philosophy with respect to religion is to display the idiosyncratic functions of religious language, loses its *raison d'être*.

Despite these criticisms, however, there is no doubt that the analyst's discussions of the 'logic' of religious language have made us much more sensitive to the complex problems of meaning that arise within the religious realm, and to the dangers of approaching religious language with a simple-minded verificationism that assumes that *scientific* meaning is paradigmatic (68). Again, the analysts emphasise how

173

important it is to enter sympathetically into the religious stream of life if we are to understand religious language.

However, as it has been remarked, 'having such an understanding of religion is perfectly compatible with asserting, as did the Swedish philosopher Axel Hägerström, that the concept of God is "nothing but a creation of our own confused thought" growing out of our need to escape "from the anxiety and wearisomeness of life" ' (69).

In order to show that the concept of God is not, as Hägerström says, an illusory one, we would need to demonstrate its instantiation in some way and not merely rest content with describing and analysing its *de facto* use in religious discourse (70). We may admit perhaps (although even this is very contentious) that the task of philosophy with regard to the sphere of morals or our knowledge of the external world is purely 'descriptive', so that philosophy does not 'justify' morality or our knowledge in the sense of demonstrating their possibility. But in the case of religion philosophy cannot escape such a justificatory role.

174

5 Conclusion

We have been concerned to isolate four main conceptions of the philosophy of religion that have appeared in the history of Western thought, and to analyse their respective logical anatomies. Each type represents an original and thorough-going attempt to reconcile the demands of philosophical reason with the demands of that which is in some way 'beyond' reason – the 'divine', the 'numinous', the 'super-natural'. Each type exhibits its own peculiar understanding of what philosophy is, on the one hand, and what religion is on the other. Each has its own philosophical and religious benefits and attractions and its own equal and opposite difficulties and drawbacks: in the philosophy of religion, as in life, you pay a price for every advantage gained.

For the most part, the religion that Western philosophy has had to confront and to come to terms with has been Judaeo-Christianity and its derivatives such as Islam. There are of course large differences between the various sectarian interpretations of Judaeo-Christianity, but their family resemblance becomes manifest when they are contrasted, for example, with Hinduism or Buddhism or Taoism. Fundamentally, the religious phenomena that religious philosophers as diverse as Augustine, Pseudo-Dionysius, Aquinas, Pascal, Kant, Kierkegaard and Tillich have to confront and 'save', are the same. Consequently, to the extent that by the 'philosophy of religion' we have understood here 'the philosophy of the Judaeo-Christian religion', our findings and conclusions are correspondingly limited in scope. If we had, for example, focused our attention on Hinduism or Buddhism instead, it might be that other quite different issues would have arisen for consideration and that the whole question of philosophy's relations with the religious order would have appeared in a rather different light.

However, as we remarked at the beginning of this work, what we know as the philosophy of religion is, as a matter of historical fact, a child of the conjunction between Greek philosophy and Judaeo-Christianity, so that our concentration upon the phenomena provided by this latter tradition is not as serious a limitation as it might appear. Certainly there has been a vast amount of quasi-philosophical speculation within both Hinduism and Buddhism, and it is salutary to be made aware of these other radically variant approaches to religion and the different range of religious phenomena with which they confront us. As Professor R. N. Smart and others have reminded us, our view of the philosophy of religion in the West has for the most part been an extremely myopic one (1).

None the less it remains true that it was with the Greeks that philosophy was first distinguished from mythical and religious speculation and achieved an autonomy and independence that it did not ever reach in Eastern cultures; and it is also true that Judaeo-Christianity lent itself to (indeed, invited) being philosophised about, so to speak, in a way in which other religions have not. Whether it be due to Providence or historical luck, it is a fact that Greek philosophy and Judaeo-Christianity have been amazingly complementary to each other. And it is from this happy conjunction, as we have said, that the philosophy of religion was born. It was within this particular context that the attempt to reconcile reason with that which is beyond reason seemed to be an urgent and possible enterprise in a way in which it has not seemed either pressing or possible in other religious contexts.

Despite the various particular criticisms made of the four views of the philosophy of religion, we have not attempted to adjudicate between them. Any such comparative judgement could only be made by reference to two distinct, though related, sets of criteria. There are, first, purely philosophical considerations arising from the specific conception of philosophy's nature and role presupposed to each type of the philosophy of religion. Thus the Platonic/neo-Platonic version of the philosophy of religion is only viable

176

if some kind of 'transcendental' metaphysics is possible. Aquinas's philosophy of religion likewise presupposes the possibility of philosophy having a metaphysical role. In the same way the Kantian and neo-Kantian view of the philosophy of religion depends for its validity upon the philosophical adequacy of Kant's 'critical' philosophy; and the Wittgensteinian view of religious language also assumes the truth of Wittgenstein's 'analytical' or 'therapeutic' (anti-metaphysical) view of philosophy's role. Which view of the nature and role of philosophy is the correct or more adequate one would have to be argued on purely philosophical grounds, and consequently any judgement between the four types of philosophy of religion would have to be argued in the same way.

There are, however, other considerations to be taken into account in making such a judgement in that any philosophical account of religion that leads to systematic theological 'reductionism' is clearly inadequate. It is extremely difficult to define exactly what constitutes 'reductionism' and what its limits are (2), but Hegel, Arnold and Santayana (to take what are, one hopes, non-contentious examples) may perhaps be considered to offer clearly reductionist accounts of religion (3). Thus for Hegel a philosophical account is given of religion which results in it being interpreted or re-described as a species of metaphysics; for Arnold the meaningfulness of religious language is 'saved' by construing the latter as a type of moral language; while for Santayana religious attitudes are identified with quasi-aesthetic attitudes. In such accounts as these religion is clearly reduced to something else that is not religion; they are philosophies of religion that effectively deny that there is such a thing as religion to be philosophised about and (unless we accept some kind of radical Logical Positivist position) they are on that account defective.

However, it is not easy to distinguish sharply between the legitimate 'interpretation' of religious phenomena that any philosophy of religion necessarily involves, and reductionism of the kind just described. If, for example, one judges Arnold to be an ethical reductionist, is it as clear that Kant's philosophy of religion may be described in the same way? Or if Hegel is said to be a metaphysical reductionist, in that for him religion becomes a species of metaphysics, is the same true of Plato and Plotinus? Or again, how are we to judge Spinoza? Is Spinoza guilty of reducing religion to philosophy, or is he attempting to give philosophy a religious dimension; is he an atheist or a 'God-intoxicated' man? There is a further difficulty when we consider accounts of specific religious traditions such as Christianity. Is it obvious, for example, that Tillich's philosophy of religion results in a reductionist denaturing of the Christian religion? It has been charged that Tillich's position violates 'essential Christian belief' and that 'the proper place for Tillich and many of his followers today is in the Hindu religion' (4). Certainly we may admit that Tillich's view of the Christian religion is at odds with traditional theology, but then Tillich is obviously concerned to proffer a reinterpretation of Christianity which will reveal its true essence, hitherto obscured by traditional theology. Once again, as we have said, it is not easy to distinguish nicely between legitimate reinterpretation of the data of Christianity and reductionism. Nevertheless, despite the difficulties of applying this criterion it remains true that a philosophy of religion that effectively evacuates religion of any specific meaning of its own by reducing it to that which is not religion, is deficient as a philosophy of religion.

These are the kinds of criteria that would have to be invoked if we were to try to adjudicate between the various types of philosophy of religion we have discussed. Fortunately, it is not our business to carry out that work of adjudication here. Our task has been the more modest one of describing and critically analysing the main ways in which philosophy and religion have been concerned with each other in the past two thousand years of Western thought.

Notes

INTRODUCTION

1. R. Otto, 'The Idea of the Holy' (Oxford, 1917). Otto attempts to show, not very successfully, that Nirvana has some analogy with the 'Wholly Other.' See R. N. Smart, 'Philosophers Speak of God' (London, 1964) p. 136: 'In early Buddhism, in the Theravada and in Jainism the mystical quest is central, and there is little place for the religion of the numinous.'

2. 'The Varieties of Religious Experience' (1902; Fontana Library, London, 1960), p. 46.

3. W. Jaeger, 'The Theology of the Early Greek Philosophers' (Oxford, 1967); Etienne Gilson, 'Reason and Revelation in the Middle Ages' (New York, 1938).

CHAPTER 1

1. G. Kaufman, 'Philosophy of Religion and Christian Theology', in 'Journal of Religion', (1957) 236.

2. R. Bultmann, 'The Question of Natural Revelation', in 'Essays: Philosophical and Theological' (London, 1955) p. 90.

3. 'Qu'est ce qu'un dogme?', in 'La Quinzaine' (16 Apr 1905) p. 517: 'Primarily a dogma (i.e. a theological statement) has a *practical* meaning. Primarily, it states a presumption of a practical kind.' p. 518: 'Christianity is not a system of speculative philosophy, but a source and rule of life, a discipline of moral and religious action, in short, a set of practical means for obtaining salvation.'

4. Cf. W. F. R. Hardie, 'Aristotle's Ethical Theory' (Oxford, 1968) p. 340: 'Aristotle was not a democratic liberal, and did not shrink from the idea that happiness, at least in its best form, is for the fortunate few not the meritorious many.'

5. Ibid., p. 523.

6. See A. D. Nock, 'Conversion: The Old and the New in Religion from Alexander the Great to Augustine of Hippo' (Oxford, 1933), esp. chap. xi, 'Conversion to Philosophy'.

7. On the medieval 'dialecticians' and 'anti-dialecticians' and St Anselm's intellectualism, see M. J. Charlesworth, 'St Anselm's Proslogion' (Oxford, 1965) pp. 25–6.

8. See Gilson, 'Reason and Revelation in the Middle Ages', pp. 55–65.

9. 'Republic', 365e; 'Laws', 885d.

10. 'Republic', 364–7.

11. 'Republic', 379a–380d.

12. A. Diès, 'Autour de Platon', ii (Paris, 1927) 591. This old but still valuable study has two excellent chapters, 'Le Dieu de Platon' (chap. iii), and 'La Religion de Platon' (chap. iv).

13. 'Philebus', 28d; 'Laws', 889e–890a; 'Gorgias', 482c–484c.

14. Cited in Diès, 'Autour de Platon', ii 533; Cf. p. 536: 'The main proofs of the existence of God are, with Plato, echoes not only of Socrates' teachings but also of an entire literature that existed before him.'

15. W. Jaeger, 'The Theology of the Early Greek Philosophers' (Oxford, 1967) p. 36.

16. Ibid., p. 54: 'He was profoundly impressed by the way in which philosophy was disturbing the old religion, and it was this that made him insist upon a new and purer conception of the divine nature.'

17. Ibid., p. 72.

18. 80a–b.

19. 'Sophist', 249a.

20. 509b.

21. See, for example, Plato's 'Seventh Letter', 341c–402, regarding the divine: 'There is no writing of mine on this subject, nor will there ever be; for it cannot be put into words like other objects of knowledge.'

22. Cf. A. J. Festugière, 'Personal Religion among the Greeks' (Berkeley and Los Angeles, 1934) p. 133: 'If *nous* is taken in its twofold meaning as both intellectual faculty and mystical faculty, there will result a philosophical contemplation leading, in its final stage, to mystical contact; here we have the true Platonic tradition, that adopted, for example, by Plotinus.' See also the same author's 'Contemplation et vie contemplative selon Platon', 2nd ed. (Paris, 1950).

23. Cf. R. Hackforth, 'Plato's Theism', in 'Studies in Plato's Metaphysics', ed. R. E. Allen (London, 1965) p. 440: 'For Plato the Demiurge is a *theos*, so is the created universe, so are the stars and planets and the gods of popular theology, and the (possible) plurality of good souls in "Laws" x; the adjective *theios* is commonly applied to the Forms.'

24. Hackforth, ibid. Cf. Diès, 'Autour de Platon', ii 592–3: 'The dialectical ascent and the mystical or religious ascent are fundamentally the same movement – the movement of the entire soul towards being, towards the intelligible, towards God.'

25. 966c–d.

26. 90a.

27. F. Solmsen, 'Plato's Theology' (New York, 1942) p. 126, claims that Plato's religious intellectualism was balanced by the influence upon him of the mystery religions and their 'general feeling of man's dependence on the gods and the atmosphere of religious awe'. Cf. also W. K. C. Guthrie, 'Orpheus and Greek Religion' (London, 1935) pp. 158–69. But it remains true, as Solmsen admits, that the ecstasy typical of the mystery cults has no place in Plato's religion. J. B. McMinn, 'Plato as a Philosophical Theologian', in 'Phronesis', (1960) 30, argues that Plato resorts to 'mythological constructs' in his philosophical theology because he recognises 'the inadequacy of rational explanation' in this sphere. McMinn concludes that Plato's acceptance of a 'noncognitive factor' in religion is akin to the views of those contemporary philosophical theologians who claim that religious knowledge is 'non-cognitive' or 'non-rational'. But it is clear that for Plato any such conception of 'non-cognitive knowledge' would be sheer nonsense, and that mythological thinking is an inferior mode of thinking incapable of really disclosing the divine.

28. Diès, 'Autour de Platon', ii 603.

29. W. D. Ross, 'Aristotle's Metaphysics' (Oxford, 1924) p. clii.

30. Ibid., p. cliv.

31. Gerald F. Else, 'Aristotle's Poetics: The Argument' (Cambridge, Mass., 1957) p. 475.

32. W. Jaeger, 'Aristotle: Fundamentals of the History of his Development', 2nd ed. (Oxford, 1948); cf. J. H. Randall, 'Aristotle' (New York, 1960) p. 7: 'This theology of the Unmoved Mover, the expression of Aristotle's early Platonistic faith, was gradually pushed into the background.' There is an enormous literature on Jaeger's thesis. For critical views see A. Mansion, 'La genèse de l'œuvre d'Aristote d'après les travaux récents', 'Revue Néoscolastique de Philosophie', (1927) 307–31, 423–66; F. Nuyens, 'L'Evolution de la psychologie d'Aristote' (Louvain, 1948). Cf. W. K. C. Guthrie, 'The Development of Aristotle's Theology', 'Classical Quarterly' (1934) p. 98: 'Aristotle's system, instead of showing a development altogether away from Platonism, might rather be described as in some respects the furnishing of logical grounds for preserving what he regarded as the essential parts of Platonism intact . . . To put this in a more general form, it was his progress in the exact sciences itself which was helping him, not to cast off Platonism, but to substantiate more and more of the Platonic position.'

33. It is not quite exact to say, as W. D. Ross does, that the object of Book viii of the 'Physics' is merely to account for 'the presence of movement in the world and for its having the characteristics it has': 'Aristotle's Physics' (Oxford, 1936) p. 85. Its object is rather to account for the mixture of potentiality and actuality that the material world exemplifies.

34. Sextus Empiricus, 'Phys.', 1. 20–3: 'Aristotle used to say that men's thoughts of gods spring from two sources – the experiences of the soul, and the phenomena of the heavens . . . . Seeing by day the sun running his circular course, and by night the well-ordered movement of the other stars, they came to think that there is a God who is the cause of such movement and order.' Cited in 'The Works of Aristotle', ed. Sir David Ross (Oxford, 1952) xii ('Select Fragments') 84.

35. 1074b 1–14; cf. W. K. C. Guthrie, in 'Classical Quarterly' (1934) p. 92. 'Astronomy had a strange but undeniable fascination for Aristotle . . . . It was one of the few outlets left to him to show his sympathy with religion. In acknowledging the supremacy of the stars he was paying homage to an age-old belief. . . . It was the one religious tenet which he felt the rationalist could retain.' I cannot agree, however, with Guthrie's implication here that Aristotle's rationalism was at odds with his sympathy for religion.

36. 'Metaphysics', x 10, 1075a 14.

37. W. J. Verdenius, 'Traditional and Personal Elements in Aristotle's Religion', 'Phronesis', v (1960) 61: 'In his strictest form the Aristotelian god is the final cause of the world, residing in his own sphere and acting on the world as a model of perfection. But the final cause sometimes develops an efficient aspect. Consequently, the Aristotelian god, who is the ultimate source of the good, brings about the order of the world, primarily as the object of the world's desire, but secondarily as a regulative force.'

38. P. Merlan, 'The Cambridge History of Later Greek and Early Medieval Philosophy', ed. A. H. Armstrong (Cambridge, 1967) p. 52. In Aristotle's actual practice in the 'Metaphysics', however, it is clear that 'theology' is a *part* of a more general inquiry.

39. 430a 20–5.

40. Merlan, 'The Cambridge History', p. 118. Alexander's interpretation of the 'De Anima' has been hotly contested by later commentators, but his reading is nevertheless a plausible one.

41. x 7, 1177a 12–18.

42. x 8, 1178b 7.

43. 1178b 18–23.

44. Cf. E. R. Dodds, 'The Greeks and the Irrational' (Berkeley, 1951) pp. 117–21.

45. 1177a 13–16; cf. W. F. R. Hardie, 'Aristotle's Ethical Theory' (Oxford, 1969) p. 345.

46. 1177a 25–32.

47. vii 15, 1249b 17–20: 'That choice, then, or possession of the natural goods – whether bodily goods, wealth, friends, or other things – which will most produce the contemplation of God, that choice or possession is best, this is the noblest standard. But any that through defect or excess hinders one from the contemplation and service of God is bad.'

48. 'De Anima', ii 5, 430a 23.

49. Cf. Nuyens, 'L'Évolution de la psychologie d'Aristote', p. 309.

50. 1074b 32.

51. 1238b 18.

52. Cf. R. Norman, 'Aristotle's Philosopher-God', in 'Phronesis', xiv (1969) 67: 'When Aristotle describes the Prime Mover as "thinking itself", he is not referring to any activity that could be called "self-contemplation", he is simply describing the same activity that human minds perform when they engage in abstract thought . . . its thinking is entirely of the "theoretic" kind and not at all of the "receptive" kind. Since "self-thinking" is the same as ordinary human abstract thought, it is not this that characterises the Prime Mover, but rather the fact that it thinks of perfection, and does so eternally.'

53. 'Metaphysics', p. cliv.

54. Ibid. Cf. also E. Gilson, 'God and Philosophy' (New Haven, 1941) p. 34: 'With Aristotle, the Greeks had gained an indisputably rational theology, but they had lost their religion.'

55. Cf. Jaeger, 'The Theology of the Early Greek Philosophers', p. 32. Speaking of Anaximander, Jaeger says: 'His first principle is immortal and without beginning. It is not only infinite but also truly eternal. It would be a mistake to blind ourselves to the religious significance implicit in this exalted conception of the Divine because of any preconceived notions of what genuine religion ought to be and what kind of knowledge it should seek. We have no right, for instance, to complain that Anaximander's god is not a god one can pray to, or that physical speculation is not true religion. Surely no one will deny that we simply cannot conceive of any advanced form of religion as lacking the idea of endlessness and eternity which Anaximander links with his new concept of the Divine.'

56. Solmsen, 'Plato's Theology', p. 177.

57. A. H. Armstrong, 'The Cambridge History of Later Greek and Early Medieval Philosophy' (Cambridge, 1967) p. 239.

58. 'Enn.' vi 7.21.

59. On Plotinus see 'Cambridge History', part iii, by A. H. Armstrong; and on Porphyry, Proclus and the later neo-Platonists, see part iv of the same work by A. C. Lloyd. See also J. M. Rist, 'Plotinus: The Road to Reality' (Cambridge, 1967).

60. Nock, 'Conversion', p. 175. On Plotinus, see Porphyry's 'Vita Plotini', in 'Enneads', trans. S. MacKenna (London, 1917) pp. 1–20. Cf. p. 17: 'Pure of soul, ever striving towards the divine which he loved with all his being, he laboured strenuously to free himself and rise above the bitter waves of this

blood-drenched life, and this is why to Plotinus – God-like and lifting himself often, by the ways of meditation and by the methods Plato teaches in the "Banquet", to the first and all-transcendent God – that God appeared, the God who has neither shape nor form but sits enthroned above the Intellectual-Principle and all the Intellectual-Sphere . . . . To this God, I also declare, I Porphyry, that in my sixty-eighth year I too was once admitted and entered into Union.' On the similarities between Plotinus and Eastern religious thought see E. Bréhier, 'La Philosophie de Plotin' (Paris, 1928) chap. vii, 'L'Orientalisme de Plotin'.

61. R. A. Markus, 'Cambridge History'. p. 343.

62. Markus, ibid., p. 344. Regarding Origen see R. A. Norris, 'God and World in Early Christian Theology' (New York, 1965) p. 133. 'However much Origen may differ from the Platonism of the Pagan schools – and his teaching in fact diverges from it widely at certain crucial points – there can be no doubt that his conception of the point and purpose of Christian teaching is shaped by the Platonist idea of the soul's intellectual quest for union with intelligible reality.' On St Gregory of Nyssa see W. Jaeger, 'Early Christianity and Greek Paideia' (Cambridge, Mass., 1961) p. 90: 'As the Greek philosopher's whole life was a process of *paideia* through philosophical ascesis, so for Gregory Christianity was not a mere set of dogmas but the perfect life based on the *theoria* or contemplation of God and on even more perfect union with him.

63. 'Confessions', iii 4.

64. See E. R. Dodds (ed.), 'Proclus: The Elements of Theology', 2nd ed. (Oxford, 1963) pp. xxvi–xxviii.

65. Cf. I. P. Sheldon-Williams, 'Cambridge History', p. 573, n. 3: 'Contemporary opinion differs as to whether the author was a pagan who prudently disguised his thorough-going neo-Platonism under a thin Christian veneer, or a sincere Christian, and even a Christian mystic, who found the neo-Platonic formularies a suitable mode of expression for his thought.'

66. See Arnaldo Momigliano, 'Cassiodorus and Italian Culture of his time', in 'Proceedings of the British Academy' (1955) 213: 'Many people have turned to Christianity for consolation. Boëthius turned to paganism. His Christianity collapsed – it collapsed so thoroughly that perhaps he did not even notice its disappearance. The God of the Greek philosophers gave peace to his mind.' For a more balanced assessment of Boëthius and the 'De Consolatione' see H. Liebeschutz, 'Cambridge History', pp. 550 ff.

67. See L. Gardet and M. M. Anawati, 'Introduction à la théologie musulmane' (Paris, 1948); R. Walzer, 'Greek into Arabic' (Oxford, 1962); R. Walzer, 'Early Islamic Philosophy', in 'Cambridge History', part viii; M. M. Sharif (ed.), 'A History of Muslim Philosophy' (Wiesbaden, 1963) i, part 3.

68. 'Rhazes on the Philosophic Life', trans, A. J. Arberry, 'Asiatic Review', xlv (1949) 703–13.

69. Cited in 'A History of Muslim Philosophy', p. 439.

70. Cited in 'Cambridge History', p. 655.

71. Cited ibid., p. 656.

72. See, for example, George Santayana, 'The Life of Reason', vol. iii; 'Reason in Religion' (New York, 1905); J. H. Randall, 'The Role of Knowledge in Western Religions' (Boston, 1956).

73. 'Al Farabi's Philosophy of Plato and Aristotle', ed. M. Mahdi (New York, 1962) pp. 44–5.

74. R. Walzer, 'Cambridge History', p. 668. See also 'A History of Muslim Philosophy', pp. 49 ff., on Ibn Sina's theory of prophecy, and A. J. Arberry, 'Avicenna on Theology' (London, 1951).

75. L. Gauthier, 'Ibn Rochd' (Paris, 1948); 'Ibn Rochd: Traité Décisif' (Algiers, 1948).

76. Ibid., p. 267.

77. Cf. Jaeger, 'Early Christianity and Greek Paideia', p. 53: 'The distinction between the "simpler" Christian minds of mere "believers" and the theologian who "knows" the true meaning of the holy books is common to both Clement and Origen. Gnosis is the fashionable word for this trend to transcend the sphere of pistis, which in Greek philosophical language always had the connotation of the subjective'.

78. 'Lectures on the Philosophy of Religion', iii, ed. E. B. Spiers and J. B. Sanderson (London, 1962) 148. On the general interest in philosophical religion or the 'religion of reason' during the Enlightenment era, and on the ideas of the various deistic thinkers such as Lord Herbert of Cherbury (1583–1648) and Lessing (1729–81), see Peter Gay, 'The Enlightenment: An Interpretation' (London, 1967), and 'Deism: An Anthology' (Princeton, 1968). See also Ernst Cassirer, 'The Philosophy of the Enlightenment' (Boston, 1951) esp. chap. 4, 'Religion'. Lessing's statement is a typical one: 'All revealed religion is nothing but a reconfirmation of the religion of reason.' See also, on the 'rational theology' of the seventeenth century 'Cambridge Platonists' (Smith, Cudworth, More), Basil Willey, 'The Seventeenth Century Background' (London, 1953) chap. viii, and the splendid anthology of texts, 'The Cambridge Platonists' ed. C. A. Patrides (London, 1969).

79. 'Pensées', ed. J. Steinmann (Monaco, 1961) p. 455.

80. H. Meynell, 'Sense, Nonsense and Christianity' (London, 1964) chap. iv, assumes that the orthodox or traditional interpretation of the Christian religion is in some way normative, so that any attempt to give Christianity a sense at variance with that interpretation ipso facto involves 'reductionism' and the denaturing of Christian doctrine.

81. J. N. Findlay, 'Hegel: A Re-examination' (London, 1958) p. 354. See also G. R. G. Mure, 'Hegel, Luther and the Owl of Minerva', in 'Philosophy', (1966) 127: 'Too little attention is now paid to the peculiar influence of his personal religion on Hegel's mature philosophical speculation.'

82. 'G. W. Leibniz: Theodicy', ed. A. Farrer (London, 1951) Introduction, pp. 9–10. Leibniz's philosophy of religion is, however, in some respects more akin to that of Aquinas than to that of Spinoza and Hegel.

83. iii 150–1.

84. 'Ethics', part iv, prop. 28, ed. J. Gutman (Hafner Library, New York , 1949) p. 207.

85. Ibid., part v, prop. 32, corollary, p. 273.

86. Ibid., corollary, p. 273.

87. 'A Theologico-Political Treatise' (Dover Publications, New York, 1951) p. 185.

88. Ibid., p. 194.

89. Ibid., p. 186.

90. Ibid., p. 190.

91. Cf. S. Hampshire, 'Spinoza' (London, 1951) p. 151. For Spinoza 'the various religious myths of the world are essentially the presentation in imaginative and picturesque terms of more or less elementary moral truths. The great majority of mankind, who are capable only of the lowest grade of knowledge,

184

will only understand, and be emotionally impressed by, myths which appeal directly to their imagination. . . . They cannot understand what is meant by the perfection and omnipotence of God, as a metaphysician understands these ideas.'

92. 'Essays and Aphorisms', trans. R. J. Hollingdale (Penguin Books, Harmondsworth, 1970) p. 96.

93. 'Phenomenology of Mind', trans. J. B. Baillie, 2nd ed. (London, 1949) pp. 780–2. Cf. Findlay, 'Hegel: A Re-examination', p. 342. For Hegel 'a religious term like "God" will, when stripped of pictorial associations, reveal itself as meaning no more than the "I" of self-consciousness, which is for Hegel also the element of universality and unity present in all thinking, which is inseparable from the finite particular self to which it may *seem* transcendent, but which uses the latter as the vehicle through which it achieves its self-consciousness.'

94. Cf. W. T. Stace, 'The Philosophy of Hegel' (London, 1924) pp. 486–7, for a useful discussion of *Vorstellung*.

95. 'Ethics', p. 19.

96. Ibid.

97. 'Lectures on the Philosophy of Religion', iii 148.

98. Ibid., pp. 87–8.

99. Letter lxxiii, 'The Correspondence of Spinoza', ed. A. Wolf (London, 1925) p. 344. Cf. Hampshire, 'Spinoza', pp. 145–6, on 'the radical lack of the idea of history' in Spinoza's thought. For Spinoza, 'We ordinarily think of the world as a mere succession of events, in the manner of the historian, only because we have not yet arrived at the eternal truths which present the true order of Nature as an unchanging system'.

100. 'Lectures on the Philosophy of Religion', pp. 78 ff. Lessing – in his religious ideas, a link between Spinoza and Hegel – has a very acute awareness of the problem that arises over the relation between the historical and necessary elements in religion. If religion is to be rational it must deal in necessary and universal truths; on the other hand religious belief is as a matter of fact always rooted in particular historical claims. How then move from the one to the other? 'Contingent historical truths can never serve as proof for necessary truths of reason. . . . To jump from historical truth to an entirely different class of truths, and to ask me to alter all my metaphysical and moral concepts accordingly. . . . if that is not a "transformation to another kind" then I do not know what else Aristotle meant by this term. . . . This is the ugly, wide ditch over which I cannot leap, however often and earnestly I try. If anyone can help me over, I pray, I conjure him to do so. God will recompense him.' 'Schriften', ed. Lachmann, Munckner (1886–1924) xiii 5. See also H. Chadwick, 'Lessing's Theological Writings' (Palo Alto, Calif., 1956).

101. Hegel's philosophy, however, is all things to all men, and it can also be interpreted in an 'historicist' sense. Thus A. MacIntyre, 'Herbert Marcuse: From Marxism to Pessimism', in 'Survey', lxii (1967) 39, claims that there is a 'spectrum' of interpretations of Hegel. 'At one end of this spectrum lies a Hegel for whom the world of historical experience is merely the phenomenal clothing of the timeless logical categories which constitute the successive phases of the self-development of the Absolute . . . . This interpretation of Hegel is fundamentally a theological interpretation and although in this Hegelian scheme the metaphysical reality behind finite experience does not enjoy the independence of its this-worldly manifestations which it does in Christian theology, nonetheless it is this element in Hegel which enabled Right Hegelianism and

Lutheranism to cement a relationship. At the other end of the spectrum lies the interpretation of Hegel according to which the categories of the logic are thought of as having no more reality than that bestowed upon them by their embodiment in historical form . . . . The history of philosophy, of categories and concepts, and the history of social transactions are but two sides of the same coin. This interpretation emphasises the empirical aspect of Hegel's thought, and especially the fact that the logical progress in both societies and conceptual schemes is something that can be discerned only after the event. We cannot discover the patterns of development without a close study of what actually happened. The owl of Minerva flies only at dusk.'

102. 'The Principles of Logic' (London, 1922), 'Terminal Essays', viii 688–9. Cf. pp. 689–70: 'I will venture once more to speak through the mouth of my supposed Christian. Imagine him asked whether, thinking as he does, he cares nothing for "the historical truth" of Christianity, any more than for the detail of Christian creeds and symbols – and possibly his answer might surprise us. "I understood you to be speaking", he might reply, "about mere temporal events and happenings, just as you might speak again about mere material things such as this crucifix or that flag. These by themselves are all abstractions, mistaken for realities by what too often is called Common Sense; and these most assuredly are not the genuine facts and beliefs of religion. Religious events and symbols, though on one side things and happenings in your "real world", are something on the other side whose essence and life is elsewhere. Identified with what is beyond, they are no mere occurrences in time or things in space. They represent, and they are the actual incarnation of eternal reality, and for the least of them a man might feel called on do die.' Bradley himself does not identify his Absolute with God nor does he argue for any kind of religious view.

103. Letter xxi, 'The Correspondence of Spinoza', p. 173.

104. F. Copleston, 'A History of Philosophy' (London, 1958) iv 245.

105. 'Dialogues concerning Natural Religion', ed. N. Kemp Smith (Oxford, 1945) p. 281. Cf. A. Seth Pringle-Pattison, 'The Idea of God' (New York, 1920) p. 22: 'How can a proposition possess any religious significance if, as Philo truly describes it here, "it affords no inference that affects human life".' It might be remarked that this kind of objection presupposes a sharp disjunction between the speculative and practical orders (à la Kant), and that it loses a good deal of its force in an Aristotelian context, for example, where the end of the moral life is primarily a contemplative one and where the 'practical reason' is dependent upon 'pure reason'.

106. Though some contemporary Christian theologians seem to deny that the notion of revelation is tied to a 'supernaturalist' understanding of it according to which revelation is a 'miraculous supernatural intervention in the natural order of existent beings'. See on this Paul Tillich, 'Revelation in the Philosophy of Religion', in 'Twentieth Century Theology in the Making', ed. J. Pelikan (London, 1970) ii 51.

107. See S. Runciman, 'The Medieval Manichee' (Cambridge, 1947).

108. See Aelred Graham, 'Conversations between Christians and Buddhists' (London, 1969) p. 44: 'Muso says that if one is going to be a Zen disciple at all he has to be of the first class.'

109. J. M. E. McTaggart, 'Some Dogmas of Religion' (London, 1906) pp. 292, 297, 298.

110. 1 Cor. 15.

111. H. Price, 'Is Theism Important?', in 'The Socratic' (Oxford, 1952) p. 41.

112. 'Some Dogmas of Religion', p. 74.

113. 'Process and Reality' (Cambridge, 1929) p. 484. On Whitehead's concept of God see W. A. Christian, 'The Concept of God as a Derivative Notion', in 'Process and Divinity', ed. W. L. Reese and E. Freeman (La Salle, Ill., 1964) pp. 181–203. See also James Collins, 'God in Modern Philosophy' (Chicago, 1959) pp. 315 ff. Cf. also the work of Whitehead's fellow-traveller, Charles Hartshorne, 'Man's Vision of God and the Logic of Theism' (Chicago and New York, 1941).

114. See C. F. Mooney, 'Teilhard de Chardin and the Mystery of Christ' (London, 1966). It is very interesting in the case of Teilhard to see how he finds himself up against the same difficulties as the philosophers of religion we have examined above – for example, how to preserve the notion of the supernatural and of revelation, and how to escape 'necessitarianism' and to allow for the dimension of historical contingency. In other words, the demands of traditional Christianity appear to conflict with the demands of his philosophy of religion.

CHAPTER 2

1. See W. Jaeger, 'Early Christianity and Greek Paideia' (Cambridge, Mass., 1961); A. H. Armstrong and R. A. Markus, 'Christian Faith and Greek Philosophy' (London, 1960) esp. chap. 10, 'Faith and Philosophy'.

2. On Philo the definitive work is 'Philo: Foundations of Religious Philosophy in Judaism, Christianity and Islam', by H. A. Wolfson (Cambridge, Mass., 1948) 2 vols. See also the old but still valuable work, 'The Christian Platonists' by Charles Bigg (Oxford, 1886) Lecture 1.

3. Wolfson, 'Philo' i 141.

4. For the history of the 'handmaid' analogy see ibid., i 145.

5. Ibid., i 115.

6. Ibid., i 116.

7. Ibid., i 125.

8. H. Chadwick, 'Early Christian Thought and the Classical Tradition' (Oxford, 1966) p. 5.

9. See R. M. Grant, 'Gnosticism and Early Christianity' (New York, 1966) esp. chap. 5, 'From Myth to Philosophy'.

10. Origen, 'Contra Celsum', trans. H. Chadwick (Cambridge, 1965) i 9; p. 12.

11. Cf. Clement of Alexandria's judgement on the simple faithful: 'The so-called orthodox believers are like beasts working out of fear; they do good works without understanding what they do.' 'Stromateis', i 45.6.

12. See Chadwick, 'Early Christian Thought', p. 3.

13. On Justin see R. A. Norris, 'God and World in Early Christian Theology' (New York, 1965) chap. 11.

14. *Apologia*, i 46: trans. 'The Library of Christian Classics' (Philadelphia, 1953) vol. i.

15. Norris, 'God and World', p. 53.

16. 'Strom.', i 30.

17. Ibid., i 94.

18. On Clement's 'Christian gnosticism' see Bigg, 'The Christian Platonists', pp. 86 ff.

19. 'Contra Celsum', vii 42; p. 430.

20. Ibid.

21. Ibid., p. 430.

22. Ibid.; J. Daniélou, 'Origen' (London, 1955) chap. v, sees Origen's rejection of Celsus's religious esotericism as a central feature of his thought. See p. 108: 'In his view, the vision of God is beyond the reach of all men without exception when they are left to their natural resources, while on the other hand it is given by God as a favour to all who ask and turn to him for it, whether they are philosophers or not.'

23. 'De Principiis', i.3.1.

24. 'Comm. Matt.', 12.5.

25. See Daniélou, 'Origen', part ii.

26. On this see J. J. O'Meara, 'The Young Augustine' (London, 1954) chaps. ix, x. The following paragraphs are taken from my book 'St Anselm's Proslogion' (Oxford, 1965) pp. 26–7.

27. 'Epist.' 120; P.L. 38, 453.

28. 'Sermo' 126; P.L. 38, 699: '... God made you a rational animal ... and formed you in His own image .... Therefore lift up your mind ... look at the things you see, and look for Him whom you do not see.'

29. 'Sermo' 43; P.L. 38, 257.

30. See E. TeSelle, 'Nature and Grace in Augustine's Exposition of Genesis 1: 1–5', in 'Recherches augustiniennes', v (1968) 114. For Augustine, 'what is required for the vision of God is not a supernatural perfection of the intellect by which it might be enabled to attain to a knowledge beyond its capabilities, but a fervour and steadfastness of the will by which the mind can be borne towards God. Augustine assumes that God is not only present to the mind but fully knowable to the pure in heart.'

31. Ibid., p. 112.

32. 'De Lib. Arbit.', II ii 5, trans. M. Pontifex, 'The Problem of Free Choice' (London, 1955) pp. 77–8.

33. Ibid., II xv; Pontifex, p. 120.

34. Ibid., II xv; Pontifex, p. 120.

35. Cf. 'De Trinitate', vi, Boëthius: 'The Theological Tractates', trans. H. F. Stewart and E. K. Rand (London, 1919) p. 31. 'If, God helping me, I have furnished some support in argument to an article which stands by itself on the firm foundation of Faith, I shall render joyous praise for the finished work to him from whom the invitation comes.'

36. See Jean Cottiaux, 'La conception de la théologie chez Abélard', in 'Revue d'histoire ecclésiastique', xxvii (1932) 248–95, 533–51, 788–828.

37. 'Tractatus', pp. 19–29.

38. Cottiaux, p. 799.

39. J. R. McCallum, 'Abelard's Christian Theology' (Oxford, 1948).

40. See A. V. Murray, 'Abelard and St Bernard' (Manchester, 1967).

41. 'Christian Theology', p. 68. Abelard goes on to cite the text from Plato's 'Timaeus' to which Origen also refers: 'Plato, greatest of philosophers, saw this point when he said in the "Timaeus": "The craftsman of the universe, and its begetter, is hard to find, and even when found, difficult to define".'

42. 'Introductio ad theologiam', P.L. 178, 1050. For a balanced view on Abelard's position on faith and reason see M. de Gandillac, 'Oeuvres choisies d'Abélard, (Paris, 1945) pp. 33 ff.

43. 'Theologia', P.L. 178, 1226A.

44. 'Introductio', 1085.

45. See the analysis of Anselm's central work 'Cur Deus Homo?' in M. J. Charlesworth, 'St Anselm's "Proslogion" ' (Oxford, 1965) pp. 30–7.

46. In I Sent.II. Cited in T. Tshibangu, 'Théologie positive et théologie spéculative' (Louvain, 1965) p. 51.

47. Ibid.

48. 'Summa Theologica', ed. Quarrachi (1924) cap.i. On the application of the Aristotelian idea of 'science' to theology see M. D. Chenu, 'La Théologie comme science au XIIIème siècle' (Paris, 1957) and Tshibangu, 'Théologie positive'.

49. See Maimonides's 'The Guide of the Perplexed', trans. S. Pines (Chicago, 1963).

50. Ibid., ii 16; pp. 293–4.

51. Ibid., ii, 22; p. 320.

52. Ibid.

53. Ibid., ii, 25; p. 328.

54. Ibid., 25; pp. 329–30.

55. Ibid., p. 329.

56. Étienne Gilson, 'Reason and Revelation in the Middle Ages' (New York, 1938) p. 83.

57. Cited in Gilson, 'Reason and Revelation in the Middle Ages', p. 64. It was ironic that some of Aquinas's own propositions were also condemned at the same time by Bishop Tempier.

58. 'Summa Theologiae', I i.

59. Ibid. See also II ii 2.3.

60. II ii 2.4.

61. See II ii 2.4. 'Whether it is necessary to believe those things which can be proved by natural reason?'

62. Ibid., ad 2.

63. I i 3.

64. I i 6.

65. I i 2. See Tshibangu, 'Théologie positive', pp. 68–96, on Aquinas's views of theology as an Aristotelian 'science'.

66. II ii 2.2

67. II ii 6.1.

68. See Y. Congar, 'La Foi et la théologie' (Paris, 1959) pp. 83 ff., on the various post-Thomistic theories of the act of faith. See also R. Aubert, 'Le problème de l'acte de foi', 3rd ed. (Louvain, 1945).

69. Heb. 11:1. In the 'Summa Contra Gentiles', iii 40, Aquinas says that *as knowledge* faith is the most imperfect act of the intellect (*operatio intellectus imperfectissima*), though with respect to its *object* it is the most perfect.

70. I 12.13. Cf. G. Van Riet, 'Y a-t-il chez saint Thomas une philosophie de la religion?', in 'Revue Philosophique de Louvain', lxi (1963) 54: 'For St Thomas, at least in his later writings, faith is not a distinct kind of apprehension due to some sort of sixth sense; it is not a knowledge of superior rank in which, thanks to a new light given by God, our intelligence might grasp supernatural meanings and truths. Despite what the term "light" naturally suggests, the *lumen fidei* or the "light" given by grace to the believer, does not directly or properly concern the order of intelligence. This light does not enable us to discover in the object of faith new aspects that would not have been discovered without it, nor to "see" this object, nor to grasp it as present, through supernatural "evidence".'

71. II ii 2.3. 'Wherever one nature is subordinate to another, we find that two things concur towards the perfection of the lower nature, one of which is in respect of that nature's proper movement, while the other is in respect of the movement of the higher nature.' Aquinas applies this principle to reason (the lower and subordinate) and faith (the higher).

72. 'The Letter on Apologetics' (1896); English trans., 'Maurice Blondel: The Letter on Apologetics and History and Dogma', by Alexandra Dru and Illtyd Trethowan (London, 1964) pp. 147–8.

73. For a highly interesting attempt to develop a coherent theory of the relationship between the natural and the supernatural on the basis of St Thomas's ideas see 'The Mystery of the Supernatural' by H. de Lubac (English trans., London, 1967).

74. I 6 ad 2. See also II ii 2.10, where Aquinas says that the adducing of reasons in support of what we believe by faith is 'consequent to the will of the believer'. 'For when a man's will is ready to believe, he loves the truth he believes, he thinks out and takes to heart whatever reasons he can find in support thereof, and in this way, human reason does not exclude the merit of faith, but is a sign of greater merit.'

75. II ii 2.10: 'When a man either has not the will, or not a prompt will, to believe, unless he be moved by human reasons . . . in this way human reason diminishes the merit of faith'.

76. I 2.2.

77. Aquinas often seems to confuse the two senses of dependence in that he seems to think that, because a person happens to believe by faith a truth (e.g. one of the preambles of faith) that can *of itself* be known by reason, the former is not logically dependent upon the latter.

78. I i 8. See also 'In Boëtium de Trinitate', IX ii 4: 'Sacred doctrine makes a threefold use of philosophy. The first is to demonstrate those truths that are preambles of faith and that have a necessary place in the science of faith . . . . The second is to give a clearer notion, by certain similitudes, of the truths of faith . . . . The third is to resist those who speak against the truth, either by showing that these statements are false, or by showing that they are not necessarily true.'

79. See I 12.7.

80. Timothy Potts, 'Theology and Philosophy', in 'The Tablet' (18 Sept 1965) p. 1026.

81. See P. T. Geach, 'Nominalism', in 'Sophia' iii 2 (1964) 3–14.

82. 'Anselm's Ontological Arguments', in 'Philosophical Review', lxix (1960) 60. Cf. Geach, 'Nominalism', p. 6. 'If all the arguments against a mystery of faith can be cleared up, then surely, people may object, the mystery ceases to be a mystery. This objection is confused. What I am maintaining is that for each single argument against faith there is a refutation, in terms of ordinary logic; not that there is some one general technique for refuting all arguments against faith, or even all arguments against a particular dogma of faith. I do not claim that we can prove, or even clearly see, that the propositions expressing mysteries of faith are consistent . . . . And as regards the doctrine of the Trinity in particular we can see that a demand for a consistency proof could never be satisfied. For the propositions expressing this dogma, relating as they do to the inner life of God without bringing in any actual or possible creatures, cannot be only possibly true; if they are possibly true they are necessarily true. So a proof that the doctrine is consistent would be a proof of its truth, which is certainly impossible.'

83. S.T., I 2.3. On the 'Five Ways' see E. L. Mascall, 'He Who Is – A Study in Traditional Theism' (London, 1943), and A. Kenny, 'The Five Ways' (Oxford, 1969).

84. Exodus iii 3:14.

85. See I 13.11: 'Whether this name, "He Who Is", is the most proper name of God?'

86. John L. McKenzie, 'God and Nature in the Old Testament', in 'Myths and Realities' (London, 1963) p. 94. Cf. p. 131: '[The Hebrews] saw nature as integrated into the moral and religious order; it was the expression of the blessing or of the wrath of Yahweh, which came as a response to human behaviour.'

87. See also K. Rahner, 'Dieu dans le Nouveau Testament', in 'Ecrits Théologiques', i (Paris, 1959) 33: 'Old Testament monotheism does not rest upon an investigation of human reason seeking the ultimate unity of the world and looking for it finally in an all-embracing principle that is transcendent to the world. It is based on the experience of the men of the Old Testament of the saving action accomplished by Jahweh at the heart of the world and in the history of their people.'

88. See J. L. McKenzie, 'The Hebrew Attitude toward Polytheism', in 'Myths and Realities', pp. 142–3: 'Even the words for "god" in Hebrew are not susceptible of refinement and precision of expression. Hebrew had no words for god except "el", "elohim"'; to express its own peculiar concept of deity which was applicable to Yahweh alone, it had no word except the name Yahweh itself. The words for god had, in Hebrew as in other Semitic idioms, a broader use than the Hebrew concept of deity, strictly speaking, would permit.

89. B. Vawter, 'The God of the Bible', in 'God, Jesus and Spirit', ed. D. Callahan (London, 1969) p. 4.

90. 'Dieu dans le Nouveau Testament', p. 64.

91. See R. Garrigou-Lagrange, 'God – His Existence and Nature' (St. Louis, 1934); E. Gilson, 'Reason and Revelation in the Middle Ages' (New York, 1938) and 'Christianisme et Philosophie' (Paris, 1936); J. Maritain, 'Approaches to God' (London, 1955).

92. See E. L. Mascall, 'He Who Is: A Study in Traditional Theism' (London, 1943); A. Farrer, 'Finite and Infinite' (London, 1943); see also 'Anglicanism: The Thought and Practice of the Church of England, Illustrated from the Religious Literature of the 17th Century', ed. P. E. More and F. L. Cross (London, 1935) sec. vi, 'Natural Theology'.

93. 1736; ed. W. E Gladstone (Oxford, 1897).

94. Ibid., p. 53.

95. Ibid., p. 162.

96. Like Aquinas also, Butler claims that revelation contains a 'republication' of the basic truths about God discoverable by philosophical reason, as well as its own proper truths that go beyond reason. The reasons that Butler gives for the practical need for such a 'republication' are almost the same as those given by Aquinas. See 'The Analogy', part ii, chap. i, p. 153.

97. Ibid., p. 295. The argument in the recent and very interesting book, 'God and Other Minds' (Ithaca, N.Y., 1967) by Alvin Plantinga, is Butlerian in mode in that it is based upon the analogy between our belief in other minds and our belief in God, and upon the analogous difficulties attending both respective beliefs.

98. See S.T., I 13, on 'The Names of God'.

99. See V. White, 'The Unknown God and Other Essays' (London, 1948) on the importance of the 'negative way' in Aquinas's conception of God.

100. On Aquinas's theory of analogy see E. L. Mascall, 'Existence and Analogy' (London, 1949).

101. It is difficult to take seriously the interpretation of Aquinas's philosophical theology advanced by Victor Preller in his book 'Divine Science and the Science of God: A Reformulation of Thomas Aquinas' (Princeton, 1967) Preller claims that the Five Ways are not really meant by Aquinas to be strict proofs of the existence of God but rather 'external and probable evidence of the truths of the theological claim that the mind of man is ordered to an Unknown God and can reflect on that order' (p. 25).

102. 'Summa Contra Gentiles', bk iii, chap. 25, 'That understanding God is the end of every intellectual substance'; chap. 37, 'That ultimate happiness consists in the contemplation of God'.

103. See Tshibangu, 'Théologie positive', part ii, for an account of the movement in late nineteenth- and early twentieth-century Catholic theology against this a-historical tendency. See also the great work of Maurice Blondel, 'History and Dogma' (1903), English trans. A. Dru and I. Trethowan (London, 1964). Criticising the a-historical approach of the Thomist school, Blondel says: 'All they ask of the facts is that they should serve as signs to the senses and as commonsense proofs. Once the signs have been supplied, an elementary argument deduces from them the divine character of the whole to which these signifying facts belong. Then, with the help of rational theses, they deduce the required universal conclusion from the premisses, and take up an embattled position in the place to which history, it would seem, has yielded up the key, thanking her for her provisional services. From then on the place belongs to others, and she has only to take her leave' (p. 226). Again, for the Thomists, 'The Bible is guaranteed *en bloc*, not by its content, but by the external seal of the divine: why bother to verify the details? It is full of absolute knowledge, ensconced in its eternal truth; why search for its human conditions or its relative meaning . . . . the ageless facts are without local colour . . . . and disappear beneath the weight of an absolute by which they are crushed' (p. 229).

104. 'The Last Years: Journals 1853–1885', ed. R. Gregor Smith (London, 1965) pp. 99–100.

CHAPTER 3

1. Pascal, 'Pensées', 273.

2. 'Mémorial', 'God of Abraham, God of Isaac, God of Jacob, not of the philosophers and scientists'.

3. Col. 2:8.

4. Rom. 1:19.

5. Matt. 11:25; Luke 10:21.

6. 'Some Dogmas of Religion', p. 298. He goes on: 'This criticism applies, naturally, not to the teacher who made the exclamation, but to the teachers who turned it into a principle. It may be remarked that the principle is applied rather capriciously. Many men would be prepared to use it as a ground for distrusting Hegel, and for trusting the peasantry of Ireland or Wales (as the case may be). But they would not admit it as a ground for accepting the peasantry of Morocco as a safer guide in religion than Thomas Aquinas. And yet Thomas Aquinas was a wise man, and the religion of a peasant in Morocco

would be eminently childish. But, of course, it is only ignorant orthodoxy that is childlike simplicity. Ignorant heterodoxy is childish superstition.'

7. Gilson, 'Reason and Revelation in the Middle Ages', p. 8.

8. 'On Prescription against Heretics', vii, in 'The Ante-Nicene Fathers' (Buffalo, 1887) iii 246.

9. 'De Carne Christi' c. 5: 'The Son of God died – this is believable because it is absurd: and he was buried and rose again – this is certain because it is impossible.'

10. 'Pensées', 267.

11. On Peter Damian, see Jean Leclercq, 'Saint Pierre Damien et la culture profane' (Louvain, 1956).

12. 'Contra quaedam capitula errorum Abaelardi, S. Bernardi Opera' (Paris, 1939) i.

13. See P. Boehner (ed.), 'William of Ockham: Selected Philosophical Writings' (London, 1957) pp. xix-xx.

14. See 'The Second Letter of Nicholas of Autrecourt to Bernard of Arezzo', trans. E. A. Moody, in 'Medieval Philosophy: Selected Readings', ed. H. Shapiro (New York, 1964) pp. 524–5. On Nicholas see J. Weinberg, 'Nicolaus of Autrecourt' (Princeton, 1948) and the interesting paper by H. Rashdall, 'Nicholas of Ultricuria: A Medieval Hume', in 'Proceedings of the Aristotelian Society', viii (1907) 1–27.

15. See R. Guelluy, 'Philosophie et théologie chez Guillaume d'Ockham' (Paris, 1947) p. 364: 'Ockham refuses to separate the domain of theology from that of metaphysics and . . . . does not seem to have as his aim the opposing of faith to reason.' On Biel, see H. A. Oberman, 'The Harvest of Medieval Theology: Gabriel Biel and Late Medieval Theology' (Harvard, 1963) p. 81: 'Biel is interested in safeguarding the peculiar character of faith and is keen not to have it subsumed under some form of higher reason. He thus makes every effort to distinguish between philosophy and theology by marking as clearly as possible where the one ends and the other begins. But there is no indication that this distinction is carried so far as to become a divorce between faith and reason.' On the Catholic orthodoxy of Ockham's and Biel's position on faith and reason, see Oberman, pp. 423–8.

16. Cited in P. Althaus, 'The Theology of Martin Luther' (Philadelphia, 1966) p. 66.

17. Ibid., pp. 69–70. 'Reason despises faith'; 'It is up to God alone to give faith contrary to nature, and ability to believe contrary to reason'. Reason is 'the greatest whore that the Devil has'; 'Philosophy is a practical wisdom of the flesh which is hostile to God'.

18. Luther admits, however, that reason has a place within theology: 'Reason enlightened by the Spirit helps us to understand the Holy Scripture'; 'Reason in godly men is something different, since it does not fight with faith but rather aids it'. Cited ibid., p. 71.

19. Calvin, 'Institutes of the Christian Religion', i 3, in Library of Christian Classics, ed. J. T. McNeill and F. L. Battles (London, 1961) p. 43.

20. Ibid., i 3; p. 44.

21. Ibid., i 4; p. 47.

22. Ibid., i 4; p. 49.

23. Ibid., i 5; p. 58.

24. Heb. 2:3.

25. Rom. 1:19.

26. 'Institutes', i 5; p. 68.

27. Ibid. i 6; p. 71.

28. W. Niesel, 'The Theology of Calvin' (London, 1956) p. 50; see chap. 2, sec. 3, 'The Question of Natural Theology'. See also E. A. Dowey, 'The Knowledge of God in Calvin's Theology' (New York, 1952).

29. Owen Chadwick, 'The Reformation' (London, 1964) p. 94.

30. A. Boyce Gibson, 'Theism and Empiricism' (London, 1970) p. 115.

31. 'Pensées', 267.

32. On Al Ghazzali see W. Montgomery Watt, 'Muslim Intellectual – A Study of Al Ghazzali' (Edinburgh, 1963); D. B. Macdonald, art. 'Al Ghazzali', in 'Encyclopedia of Islam' (London, 1927) ii 146–9; 'Al Ghazzali', by M. Saeed Sheikh in 'A History of Muslim Philosophy', ed. M. M. Sharif, i (Wiesbaden, 1963) chaps xxx, xxxi.

33. English trans. W. Montgomery Watt, 'The Faith and Practice of Al Ghazzali' (London, 1963).

34. Ibid., pp. 37–8.

35. Ibid., p. 34.

36. Macdonald, art. 'Al Ghazzali', p. 146.

37. English trans. by Sabih Ahmad Kamali (Lahore, 1958). See the analyses of this work in Montgomery Watt, 'Muslim Intellectual', pp. 57–65, and 'A History of Muslim Philosophy', pp. 588–616.

38. 'The Inconsistency', p. 181.

39. 'The Inconsistency', p. 186. See the discussion of Al Ghazzali's theory of causality in 'A History of Muslim Philosophy', pp. 614–15.

40. Ibid., p. 189.

41. 'The Deliverance', p. 61.

42. Ibid., p. 54.

43. 'Pensées', 469.

44. Ibid., 347.

45. Ibid., 273.

46. Ibid., 72.

47. Ibid.

48. Ibid., 470.

49. Ibid., 233.

50. Ibid.

51. Ibid., 241. On the 'wager' see J. Chevalier, 'Pascal' (London, 1970) pp. 242–53 and appendix iv, 'Historical and Critical Note on Pascal's "wager".'

52. 'Pensées', 83.

53. Ibid., 229.

54. Ibid., 230.

55. Ibid., 555.

56. Ibid., 278.

57. Ibid., 277.

58. Ibid., 282.

59. See the 'Mémorial', cited in Chevalier, 'Pascal', pp. 94–5.

60. 'Pensées', 587.

61. Ibid., 267, 268, 269, 270, 271, 272.

62. For a brief analysis of these early works of Kant see A. E. Taylor, art. 'Theism', in 'Encyclopedia of Religion and Ethics', ed. Hastings (1921) xii 275–6. See also Kant, 'Selected Pre-Critical Writings', translated and introduced by G. R. Kerferd, and D. E. Walford (Manchester, 1965) for Kant's 'Enquiry Concerning the Clarity of the Principles of Natural Theology and Ethics' (1763).

194

63. Taylor, 'Theism', p. 276.

64. See N. Kemp-Smith, 'Hume's Dialogues Concerning Natural Religion' (Oxford, 1935) pp. 38–9.

65. See 'Dialogues', p. 234. On this see A. Flew, 'Hume's Philosophy of Belief' (London, 1961) pp. 230–1.

66. 'Dialogues', p. 230.

67. Ibid., pp. 232–3.

68. Ibid., p. 282.

69. J. Collins, 'The Emergence of Philosophy of Religion' (New Haven, 1967) p. 76. The same author goes on to say: 'To Holbach and other atheistic friends of Hume, the reasonable expectation was that, upon exposure of the frailties and fallacies involved in natural theology and upon presentation of an areligious moral humanism as the social ideal, religious belief would shrivel up and disappear. It was freely predicted that this result would follow at least for those honest minds who gave sufficient time, study, and reflection to the problem of the intellectual standing of theism. But Hume's own experience ran counter to this prediction, even though he did not care to give any comfort to the proponents of traditional theism and the institutional forms of religion. One's assent to God's reality may be deprived of many customary supports in argument, without thereby being annihilated or reduced merely to an uncommonly stubborn social custom, destined for eventual disappearance.'

70. On Hume's attitude to religion see Kemp Smith, 'Hume's Dialogues'. Kemp Smith cites Boswell's interview with Hume in 1777: 'He [Hume] said he never had entertained any belief in Religion since he began to read Locke and Clarke.' However, while rightly stressing Hume's philosophical and personal antagonism to religion, Kemp Smith perhaps underestimates the strength of Hume's lifelong fascination with the phenomenon of religion. This is brought out very well by Collins, 'The Emergence of Philosophy of Religion', pp. 3–4, 76–7.

71. 'Dialogues', p. 282. Cf. p. 162: 'You propose then, Philo, said Cleanthes, to erect religious faith on philosophical scepticism; and you think, that if certainty or evidence be expelled from every other subject of enquiry, it will all retire to these theological doctrines, and there acquire a superior force and authority.'

72. 'Essays: Moral, Political and Literary', ed. T. H. Green and T. H. Grose (London, 1875), II 107.

73. Ibid., II 399.

74. Ed. L. A. Selby-Bigge (Oxford, 1894) p. 131.

75. 'Dialogues', p. 166.

76. Ibid.

77. Ibid., p. 230.

78. Ibid., p. 158.

79. Ibid., pp. 172–3.

80. A. Leroy, 'David Hume' (Paris, 1953) pp. 308–9, argues that Hume's position differs from that of the Christian fideists such as Pascal, Hamann and Kierkegaard, in that his scepticism is not directed to arousing an act of supernatural faith, nor does it abase human reason to make room for revelation. This is true enough as far as Hume's own personal intentions go. But the intrinsic logic of Hume's position – philosophical agnosticism making room for faith – is nevertheless very similar to that of the fideists mentioned.

81. 'To Christian Garve, 21 Sept 1798', in 'Kant: Philosophical Correspondence, 1759–99', ed. A. Zweig (Chicago, 1967) p. 252: 'It was not the

investigation of the existence of God, immortality, and so on, but rather the antinomy of pure reason – "the world has a beginning; it has no beginning, and so on", right up to the 4th (*sic*): "There is freedom in man, versus there is no freedom, only the necessity of nature" – that is what first aroused me from my dogmatic slumber and drove me to the critique of reason itself . . . .'

82. P. F. Strawson, 'The Bounds of Sense: An Essay on Kant's Critique of Pure Reason' (London, 1966) p. 16; cf. 'Critique of Pure Reason', trans. N. Kemp Smith (London, 1929) B 195: 'All concepts, and with them all principles, even such as are possible *a priori*, relate to empirical intuitions, that is, to the data for a possible experience. Apart from this relation they have no objective validity.'

83. Ibid., B 76; A 52.

84. Ibid., A 619; B 647: 'The ideal of the supreme being is nothing but a regulative principle of reason, which directs us to look upon a connection in the world *as if* it originated from an all-sufficient necessary cause. We can base upon the ideal the rule of a systematic and, in accordance with universal laws, necessary unity in the explanation of that connexion; but the ideal is not an assertion of an existence necessary in itself.'

85. Ibid., A 483; B 511.

86. Ibid., A 636; B 664.

87. Cf. Hume, 'Letters', i 157: 'All our inference [from design in nature to God] is founded on the similitude of the works of nature to the usual effects of the mind. Otherwise they must appear a mere chaos. The only difficulty is, why the other dissimilitudes do not weaken the argument. And indeed it would seem from experience and feeling, that they do not weaken it so much as we might naturally expect. A theory to solve this would be very acceptable.'

88. 'Critique of Pure Reason', A 638; B 666.

89. Ibid., A 639; B 667.

90. D. P. Dryer, 'Kant's Solution for Verification in Metaphysics' (London, 1966) p. 526. Despite its formidable style this is one of the most perceptive commentaries on the 'Critique of Pure Reason'.

91. 'Critique of Pure Reason', A 641; B 669.

92. Ibid., B xxx.

93. On Kant's notion of 'faith' see L. W. Beck, 'Studies in the Philosophy of Kant' (New York, 1965) p. 51. Rational faith is 'a faith which demands the same degree of assent required for theoretical knowledge and yet avoids the speculative claims of those who believe metaphysics to be a theoretical science'.

94. Cf. Strawson, 'The Bounds of Sense', p. 15: 'Wherever he [Kant] found limiting or necessary features of experience, he declared their source to lie in our own cognitive constitution; and this doctrine he considered indispensable as an explanation of knowledge of the necessary structure of experience. Yet there is no doubt that this doctrine is incoherent in itself . . . .'

95. 'Émile', trans. B. Foxley (Everyman's Library, London, 1911) p. 228.

96. Ibid., p. 272.

97. Ibid., p. 254.

98. Ibid., p. 277. On Rousseau's view of religion see R. Grimsley, 'Rousseau and the Religious Quest' (Oxford, 1968); P. M. Masson, 'La Religion de J.-J. Rousseau', 3 vols (Paris, 1916); K. Barth, 'From Rousseau to Ritschl' (London, 1959) chap. ii. See also the valuable annotations in the Pléiade edition, 'Jean-Jacques Rousseau: Œuvres Complètes', vol. iv (Paris, 1969). Judith Shklar, 'Men and Citizens: A Study of Rousseau's Social Theory' (Cambridge, 1969)

pp. 113–20, has some acute observations on Rousseau's religious ideas. On Rousseau's influence on Kant see E. Cassirer, 'Rousseau, Kant, Goethe' (Princeton, 1945) and Beck, 'Studies in the Philosophy of Kant', pp. 5–10.

99. Cited by H. J. de Vleeschauwer, 'The Development of Kantian Thought' (London, 1969) pp. 39–40. Vleeschauwer argues (p. 42) that Rousseau's influence was crucial in Kant's change from his Wolffian beginnings: 'I believe that Rousseau must be held responsible for this change of tone, for he revealed to Kant the superiority of morality to knowledge.'

100. 'Émile', p. 245.

101. To J. C. Lavater, 1775; Zweig, 'Philosophical Correspondence', pp. 79–82.

102. Ibid.

103. 'Critique of Pure Reason', B xxiv–vi.

104. Ibid., B xxvi.

105. 'Critique of Practical Reason, and Other Writings in Moral Philosophy', trans. L. W. Beck (Chicago, 1950).

106. Ibid., bk ii, chap. ii, sec. v, p. 227.

107. Ibid., p. 229.

108. Ibid., p. 232: 'Morals is not really the doctrine of how to make ourselves happy, but of how we are to be *worthy* of happiness. Only if religion is added to it can the hope arise of some day participating in happiness in proportion as we endeavoured not to be unworthy of it.'

109. Ibid., A 811; B 839.

110. Cf. W. H. Walsh, 'Kant's Moral Theology', in 'Proceedings of the British Academy', xlix (1963) 266: 'This is simply a causal argument which attempts to infer God's existence from the particular way in which things are constituted; in form it is identical with Descartes's argument from the fact that we possess the idea of God, or again with the teleological argument itself. And it shares all the weaknesses of these purported demonstrations, as Kant himself would have been the first to point out.'

111. 'Critique of Practical Reason', p. 229.

112. Ibid., pp. 229–30.

113. Ibid., p. 231.

114. Ibid., p. 232. Cf. Walsh, 'Kant's Moral Theology', p. 285: 'Interpreted on these lines, the theology of Kant becomes identical in essentials with the theology of Professor Braithwaite as expressed in his well-known lecture "An Empiricist's View of the Nature of Religious Belief". . . . Though Braithwaite and Kant follow somewhat different lines in working this alternative out, they end up with what is fundamentally the same view, namely that the whole force of a declaration of belief in God's existence is to be found in the adoption of a practical attitude. Braithwaite virtually identifies belief in God with acceptance of the command that we love one another; Kant equates it more generally with manifest confidence that the moral struggle will not be in vain.'

115. Ibid., p. 245.

116. Cf. Beck, 'Studies in the Philosophy of Kant', p. 52: 'Since it is practical and not speculative reason which finally warrants Kant's use of the concept of God, theology for him can have no theoretical content, and religion is only the attitude of performing all duties as divine commands. The judgement, "There is a God" is not a theoretical judgement; it is not a hypothesis in a theoretical context. It is a practical postulate, a point of orientation. In the ordinary sense of the word "know" we do not know that it is true, yet there is an *a priori* guaranty for it.'

117. In the manner of J. H. Newman's argument in 'A Grammar of Assent' (London, 1901) pp. 109–10; see also 'The Argument from Conscience to the Existence of God According to J. H. Newman', by A. J. Boekraad and H. Tristram (Louvain, 1961), and A. E. Taylor's thesis in 'The Faith of a Moralist' (London, 1930). See also H. P. Owen, 'The Moral Argument for Christian Theism' (London, 1965).

118. 'The Limits of Religious Thought', 4th ed. (London, 1859) p. 70.

119. Kant's oscillations on this point are vividly exemplified in 'Critique of Practical Reason', bk ii, chap. ii, sec. vii, pp. 236–43: 'How is it possible to conceive of extending pure reason in a practical respect without thereby extending its knowledge as speculative?" '

120. A. R. C. Duncan, 'Practical Reason and Morality' (London, 1957) pp. 134–5.

121. For a full discussion of this work see C. C. J. Webb, 'Kant's Philosophy of Religion' (Oxford 1926) chap. v.

122. Ibid., p. 151.

123. Cited ibid., p. 169. An English translation of part of this work is included in 'Kant's Political Writings', ed. H. Reiss (Cambridge, 1970).

124. Cited in Webb, 'Kant's Philosophy of Religion', p. 171.

125. Ed. E. Adickes (Berlin, 1920) p. 819.

126. Ibid., p. 820; cf. p. 824: 'There is a Being in me, distinguished from myself as the cause of an effect wrought upon me, which freely – that is without being dependent on laws of nature in space and time – judges me within, justifying or condemning me; and I as man am myself this being, and it is no substance external to me, and – what is most surprising of all – its causality is no natural necessity but a determination of me to a free act.'

127. Adickes, p. 781. See the discussion of these passages in F. E. England, 'Kant's Conception of God' (London, 1929) pp. 198–200.

128. 'Kant: Philosophical Correspondence 1759–99', ed. A. Zweig, pp. 217–20. In this letter, however, it is clear that Kant sees the essence of Christianity to consist in its moral content, the theoretical articulation of Christian doctrine being accidental and dispensable. 'It was, I maintain, my duty to make clear the status of rational religion. It should have been incumbent on my accusers to point out a single case in which I depreciated Christianity either by arguing against its acceptance as a revelation or by showing it to be unnecessary. For I do not regard it as a depreciation of a revealed doctrine to say that, in relation to its practical use (which constitutes the essential part of all religion), it must be interpreted in accordance with the principles of pure rational faith and must be urged on us openly. I take this rather as a recognition of its morally fruitful content, which would be deformed by the supposedly superior importance of merely theoretical propositions that are to be taken on faith . . . . I have insisted on the holy, practical content of the Bible, which, with all the changes in theoretical articles of faith that will take place in regard to merely revealed doctrines, because of their coincidental nature, will always remain as the inner and essential part of religion.'

129. Cited in Barth, 'From Rousseau to Ritschl', p. 195. While recognising that Kant wished to limit theology to the study of the accidental and dispensable historical expression of religion, Barth sees a genuine insight in Kant's sharp distinction between theology and philosophy. Cf. p. 196: 'It is only necessary to take quite seriously what Kant said half in mockery, in order to hear something very significant, even though we reserve in every respect our right to object to his formulations. Or is it not the case that the philosopher of

pure reason has said something very significant to the theologian in telling him in all succinctness that "The biblical theologian proves that God exists by means of the fact that He has spoken in the Bible"?' Barth's view of the Bible as the self-authenticating word of God, however, is profoundly different from Kant's.

130. Cf. Mansel's criticism of Kant in 'The Limits of Religious Thought', p. 14. 'Throughout every page of Holy Scripture God reveals Himself not as a Law but as a Person . . . . By what right do we venture to rob the Deity of half his revealed attributes, in order to set up the other half, which rest on precisely the same evidence, as a more absolute revelation of the truth? By what right do we enthrone, in the place of the God to whom we pray, an inexorable Fate or immutable Law?'

131. Though Kierkegaard, despite his continued sarcasms at Hegel's expense, always retained a reluctant admiration for him. In a footnote written for the 'Postscript', Kierkegaard wrote: 'I cherish a respect for Hegel which is sometimes an enigma to me; I have learnt much from him, and I know that on returning again to him I could still learn much more . . . . His philosophical knowledge, his astonishing learning, the sharpsightedness of his genius, and whatever else can be alleged to the advantage of a philosopher, I am as ready as any disciple to concede – but no, not to concede, that is too proud an expression; I would say rather, willing to admire, willing to let myself be taught. But for all that, one who is thoroughly tried in life's vicissitudes and has recourse in his need to the aid of thoughts, will find him comic – in spite of the great qualities which are no less certain.' Cited by W. Lowrie, 'Kierkegaard's Concluding Unscientific Postscript', trans. D. F. Swenson and W. Lowrie (Princeton, 1944) p. 558. For a balanced assessment of Kierkegaard's attitude to Hegel see J. Collins, 'The Mind of Kierkegaard' (London 1954) chap. 4.

132. 'Søren Kierkegaard – The Last Years: Journals 1853–55', ed. and trans. by R. Gregor Smith (London, 1965) p. 30.

133. p. 54.

134. Ibid., p. 504.

135. 'Philosophical Fragments', trans. D. F. Swenson (Princeton, 1936) p. 35. Cf. 'Concluding Unscientific Postscript', p. 495: Every man can distinguish 'between what he understands and what he does not understand . . . . and he can discover that there is something which is, in spite of the fact that it is against his understanding and way of thinking'.

136. 'Philosophical Fragments', p. 35.

137. 'The Last Years', p. 246.

138. 'Philosophical Fragments', p. 37.

139. 'The Last Years', p. 100.

140. 'Concluding Unscientific Postscript', p. 55: 'The subject is in passion infinitely interested in his eternal happiness . . . . But in order to philosophise he must proceed in precisely the opposite direction, giving himself up and losing himself in objectivity, thus vanishing from himself . . . . Christianity does not lend itself to objective observation, precisely because it proposes to intensify subjectivity to the utmost . . . .'

141. Ibid., p. 23.

142. Ibid., p. 124.

143. 'Philosophical Fragments', pp. 31–2. Cf. 'Concluding Unscientific Postscript', p. 107: 'An existential system is impossible . . . . System and existence are incapable of being thought together; because in order to think

existence at all, systematic thought must think it as abrogated, and hence as not existing. Existence separates, and holds the various moments of existence discretely apart, the systematic thought consists of the finality which brings them together.'

144. 'Papirer', X2 a 354, cited by J. Heywood Thomas, 'Subjectivity and Paradox' (Oxford, 1957) p. 121.

145. Kierkegaard suggests that even speculative thought presupposes 'a resolution of the will' in order to get it going. Cf. 'Concluding Unscientific Postscript', p. 103: 'Only when reflection comes to a halt can a beginning be made, and reflection can be halted by something else, and this something else is something quite different from the logical, being a resolution of the will'.

146. Cf. ibid., p. 53: 'The comical inheres precisely in the incommensurability between his [the speculative philosopher's] interest and the speculative objectivity . . . . If, therefore, he says that he bases his eternal happiness on his speculation, he contradicts himself and becomes comical, because philosophy in its objectivity is wholly indifferent to his and my and your eternal happiness.'

147. 'Philosophical Fragments', p. 52.

148. 'Concluding Unscientific Postscript', p. 497.

149. Ibid.

150. 'The Last Years', p. 354. On Kierkegaard's ideas on grace see L. Dupré, 'Kierkegaard as Theologian' (London, 1964) chap. iii.

151. Trans. D. F. and L. Swenson (Princeton, 1946) p. 248.

152. Heywood Thomas, 'Subjectivity and Paradox', p. 16.

153. 'Concluding Unscientific Postscript', p. 196.

154. Ibid., p. 339.

155. 'The Last Years', pp. 354–5.

156. 'Concluding Unscientific Postscript', p. 514.

157. Cf. on this Dupré, 'Kierkegaard as Theologian', p. 146: 'Since faith is paradoxical, reason is assigned the negative but indispensable task of pointing up the incomprehensibility of faith. Consequently, reason must know precisely what is and what is not outside its competence, and such knowledge is a prerequisite for defining with accuracy the sphere of faith. Instead of dispelling the mysteriousness of faith, reason must set itself the task of bringing it into relief. This requires that it be able to distinguish between the contradictory and the incomprehensible.'

158. Cf. 'Fear and Trembling', p. 85: Abraham, the man of faith *par excellence*, 'cannot be mediated; in other words, he cannot speak. As soon as I speak, I express the universal, and when I remain silent, no one can understand me.'

159. 'Concluding Unscientific Postscript', p. 181.

160. Ibid., pp. 179–80.

161. Boyce Gibson, 'Theism and Empiricism', p. 117.

162. Cf. Collins, 'The Mind of Kierkegaard', p. 155: 'Existential thoughts . . . always retain this orientation to a free plan about one's personal existence and moral condition. But if this accounts sufficiently for existential thinking, then the latter does not differ *in the cognitive order* from other sorts of thinking. Only the use and personal reference of the thinking are different. The conclusion is inescapable that only a non-cognitive shift of attitude is needed to convert abstract thinking . . . . into existential thinking.'

163. H. L. Mansel, 'The Limits of Religious Knowledge', 4th ed. (London, 1859) p. xliv.

164. Ibid., p. 48.

165. Ibid., p. 153. On Mansel's undeservedly neglected work, see Kenneth D. Freeman, 'The Role of Reason in Religion – A Study of Henry Mansel' (The Hague, 1969). J. S. Mill has a rather external critique of Mansel's book in 'An Examination of Sir William Hamilton's Philosophy', 2nd ed. (London, 1865) chap 7. Mill alleges (p. 89) that Mansel's position involves that 'no argument grounded on the incredibility of the [religious] doctrine, as involving an intellectual absurdity, or on its moral badness as unworthy of a good or wise being, ought to have any weight, since of these things we are incompetent to judge'. And Mill goes on to say (p. 90): 'My opinion of this doctrine, in whatever way presented, is, that it is simply the most morally pernicious doctrine now current.'

166. Richard R. Niebuhr, 'Schleiermacher on Christ and Religion' (New York, 1964) p. 195: 'A silent assumption of the attack on natural theology by recent Protestant theology is that knowledge is a form of power. This assumption no doubt reflects the extent to which technological science has become the norm of all our conceptions of knowing. In any case, a natural knowledge of God seems to represent some form of human power over, or claim upon, God, according to this way of thinking, and this in part accounts for the vehemence with which crisis theology rejects the notion of a seed of religion present in all men, an innate idea of God, obscured and vitiated, but still abiding in human nature.'

167. 'The Idea of the Holy' (Penguin Books, Harmondsworth, 1959) p. 129.

168. Ibid., p. 33.

169. 'Die Kategorie des "Heiligen" bei Rudolf Otto', cited in J. L. Adams, 'Paul Tillich's Philosophy of Culture, Science and Religion' (New York, 1965) p. 220.

170. See K. Barth, 'From Rousseau to Ritschl' (London, 1959) pp. 195–6.

171. See H. Zahrnt, 'The Question of God' (London, 1969) pp. 27–8, for a discussion of Kierkegaard's influence on Barth.

172. Cf. the attack on Barth's supposed 'irrationalism' by Brand Blandshard, 'Critical Reflections on Karl Barth', in 'Faith and the Philosophers', ed. J. Hick (London, 1964) pp. 159 ff.

173. See K. Barth, 'Fides Quaerens Intellectum', English trans. (London, 1960).

174. R. Bultmann in 'The Theology of Rudolf Bultmann', ed. C. W. Kegley (London, 1966) p. 276.

175. Ibid., p. 274. The essay 'Philosophy and Theology in Bultmann's Thought', by John Macquarrie, in 'The Theology of Rudolf Bultmann', is the clearest account in English of Bultmann's implicit philosophy of religion.

176. Cf. 'The Historicity of Man and Faith', in 'Existence and Faith', trans. S. M. Ogden (London, 1961) p. 95: 'A philosophy would be unusable if it undertook to ascertain the "meaning" of human existence in the sense of trying to show that the latter is "meaningful" (or, on the contrary, as in Nietzsche, that it is "meaningless"). It would then try to take from the concrete man the question as to his "meaning", a question that is posed uniquely to him and can only be answered by him as an individual person; it would try to give a universal answer to man's question, "What is truth?" which as his question is a question of the moment. On the other hand, a legitimate philosophical analysis of human existence shows precisely that it is the concrete man himself who must alone pose the question about his "meaning", the question, "What is truth?" and give an answer to it. And just this is what it

means for such an analysis to exhibit the "meaning" of human existence, i.e. to show what man means, what *meaning* "being" has when one speaks of man. If philosophy by no means deceives itself into thinking that its work as inquiry leads to absolute knowledge, then naturally theology also ought not to suppose that philosophy provides it with a normative ontology with which it is then able to work as it pleases.'

177. 'Symbol and Knowledge', in 'Journal of Liberal Religion', ii (1941) 203.

178. On Tillich's position, see Adams, 'Paul Tillich's Philosophy of Culture, Science and Religion', p. 215: 'All in all the epistemological method presented is a way of faith whereby one through decision puts his trust in that effulgent and powerful mystery which vibrates through every part of creation, supporting and threatening, form-creating, form-bursting, form-transforming. One cannot prove or disprove its reality. One can only recognise that in it and through it we live and move and have our being. This is rather an affirmation about the ultimate, a decision for that without which being and meaning and truth lose their life-blood. It is, in short, a method that presupposes the reality it is supposed to lead to. Tillich himself calls it an "original decision" in response to grace.' Adams' study, at once sympathetic and discerningly critical, is the best account in English of Tillich's philosophy of religion. See also Stuart C. Brown, 'Do Religious Claims Make Sense?' (London, 1909) pp. 154 ff., on 'Tillich's A-Theism'.

179. 'The Limits of Religious Knowledge', p. xxxii.

CHAPTER 4

1. K. Nielsen, 'Wittgensteinian Fideism', in 'Philosophy', xlii (1967) 193.

2. See, for example, the conclusion to Stuart C. Brown's book, 'Do Religious Claims Make Sense?' (London, 1969) pp. 182–3: 'The question to which this essay has been addressed is whether religious claims can be said to make sense. It has been argued that there is no basis for a general negative or a general affirmative to this question. If, however, a general negative may be ruled out, then some account is required of how it is possible for some people to make sense of such claims whereas others do not. I have been concerned to explore the implications of saying that it is in some way a necessary matter that the non-believer should find the claims of religion unintelligible. No conclusion follows from the arguments offered as to whether or not there is anything to learn from this or that religion . . . . I have thus left open what many would regard as the crucial question about religion. My argument has been that, *so far as epistemology is concerned*, this question *should* be left open.'

3. See G. E. Hughes, 'Critical Notice of "Religious Belief", by C. B. Martin', in 'Australasian Journal of Philosophy', xl (1962) 216: 'When a phenomenalist offers an account of statements about sense-data, he is not usually accused even by his opponents of not believing in the existence of chairs and tables. When two philosophers differ in their account of what it is to make a moral judgement, they do not usually accuse each other of not making any genuine moral judgement; they may even be, and recognize themselves to be, in complete accord on every moral issue. Does the parallel not hold in the theological case?'

4. See J. O. Urmson, 'Philosophical Analysis: Its Development between the Two World Wars' (Oxford, 1956); G. J. Warnock, 'English Philosophy

since 1900' (Oxford, 1958); M. J. Charlesworth, 'Philosophy and Linguistic Analysis' (Pittsburgh, 1959).

5. See A. J. Ayer (ed.), 'Logical Positivism' (London, 1959).

6. 'Tractatus Logico-Philosophicus' (London, 1922) 6.432.

7. Ibid., 6.44. Cf. E. Stenius, 'Wittgenstein's Tractatus' (Oxford, 1960) p. 223: 'In a logical empiricist's vocabulary "nonsensicality" means something purely negative. Wittgenstein's identification of the inexpressible with the mystical seems to show that to him "nonsensicality" has a rather positive ring. The German word *Unaussprechlich* means not only "inexpressible" but also "ineffable".'

8. G. E. M. Anscombe, 'An Introduction to Wittgenstein's Tractatus' (London, 1959) p. 173.

9. N. Malcolm, 'Ludwig Wittgenstein, A Memoir' (London, 1958) p. 70: 'Wittgenstein did once say to me that he could understand the conception of God, in so far as it is involved in one's awareness of one's own sin and guilt', though whether he thought of God being transcendent to the world is not at all clear. A. Flew, 'Tolstoi and the Meaning of Life', in 'Ethics', lxxiii (1963) 118, claims that in Wittgenstein 'we can find suggestions of a religion without reference to any world beyond the world', and he cites Wittgenstein's 'Notebooks, 1914–1916' (Oxford, 1961) p. 74: 'To believe in God means to see that life has a meaning. The world is *given* me, i.e. my will enters into the world completely from the outside as into something that is already there . . . . That is why we have the feeling of being dependent on an alien will. *However* this may be, at any rate we *are* in a certain sense dependent, and what we are dependent on we can call God.'

10. See Eddy Zemak, 'Wittgenstein's Philosophy of the Mystical', in 'Essays on Wittgenstein's Tractatus', ed. I. M. Copi and R. W. Beard (London, 1966). Cf. p. 362: 'Since the form of all facts, i.e. factuality, is not a fact, it is not *in* the world. It is the *limit* of the world of facts. Thus it can be named "Fate" or "Alien Will", because there can be no reason *why* these are the facts. God is exactly this essence of the facts, their factuality. He is not, therefore, *in* the world.' Cf. p. 363: 'God, the inexpressible, the mystical, is a formal "fact". The formal "fact" *that* the world is, namely, that there is the totality of facts, is God.' And p. 368: 'The willing I, the value-endower, cannot exist *in* the world, which is nothing but the totality of facts . . . . To occupy the ethical standpoint is, consequently, to place oneself outside the world, so to speak, at a place where no facts may hold.'

11. Cited by G. E. M. Anscombe, 'What Wittgenstein Really Said', in 'The Tablet' (17 Apr 1954) p. 373. Miss Anscombe continues: 'I do not know whether he was right about this. I am certain that if he was wrong it was not because of some initial doctrine about the impossibility of metaphysics: he had no such initial doctrine.' Cf. also Malcolm, 'Ludwig Wittgenstein', p. 72: 'I think that there was in him [Wittgenstein], in some sense, the possibility of religion. I believe that he looked on religion as a "form of life". . . in which he did not participate, but with which he was sympathetic and which greatly interested him.'

12. Oxford, 1953.

13. Hughes, 'Critical Notice of "Religious Belief",' p. 215.

14. London, 1936.

15. On the relations between Logical Positivism and linguistic analysis see Charlesworth, 'Philosophy and Linguistic Analysis', chap. iv; J. Wisdom,

'Note on the New Edition of Professor Ayer's "Language, Truth and Logic",
in 'Philosophy and Psychoanalysis', pp. 230 ff.

16. 'Language, Truth and Logic', p. 48.

17. Ibid., p. 107.

18. Ibid.

19. 'On the Analysis of Moral Judgements', reprinted in 'Philosophical
Essays' (London, 1954) pp. 231–49. Concerning the 'emotive theory of ethics'
see M. Warnock, 'Ethics since 1900' (Oxford, 1960) pp. 79–93.

20. See A. Gewirth, 'Meta-Ethics and Normative Ethics', in 'Mind', lxix
(1960) 187–205.

21. 'Theology and Falsification', in 'New Essays in Philosophical Theology',
ed. A. Flew and A. MacIntyre (London, 1955) p. 98. See also R. W. Hepburn,
'Christianity and Paradox: Critical Studies in 20th Century Theology'
(London, 1958) and C. B. Martin, 'Religious Belief' (Ithaca, N.Y., 1959).

22. See J. A. Passmore, 'Christianity and Positivism', in 'Australasian
Journal of Philosophy', xxxv (1957) 125–36: ' "Logical Positivism is dead",
so they say. Rightly too, in the sense that few would now wish to subscribe
themselves "logical positivists". Yet the deadness of logical positivism is
more like the deadness of a dead metaphor than it is like the deadness of
phlogiston theory: if it no longer lives, this is because a weakened version of
the main positivist thesis – in some such form as "an empirical proposition is
meaningless unless it can in principle be falsified" – has come quietly to be
taken for granted.' Cf. A. Plantinga's devastating attack on this kind of verificationism in 'God and Other Minds' (Ithaca, 1968) chap. 2.

23. Cambridge, 1955. See also Braithwaite's earlier article, 'Belief and
Action', in 'Proceedings of the Aristotelian Society', supp. vol. xx (1946) 1–19.
As Braithwaite himself admits, his position is very close to that of Matthew
Arnold in 'Literature and Dogma' (London, 1874).

24. Ibid., p. 14.

25. Ibid., p. 27.

26. As the late G. C. Colombo, S.J., has pointed out in his article 'The
Analysis of Belief', in 'The Downside Review' (1958–9) p. 23, Braithwaite's
position is at bottom identical with that of the nineteenth-century modernists,
and he cites a revealing extract from a letter written by George Tyrrell to von
Hügel in 1904: 'It is not, as they [the traditional theologians] suppose, about
this or that article of the creed that we differ; we accept it all; but it is the
word "credo", the sense of "true" as applied to "dogma", the whole course
of revelation that is at stake'. H. Meynell, 'Sense, Nonsense and Christianity'
(London, 1964) p. 73, notes the similarity between Braithwaite's theory and
that of Kant's 'Religion within the Limits of Mere Reason' which attempts
'to make religion strictly and exclusively ancillary to morality'. Meynell says,
however, that Kant 'never goes so far as to *identify* religious belief with adherence
to a moral programme, as Professor R. B. Braithwaite does'.

27. Cf. J. A. Passmore, 'Christianity and Positivism', in 'Australasian
Journal of Philosophy', xxxiv (1956) 133: 'I heard Braithwaite give his lecture
at Oxford. Afterwards I spent half an hour trying to persuade an intelligent,
newly arrived American graduate student that it was not intended as a defence
of atheism. His final conclusion: "Well, the English sure are queer!" should
perhaps have been met by the reply, "Non Angli, sed Anglicani!" '

28. 'Theology and Falsification', in 'New Essays', p. 99.

29. Ibid., p. 102.

30. 'Religion and Morals', in 'Faith and Logic', ed. B. Mitchell (London, 1957) pp. 189–90.

31. Ibid., p. 190.

32. In 'Faith and the Philosophers', ed. J. Hick (London, 1964) pp. 103–10.

33. Ibid., p. 107.

34. Ibid.

35. Ibid., p. 110.

36. See also R. W. Coburn, 'A Neglected Use of Religious Language', in 'Mind', lxxii (1963) 369–85.

37. Hughes, 'Critical Notice of "Religious Belief",' p. 216: 'Braithwaite, it could be argued . . . . is not offering us a religion or a substitute for one but something quite different, namely an account of what it is to have a religious belief. . . . Why should the fact that a Braithwaitean gives the account he does of what it is to have a religious belief be taken to show that he does not have any religious beliefs? Must someone hold a view of what it is to believe statements of a certain type (or a certain view of the function of statements of that type) before he can properly be said to believe any of them?'

38. 'Philosophical Investigations', secs. 23, 290, 184.

39. Ibid., secs. 19, 23.

40. Ibid., p. 223.

41. Cf. G. Pitcher, 'The Philosophy of Wittgenstein' (Englewood Cliffs, N.J., 1964) p. 243: 'We could not tell what, if anything, he has asserted, for the modes of behaviour into which his use of words is woven are too radically different from our own. We would not understand him, since he does not share the relevant forms of life with us.'

42. Ibid., p. 226.

43. 'Lectures and Conversations on Aesthetics, Psychology and Religious Belief', ed. C. Barrett (Oxford, 1966) pp. 53–4.

44. Hughes, 'Critical Notice of "Religious Belief",' p. 215.

45. Ibid., pp. 55–6.

46. Ibid., p. 61: 'When we encounter this concept [of necessary being] as a problem in philosophy, we do not consider the human phenomena that lie behind it. It is not surprising that many philosophers believe that the idea of a necessary being is an arbitrary and absurd construction.'

47. Ibid., p. 214.

48. 'Ludwig Wittgenstein: The Bearing of His Philosophy upon Religious Belief' (London, 1968) p. 67.

49. Ibid., p. 71: 'Could it be argued that there is a dimension, at once mysterious and magnificent, which religious language, and the kind of experience which goes with it, add to human life; and that if this dimension were lost something essential to what we mean by calling our life "human" would be lost also?'

50. 'American Philosophical Quarterly' i (1964) 307–24.

51. Ibid., p. 309.

52. Ibid., pp. 308–9.

53. Ibid., p. 313.

54. 'The Idea of a Social Science and Its Relation to Philosophy' (London, 1958) p. 102.

55. Cf. D. Z. Phillips, 'The Concept of Prayer' (London, 1966) p. 25: 'The possibility of the unreality of God does not occur *within* any religion, but it arises in disputes *between* religions' or between religion and irreligion. 'It is logically proper to say "There is no God" if this means that the theistic

language game and form of life is being rejected on the grounds that one cannot make sense of it or that one finds it morally objectionable.'

56. Ibid., p. 309.

57. See J. R. Jones and D. Z. Phillips, 'Belief and Loss of Belief: A Discussion', in 'Sophia', ix 1 (1970).

58. Ibid., p. 2.

59. Ibid., p. 5.

60. Ibid., p. 6.

61. 'Faith, Scepticism and Understanding', in 'Religion and Understanding', ed. D. Z. Phillips (London, 1967) p. 60.

62. 'Critical Notice of "Religious Belief"', p. 215.

63. Cf. the same conflation in Jones and Phillips, 'Belief and Loss of Belief', p. 2: 'I think, that if we do look at the role this belief plays in at least many believers' lives, we find that it is not a hypothesis, a conjecture, that some dreadful event is going to happen so many thousand years hence. We see this by recognising that a certain range of reactions is ruled out for the believer. What I mean is this: if it were a conjecture about a future event, he might say, "I believe it is going to happen" or possibly "It might happen" or "I'm not sure; it may happen", and so on. But that range of reactions plays no part in the believers' belief in the last judgement.' Does Phillips mean to say here that as a matter of ascertainable fact most believers do not think of the Last Judgement as a future event that will happen; or is he saying that they could not really think this (regardless of what they say they think) for they would then be confusing religious beliefs with scientific conjectures?

64. Cf. Hudson, 'Ludwig Wittgenstein', p. 71: if this religious dimension were lost, 'something essential to what we mean by calling our life "human" would be lost also'.

65. A. MacIntyre, 'Is Understanding Religion Compatible with Believing?', in 'Faith and the Philosophers', ed. J. Hick (London, 1964) p. 122. MacIntyre's essay is an extended critique of Winch's article.

66. The term is K. Nielsen's. See his 'Wittgensteinian Fideism', in 'Philosophy', xlii (1967) 191–209, for a vigorous attack on this whole position.

67. Ibid., p. 196.

68. A good example of analytic illumination in this sphere is provided by Stuart C. Brown's book, 'Do Religious Claims make Sense?' (London, 1969).

69. Nielsen, 'Wittgensteinian Fideism', p. 192; Axel Hägerström, 'Philosophy and Religion' (London, 1964) p. 216.

70. There is some resemblance between the approach of the analysts and the 'phenomenological' approach of M. Henry Duméry in 'The Problem of God in Philosophy of Religion' (Evanston, Ill., 1964). The notion of God, Duméry says, comes from religion and 'the philosopher *encounters* it; he is not the author of it' (p. 7). The philosopher of religion passes 'concrete theism' through 'the sieve of criticism' (p. 13), but he must 'take care in criticising concrete theism to respect its specificity' (p. 10). See the illuminating review of Duméry's book by A. Boyce Gibson in 'Australasian Journal of Philosophy', xliii (1965) 239–45. Gibson notes (p. 240) that for Duméry 'God is a datum to be sifted, not a conclusion to be argued'; and again (p. 244): 'In the philosophy of religion, analysts claim to be tidying up religious discourse, not replacing it; and in the same way M. Duméry insists on respecting religion "in its specificity" and showing it its own implications'. On Duméry's phenomenology of religion see also Gerald A. McCool, 'Duméry and the Dynamism of the Spirit', in 'Theological Studies', xxx (1969) 178–206; and Georges Van Riet,

'Idéalisme et Christianisme', in 'Revue Philosophique de Louvain', lvi (1958) 361–428, and 'Philosophie de la religion et théologie', in 'Revue Philosophique de Louvain', lvii (1959) 415–37.

CHAPTER 5

1. Cf. R. N. Smart, 'Reasons and Faiths' (London, 1958).
2. See J. C. Thornton, 'Religious Belief and "Reductionism",' in 'Sophia', v (1966) 3–16.
3. For Hegel, see above; for Matthew Arnold, see 'Literature and Dogma' (London, 1874); for Santayana, see 'Reason in Religion', vol. iii: 'The Life of Reason' (New York, 1905).
4. H. D. Lewis, 'The Study of Religions' (London, 1969) p. 209.

Bibliography

GENERAL

A. H. Armstrong and R. A. Markus, 'Christian Faith and Greek Philosophy' (London, 1960).
J. Collins, 'The Emergence of the Philosophy of Religion' (New Haven, 1967).
A. Boyce Gibson, 'Theism and Experience' (London, 1970).
E. Gilson, 'God and Philosophy' (New Haven, 1941).
J. Hick, 'The Philosophy of Religion' (New York, 1963).
R. N. Smart, 'Historical Selections in the Philosophy of Religion' (London, 1962).
H. D. Lewis, 'Teach Yourself Philosophy of Religion' (London, 1965).
'The Study of Religions' (London, 1969).
George I. Mavrodes and Stuart C. Hackett, 'Problems and Perspectives in the Philosophy of Religion' (Boston, 1967).

CHAPTER 1

The Greeks
W. Jaeger, 'The Theology of the Early Greek Philosophers' (Oxford, 1967).
A. Festugière, 'Personal Religion among the Greeks' (Berkeley and Los Angeles, 1934).

Plato
A. Festugière, 'Contemplation et vie contemplative selon Platon' (Paris, 1950).
R. Hackforth, 'Plato's Theism', in 'Studies in Plato's Metaphysics', ed. R. E. Allen (London, 1965).
F. Solmsen, 'Plato's Theology' (New York, 1942).
A. Diès, 'Autour de Platon', vol. ii (Paris, 1927).

Aristotle
W. Jaeger, 'Aristotle: Fundamentals of the History of His Development', 2nd ed. (Oxford, 1948).
W. K. C. Guthrie, 'The Development of Aristotle's Theology', in 'Classical Quarterly' (1934).
W. J. Verdenius, 'Traditional and Personal Elements in Aristotle's Religion', in 'Phronesis', v (1960).
R. Norman, 'Aristotle's Philosopher-God', in 'Phronesis', xiv (1969).

Plotinus and neo-Platonists
A. H. Armstrong, 'The Cambridge History of Later Greek and Early Medieval Philosophy' (Cambridge, 1967) part iii.
J. M. Rist, 'Plotinus: The Road to Reality' (Cambridge, 1967).
E. Bréhier, 'La Philosophie de Plotin' (Paris, 1928).
A. D. Nock, 'Conversion: The Old and the New in Religion from Alexander the Great to Augustine of Hippo' (Oxford, 1933).

209

Early Christian thinkers

R. A. Norris, 'God and World in Early Christian Theology' (New York, 1965).
W. Jaeger, 'Early Christianity and Greek Paideia' (Cambridge, Mass., 1961).

Islamic thought

L. Gardet and M. M. Anawati, 'Introduction à la théologie musulmane' (Paris, 1948).
R. Walzer, 'Early Islamic Philosophy', in 'Cambridge History of Later Greek and Early Medieval Philosophy', part viii.
L. Gauthier, 'Ibn Rochd' (Paris, 1948).

The Enlightenment

E. Cassirer, 'The Philosophy of the Enlightenment' (Boston, 1951).
P. Gay, 'The Enlightenment – An Interpretation' (London, 1967).

Hegel

J. N. Findlay, 'Hegel: A Re-examination' (London, 1958).
G. R. G. More, 'Hegel, Luther and the Owl of Minerva', in 'Philosophy', xli (1966).

Spinoza

S. Hampshire, 'Spinoza' (London, 1951).
H. Wolfson, 'The Philosophy of Spinoza' (New York, 1948).

CHAPTER 2

Philo

H. A. Wolfson, 'Philo: Foundations of Religious Philosophy in Judaism, Christianity and Islam' (Cambridge, Mass., 1948).

Christian Platonists

H. Chadwick, 'Early Christian Thought and the Classical Tradition' (Oxford, 1966).
R. M. Grant, 'Gnosticism and Early Christianity' (New York, 1966).
J. Daniélou, 'Origen' (London, 1955).

St Augustine

J. J. O'Meara, 'The Young Augustine' (London, 1954).
E. Gilson, 'The Christian Philosophy of St Augustine' (New York, 1960).

Early Medieval thinkers

J. Cottiaux, 'La conception de la théologie chez Abélard', in 'Revue d'histoire ecclésiastique', xxviii (1932).
M. de Gandillac (ed.), 'Œuvres choisies d'Abélard' (Paris, 1945).
M. J. Charlesworth, 'St Anselm's "Proslogion" ' (Oxford, 1965).
M. D. Chenu, 'La Théologie comme science au XIIIème siècle' (Paris, 1957).
T. Tshibangu, 'Théologie positive et théologie spéculative' (Louvain, 1965).

St Thomas Aquinas

E. Gilson, 'Reason and Revelation in the Middle Ages' (New York, 1938).
  'The Christian Philosophy of St Thomas Aquinas' (New York, 1956).
G. Van Riet, 'Y a-t-il chez saint Thomas une philosophie de la religion?', in 'Revue Philosophique de Louvain', lxi (1963).
H. de Lubac, 'The Mystery of the Supernatural' (London, 1967).
E. L. Mascall, 'He Who Is – A Study in Traditional Theism' (London, 1943).
R. Garrigou-Lagrange, 'God: His Existence and Nature' (St Louis, 1934).

CHAPTER 3

Al Ghazzali
W. Montgomery Watt, 'Muslim Intellectual: A Study of Al Ghazzali' (Edinburgh, 1963).

Pascal
J. Chevalier, 'Pascal' (London, 1970).

Hume
N. Kemp Smith (ed.), 'Hume's Dialogues Concerning Natural Religion' (Oxford, 1935).
A. Leroy, 'David Hume' (Paris, 1953).

Rousseau
R. Grimsley, 'Rousseau and the Religious Quest' (Oxford, 1968).

Kant
L. W. Beck, 'Studies in the Philosophy of Kant' (New York, 1965).
W. H. Walsh, 'Kant's Moral Theology', in 'Proceedings of the British Academy', xlix (1963).
C. C. J. Webb, 'Kant's Philosophy of Religion' (Oxford, 1926).
F. E. England, 'Kant's Conception of God' (London, 1929).

Kierkegaard
J. Collins, 'The Mind of Kierkegaard' (London, 1954).
L. Dupré, 'Kierkegaard as Theologian' (London, 1964).

Barth, Bultmann, Tillich
H. Zahrnt, 'The Question of God' (London, 1969).
C. W. Hegley (ed.), 'The Theology of Rudolf Bultmann' (London, 1966).
J. L. Adams, 'Paul Tillich's Philosophy of Culture, Science and Religion' (New York, 1965).

CHAPTER 4

General
J. O. Urmson, 'Philosophical Analysis: Its Development Between the Two World Wars' (Oxford, 1956).
J. Hick (ed.), 'Faith and the Philosophers' (London, 1964).
A. Flew and A. MacIntyre (eds), 'New Essays in Philosophical Theology' (London, 1955).
Stuart C. Brown, 'Do Religious Claims Make Sense?' (London, 1969).
M. J. Charlesworth, 'Linguistic Analysis and Language about God', in 'International Journal of Philosophy', xxv (1957).

Wittgenstein
D. Pears, 'Wittgenstein' (Fontana Modern Masters, London, 1970).
E. Zemak, 'Wittgenstein's Philosophy of the Mystical', in 'Essays on Wittgenstein's Tractatus', ed. I. M. Copi and R. W. Beard (London, 1966).

Verficationism
J. A. Passmore, 'Christianity and Positivism', in 'Australasian Journal of Philosophy', xxxv (1957).
A. Plantinga, 'God and Other Minds' (Ithaca, N.Y., 1965).

Reductionism

R. B. Braithwaite, 'An Empiricist's View of the Nature of Religious Belief' (Cambridge, 1955).

H. Meynell, 'Sense, Nonsense and Christianity' (London, 1964).

R. M. Hare, 'Religion and Morals', in 'Faith and Logic', ed. B. Mitchell (London, 1951).

Wittgensteinian fideism

W. D. Hudson, 'Ludwig Wittgenstein: The Bearing of His Philosophy upon Religious Belief' (London, 1965).

P. Winch, 'Understanding a Primitive Society', in 'American Philosophical Quarterly', i (1964).

D. Z. Phillips, 'Faith, Scepticism and Understanding', in 'Religion and Understanding', ed. D. Z. Phillips (London, 1967).

K. Nielsen, 'Wittgensteinian Fideism', in 'Philosophy' xlii (1967).

Index